THINKING ABOUT TRAFFIC IN WEST MAUI

THINKING ABOUT TRAFFIC IN WEST MAUI

Edited by

Bianca K. Isaki and Lance D. Collins

North Beach-West Maui Benefit Fund Inc.

Lahaina, Maui, Hawai'i

Printed in the United States of America

26 25 24 23 22 21 6 5 4 3 2 1

ISBN 978-1-9524-6100-2 (pbk : alk. paper)

Published by the North Beach-West Maui Benefit Fund, Inc.
P O Box 11329
Lahaina, Hawai'i 96761

Distributed by University of Hawai'i Press
2840 Kolowalu Street
Honolulu, HI 96822-1888

This book is printed on acid-free paper and meets the guidelines for permanence and durability of the Council on Library Resources.

Print-ready files provided by North Beach-West Maui Benefit Fund, Inc.

Contents

Introduction

Lance D. Collins and Bianca K. Isaki

On Saturday March 31, 2012, North Beach-West Maui Benefit Fund sponsored a workshop at which community members would work on preferred visions for West Maui's future. The day-long workshop was conducted by the Hawai'i Research Center for Futures Studies of the University of Hawai'i at Mānoa at the Lahaina Educational Center. West Maui workshop participants and University Futures Studies graduate students worked out what different futures would look like for West Maui. The workshop produced a report and a website. Through the working out of alternative futures, the ways community participants thought about West Maui's present and future changed in notable ways.

The West Maui participants were divided into four groups that considered four broad images of alternative futures first described by University of Hawai'i Professor Emeritus Jim Dator: continued growth, societal collapse, managed shrinkage, and transformational society.

The groups involved in societal collapse and transformational society seemed to have the most productive and creative discussions. "Societal collapse" scenarios, however, involved a series of major undesirable events that put a damper on the highly creative ideas for the "day after tomorrow." For these groups, it seemed that natural disasters like a devastating hurricane or destructive tsunami would occur, but would not cause societal collapse. Rather, the participants all believed that societal collapse would only occur if tourism, the main economic engine of Maui, were to cease operations. For instance, there seemed to be near unanimity that a collapse would likely occur only if there were something like a terrorist attack on a hotel. All four groups also looked at traffic as a node in thinking about the future for West Maui. Because of this, collapse and transformation both looked at alternative futures after tourism. The following two vision statements proceeded from workshop participants:[1]

Vision No. 1. The future lies in the past: West Maui 2042. Vision No. 1 sought to build a more tranquil West Maui by embracing Hawaiian culture and values:

Maui in 2042 will be a far different place than it is today. The tranquil and calm atmosphere of Hawaii, namely Maui, can and must be restored if everything is Hawaiian-based. Think Hawaii. What fits and what does not in/on island life. If a tranquil and calm Hawaii consists of less cars, less hotels and controlled tourism—and more beach access, waterfalls and a thriving natural environment, then everyone should move in that direction. Mayor Charmaine Tavares said it well: "The environment is the economy."

The future, 2042, has to revert back to the islands' identity. In Hawaiian thinking, island first. The islands have the priority.

Imagine being on a cruise ship with over 2,000 passengers. One might ask: which is more important, the ship or its passengers? The answer is both. But one must have the priority. To Western civilization, people matter because they pay a high price to cruise. However, Hawaiians would say the ship because if it sinks, everyone dies.

When things go back to being Hawaiian-based, everyone wins, both native and non-native. And when everyone wins, only then will tranquility and serenity exist.

West Maui will be a place that embraces Hawaiian cultural values. We will do right by the land and sea.

We will encourage natives and non-natives to learn about the culture, and we will take advantage of increased interest in Hawaiian language immersion schools and the knowledge acquired to make West Maui the place it can and should be for the benefit of not only Kanaka Maoli, but the many residents and visitors who can learn from the Hawaiian experience.

In 2042, Maui and West Maui will have evolved beyond timeshares and concepts of greed. It will be a thriving place for those who seek Hawaiian spiritual values and knowledge of renewed Hawaiian culture. The economy and the Hawaiian government will be strong, a government of the people for the people. It will be a peaceful, tranquil, and calm place to live with a strong sense of community.

We will:

- emphasize the development of transportation systems such as light rail that will take the pressure off overcrowded highways
- support the revitalization of the ocean, its fishes and reefs
- reject the concept of unbridled growth at any cost and support only those new initiatives that will foster preservation of land and sea
- By creating a more self-governed local community, we will achieve:

- higher educational standards
- excellent public transportation
- other systems that support all the people and encourage them to create an ever-better future.

We will be a community that:

- employs renewable energy
- stresses local food production
- provides a living wage for workers
- increases ocean productivity—the Ahupuaʻa from the Mountains to the Sea

Vision No. 2 narrated a possible future stemming from radical environmental and economic change.

> In 2016, crises hit West Maui environmentally and economically. As a result, the island's transient population declines, leaving those who remain to focus on solutions. Immediate actions are taken to resolve deteriorating water infrastructure, and the water systems are redesigned to meet the needs of the residents. New technologies are pioneered, leading to a greater focus on total sustainability.
>
> In 2027, the island's natural streamflows are restored, leading back to traditional farming for self-sufficiency. This movement causes improved health of the land, ocean, and the people, who can live, work, and learn without having to leave their community. Thus, community life is strengthened.
>
> By 2042, we have learned to share with global communities without losing our identity and sense of what is really important to us, the residents of Maui. The children who have grown up in West Maui are secure in their spirituality and culture. They will go out into the world and share their values, then return and share their experiences with the rest of us because . . . there's no place like home!

Both of these visions sought a hopeful balance between technology, infrastructural development and quality of life at least in part by seeking answers in Hawaiian culture for an economic plan.

Five years later, in 2017, as the economy had recovered from the Great

Recession and tourism was booming, West Maui's traffic problems of the pre-recession period had returned with a vengeance. The board of directors of the North Beach-West Maui Benefit Fund decided to commission a telephone poll of West Maui residents (both Lahaina district and Kāʻanapali district) to get an idea of what the community believed were the solutions to West Maui's traffic problems.

A total of 322 telephone surveys were conducted from July 17, 2017, to August 12, 2017, by Anthology Marketing Group using their Random Digit Dialing software. The margin of error for their sample was +/- 5.57 percentage points with a 95 percent confidence level.

First, survey participants were asked to identify the most important issues currently facing West Maui. By far, they identified traffic as the most important issue facing West Maui residents. Seventy percent prioritized traffic. The next four most important issues were: affordable housing (25%), lack of infrastructure (23%), lack of adequate health care (14%), and too much development (12%). At the end of the survey, all participants were asked how important traffic was as an issue. Six percent said they cared little or not at all about it, while 72 percent said they cared strongly and 21 percent cared somewhat. Only ten percent of participants said they did not alter their behavior due to traffic.

Participants who stated traffic was a major or moderate concern were asked why they felt traffic was a concern. The top five answers were: that there were no alternative routes (29%), there were too many cars/drivers (22%), there was a need for additional lanes and road widening (21%), there was a lack of planning or leadership (18%), and there were too many tourists and rental cars (16%).

Participants were then presented with a list of possible causes of traffic and whether it was a major, significant, or minor contributor, or not a contributor at all. The top answers were: insufficient number of lanes on highway between West and Central Maui (79%), visitors staying in West Maui visiting other areas and visitors staying in other areas visiting West Maui (58%), visitors coming from and going to Kahului Airport (56%), residents going to and from work outside West Maui (52%), West Maui is overpopulated (41%), visitors' driving habits (35%), and residents going to and from non-work activities outside West Maui (37%).

Participants were then asked to list what they thought were "solutions" to traffic that they would like to see employed to help the overall situations. The solutions proposed were diverse: extending the bypass to The Pali, widening Kahekili Highway, adding lanes to Honoapiʻilani Highway, moving the Honoapiʻilani Highway away from the coastline, offering/increasing mass transit options, organizing ridesharing and carpools, constructing a tunnel through the West Maui mountains, imposing a moratorium on all non-affordable housing construction, expanding Kapalua Airport, expanding bicycling as a transportation option, and limiting the number of rental cars permitted in West Maui.

Younger participants were much more supportive of expanding express bus options. Older participants were much more interested in constructing a tunnel through the West Maui mountains, which had little support from younger participants.

Constructing a tunnel was the top response for what participants thought would have the most impact when rated on an individual basis. However, it also had the strongest and widespread opposition, making it a highly polarizing solution. The second-highest response for most impact was extending the bypass to The Pali. The rest of the proposed solutions did not gain widespread support for having the most impact, but they were felt to have some impact.

Only four percent of participants felt that local government planners were doing a very good job of addressing traffic. Twenty-one percent felt planners were doing a somewhat good job, 30 percent a somewhat poor job, and 39 percent felt they were doing a very poor job.

Based upon the survey results, North Beach-West Maui Benefit Fund decided to have experts in traffic, transportation planning, and other related fields each look at one of the more popular solutions to traffic issues in West Maui and examine and explore that solution. These investigations were not intended to provide long-term traffic plans. Rather, these experts were tasked with producing more open investigations of potential solutions, in either quantitative or qualitative ways. Since this project was initiated, the Maui Metropolitan Planning Organization (MMPO) has put together Hele Mai Maui 2040, which is intended to be a long-range transportation plan for the county. This MMPO report provides additional information and analysis of traffic and transportation issues important to West Maui.

One limitation of the telephone survey, which sought to obtain the views of the people of the Lahaina and Kāʻanapali districts through a scientific random sample, is that it did not ask participants for solutions that were "outside the box." Many answers, however, were unaided in that the participants were not given a list of choices to pick from and rather were able to freely give what they thought was the right answer. The survey was formulated within the Futures Studies rubric of "continued growth" or "managed shrinkage," in Professor Dator's terms.

One of the limitations of traffic planning and the decisions that go into what gets funded are the assumptions about the nature of what is being planned and the context. For example, if cheap and abundant oil or other factors stop automobiles from being the primary mode of transportation, spending hundreds of millions of dollars on building bigger, wider roads designed for automobiles is a questionable investment. A different question that can be asked is whether solutions should reinforce or encourage automobiles as the primary mode of transportation, and how each of those solutions adequately account for hidden costs to communities, ecological resources, and future options.

This introduction is being written during the time of the COVID-19 pandemic, when all Hawai'i residents are ordered to stay in their places of residence. With the mandatory fourteen-day quarantine for all persons arriving from off-island, hotels and tourism-related businesses have closed or severely narrowed the extent of their operations. This has led to nearly half of Hawai'i workers filing claims for unemployment insurance benefits. Nearly 20,000 rental cars are parked on lands surrounding Kahului Airport. The only contribution to traffic right now on Maui are the roving roadblocks of the Maui Police Department and the Hawai'i National Guard, and minor road construction activities. The amount of automobile travel has plummeted. Oil futures contracts have been trading in negative territory for months—producers were paying buyers to take their oil. Car insurance companies have been partially refunding premiums to reflect the massive drop in travel and the accidents that occur in relation to the amount of travel.

Were this present state of things to become permanent, and tourism were not to return at all, it would seem that none of the solutions proposed for traffic would be necessary or appropriate. Funding committed to a vision of continuing growth such as the $350 million car rental facilities at Honolulu and Kahului airports would seem like a huge waste of money or misplaced priorities.

Yet, continued economic growth or even maintaining the present level of economic activity is never certain. Authors, tasked with their topics over a year ago, were given flexibility in how they explored the topic they covered. They were supposed to the help think about exactly what each solution would look like. If growth or maintenance was not a key assumption, sometimes the thinking of the solution required discussion of that alternative. The authors are not proposing the solutions they explore. In some explorations, it becomes readily apparent that the solution will never happen in any way remotely similar to what was likely envisioned by the survey participants. Authors also explore thematically similar alternatives to expand the scope of solutions.

Mason M. Yamaki's "Tunneling through the West Maui Mountains" opens by affirming that while a tunneled highway through the West Maui mountains is "feasible," such a project would take decades; significant financial support from many sources, including federal funding; and require research; planning in coordination with multiple levels of government; and mitigation measures for protected plant and animal species, historic properties and burials, and water quality impacts. Even assuming that county, state, and federal agencies coordinated efforts to construct a tunneled highway, "it may take decades to include a West Maui mountains highway project within" their respective planning horizons. Yamaki methodically details regulatory requirements as well as other issues that would likely arise even before construction. The chapter closes by assessing three potential West Maui mountains highway routes: Kāʻanapali to Waiheʻe, Lahaina to Waikapū, and ʻĪao Valley to Lahaina. Each option, particularly the one through ʻĪao Valley, would require significant examination of historic properties and environmental impacts. Therefore, while "feasible," a tunneled highway would take decades to accomplish and cost billions in the process.

Lauren Armstrong's "Managed Retreat of Coastal Roads" is unique in this collection in that its explicit aim is not to explore solutions to existing traffic problems, but to head off the coming collapse of West Maui's coastal roads by discussing managed retreat. Armstrong details ongoing efforts to implement managed retreat for West Maui's critically threatened roadways, and to identify paths forward for near- and long-term solutions. These efforts arose from the historical, social, and geographic context of transportation in West Maui. Armstrong also examines current impacts of coastal hazards to roadways, and the anticipated impacts as hazards worsen over time with climate change and sea level rise. Armstrong then uses this lens to present thoughts on implementation: how to pull together funding and community support to realize the vision of a realigned Honoapiʻilani Highway with open space along the oceanfront for the benefit of present and future generations.

In her chapter, "Congestion, Commuting, and Carpooling," Dawn Hegger-Nordblom of Ke Kai Planning considers both some of the causes of congestion and then carpooling and ridesharing as one of the proposed solutions to West Maui traffic. Hegger-Nordblom highlights the connection between lack of affordable housing for workers, the consequent number of daily commuters to and from West Maui, and West Maui traffic. The chapter reviews Traffic Network Companies (TNCs) or TNC-like applications for coordinating transportation needs and riders under popular trade names like Charley's Taxi, Lyft, and Uber, and Hawaiʻi governmental efforts to regulate them for local needs to explore facets of a ride-sharing program run under municipal government, a nonprofit organization, or a public-private partnership.

Benjamin Treviño and Victoria Larson Treviño's "The Ahupuaʻa and the Housekeeper" investigates various community biking programs as a form of transportation that could alleviate traffic—but also, and not incidentally, rework West Maui society, economies, and technology. Treviño and Larson Treviño propose "island urbanism," defined as "an urban form based on the technology of the ahupuaʻa [. . .] achieved through their repair and recovery," to be a necessary predicate to the progressive visions of West Maui that are simultaneously rooted in Hawaiian traditional cultures and systems. What is urban and immanent about West Maui includes the large segment of the population who work in service industries. Providing service industry workers within West Maui would "contain West Maui's intensity" and also make biking a more feasible means of transportation. Treviño and Larson Treviño write:

> Much of what West Maui experiences as congestion is induced by this intense economic activity. Housekeepers, groundskeepers, service associates, cooks, bartenders, engineers, and managers that live in south or central Maui come to these lands to work on them. The modern system of transportation has intensified along with it, but it has not been contained to the ahupuaʻa.

Ryan Tam similarly takes expansive approaches to the proposed solution of light rail connecting Kahului and West Maui in his chapter, "Using Light Rail to Shape a More Sustainable Future for West Maui." A fast light rail system running on its own dedicated tracks could whisk riders between the Kahului Airport and Lahaina in about 30 minutes, with another 15–20 minutes to get up to Kapalua. The potential of light rail and other mass transit to create more reliable mobility and shape a more sustainable future for Maui will pivot on several considerations, many of which are examined in Tam's chapter explicitly and through comparison with light-rail projects constructed in other states.

Finally, Albert Perez reviews the concept of widening Kahekili Highway from Honokōhau through Kahakuloa to Waiheʻe in his chapter, "Around Kahakuloa." Much of Kahekili Highway is a one-lane road on which drivers may have to back up along a cliff and has a reputation for being one of the most dangerous roads in the world. Nevertheless, it is an actual existing route from West Maui to Central Maui. Perez, the director of the community-based Maui Tomorrow Foundation, prefaces his discussion of the physical practicalities of widening Kahekili Highway with a stern recitation of the important social, cultural, and equitable considerations.

> Kahekili Highway was one of the last roads to be built on Maui. Kahakuloa, the only real village in this vicinity, is one of the last remaining places on Maui where a Hawaiian subsistence lifestyle is practiced. There are many cultural sites in the area, and there is a good likelihood that additional cultural features would be disturbed during any roadway expansion. Given the known opposition by local residents to improvement of the roadway, impact to cultural impacts would surely be an issue during environmental review. Many residents value the fact that the roadway is difficult to traverse, because it reduces the amount of traffic, and makes it less likely that outsiders will be willing to try to buy land and/or build houses in the area.

A myopic focus on reducing traffic in West Maui cannot be allowed to stamp out the needs and wishes of its unique communities. After a careful analysis of Kahekili Highway-widening construction, Perez notes that, all things considered, a no-action alternative makes the most sense.

Each exploration of traffic solutions in these chapters not only describes regulatory compliance and construction considerations, but also attends to the ways proposed traffic mitigation are appropriate to the place that West Maui is and has been in history. This attention to the Hawaiian history and culture that conditions the contemporaneous community of West Maui is appropriate to the ways participants in 2012 envisioned a future for West Maui: "West Maui will be a place that embraces Hawaiian cultural values. We will do right by the land and sea." Traffic solutions will not be embraced unless they also protect, preserve, and restore West Maui lands and nearshore environments as a legacy of Hawaiian culture.

Notes

1. See Futures for West Maui website (accessed May 23, 2020). *Available at*: https://futuresofwestmaui-blog.tumblr.com/.

Chapter 1

TUNNELING THROUGH THE WEST MAUI MOUNTAINS

Mason M. Yamaki

This chapter addresses whether a West Maui tunneled mountain highway to connect Wailuku to Lāhainā/Kāʻanapali is feasible. The quick answer to this question is "yes"; however, even if planning a West Maui mountain highway were to begin today, the project would require significant political and financial support and take decades to plan and build. The following discussion is a broad-brushed analysis addressing expected challenges that project proponents will likely face from a pragmatic perspective. Topics that will be discussed in detail here include sensitive Native Hawaiian sites, protected native Hawaiian species, and island water quality concerns. A tunnel may be the only feasible way to address said concerns. Lessons learned from constructing the H-3 Highway on Oʻahu may be applied to a West Maui Mountains highway, and although costs may be in the multibillion-dollar range, the physical construction of a tunneled highway will probably be straightforward. Lastly, potential routes for a West Maui Mountains highway include, without limitation, Kāʻanapali to Waiheʻe, Lāhainā to Waikapū, and ʻĪao Valley to Lāhainā, with the ʻĪao Valley-to-Lāhainā route as the least attractive of these routes.

Background

The first step in assessing a West Maui Mountains highway project requires understanding the physical features of the island. The Island of Maui is made up of two mountain regions: the West Maui Mountains, which include Mauna ʻEke and Puʻu Kukui, and Haleakalā to the east. Native Hawaiians once referred to Haleakalā as the entire mountain and to Halemahina as the West Maui

Mountains. Haleakalā was thought of as the house of the male, and Halemahina the house of the female or the house of the moon.[1] The whole of the West Maui Mountains was considered the *piko ka honua*, the navel of the earth, or the woman.[2] Halemahina is derived from Hina, goddess of the moon, who resided in ʻĪao Valley.[3] The West Maui Mountains have also been referred to as Mauna Kahalawai, House of Water. *Wai*, meaning water in Hawaiian, is the "staff of life" and is protected by the *Moʻo Akua*, or lizard gods. The ancient Hawaiians recognized the significance of the forest as the main source of water and perpetuated this knowledge in a proverb: *Hahai no ka ua i ka ululāʻau*—the rain follows the forest. *Wai* was synonymous with wealth, such that the areas that contained the most water were prized above all others. Thus, Mauna Kahalawai, with its steady rainfall, misty cloud cover, and bountiful streams was highly regarded. Near the summit of ʻEke Crater and Puʻu Kukui is Kiʻowaiokihawahine (Violet Lake), a Hawaiian montane lake that formed in the highland bogs. This small lake is an extremely rare gem, part of the larger *kapu* (forbidden) area of the summit, where heaven and earth were believed to meet.[4] The west end of the island is composed of large, heavily eroded amphitheater valleys that contain well-developed permanent stream systems that watered fertile agricultural lands extending to the coast.[5]

The next step includes understanding the historical political divisions of the island, which will be referenced by name throughout the rest of the chapter. The division of Maui's lands into *moku* (districts) and *ahupuaʻa* (subdistricts) was performed by a *kahuna* (priest, expert) named Kalaihaʻōhia, during the time of the *aliʻi* (chief) Kakaʻalaneo. A moku contained ahupuaʻa that customarily continued inland from the ocean and upland into the mountains. Extended household groups living within the ahupuaʻa were therefore able to harvest from both the land and the sea. Ideally, this situation allowed each ahupuaʻa to be self-sufficient by supplying needed resources from different environmental zones.[6] West Maui was once divided into three moku: Lāhainā, Kāʻanapali, and Wailuku.[7] In 1859, the Hawaiian Legislature combined Kāʻanapali with Lāhainā to form the present-day Lāhainā District (see Figure 1.1).[8] The present-day towns of Lāhainā and Kāʻanapali are located along the coast within the district of Lāhainā, and the town of Wailuku is within the district of Wailuku.

Maui residents and visitors commuting between Wailuku and Lāhainā/Kāʻanapali have long coveted a highway through the West Maui Mountains connecting both communities. The current route for travelers typically starts in downtown Wailuku, continues along Hawaiʻi State Highway 30, also known as the Honoapiʻilani Highway, travels south around the West Maui Forest Reserve,

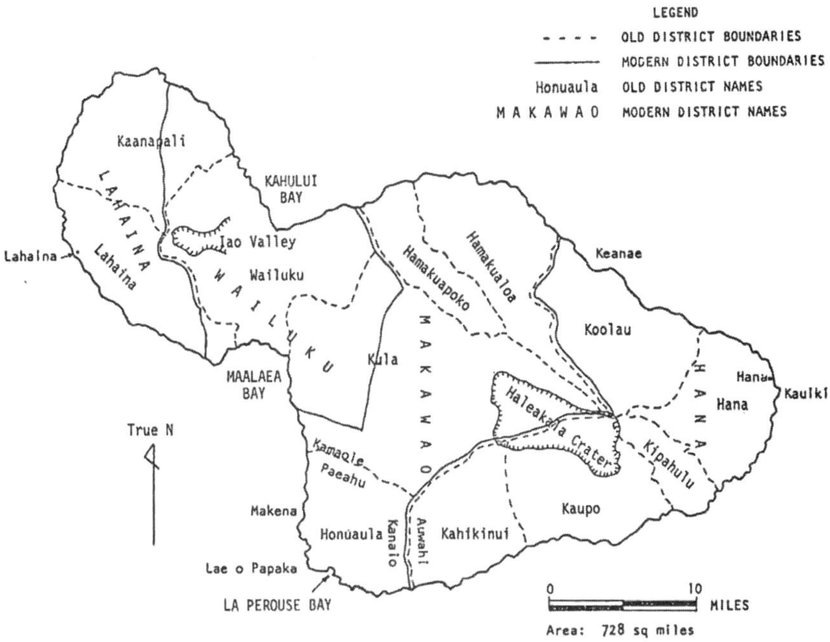

Figure 1.1. Traditional and Modern Districts of Maui. Colleen Dagan, Robert Hill, Tanya L. Lee-Greig, and Hallett H. Hammatt, *Supplemental Cultural Impact Assessment for the Proposed Advanced Technology Solar Telescope (ATST) at Haleakalā High Altitude Observatories Papaʻanui Ahupuaʻa, Makawao District, Island of Maui TMK: (2) 2-2-2-07:008*, Cultural Surveys Hawaiʻi, Inc., 2007:26

and then in a northwest direction along the southern coast of the island to Lāhainā/Kāʻanapali. An alternate route exists along the northern coastline of the island using Hawaiʻi State Highway 340, also known as Kahekili Highway, which ultimately connects to the Honoapiʻilani Highway then travels along the northwest coast of Maui to Kāʻanapali/Lāhainā; however, the State of Hawaiʻi Department of Transportation (DOT) does not maintain a significant portion of this route. This portion, which is maintained by the County of Maui, contains many one-lane stretches, lacks guardrails in some places, and the DOT requires vehicles traveling this road to have four-wheel drive capabilities (see Figure 1.2).

The daily average vehicle trip time between Lāhainā and Wailuku is estimated at 59 minutes in 2020 and is expected to increase to 83 minutes by 2035.[9] It is also common knowledge to Maui residents that the Honoapiʻilani Highway has a history of traffic stoppages caused by auto accidents and no comparable alternate route. Portions of the Honoapiʻilani Highway are along the coast and

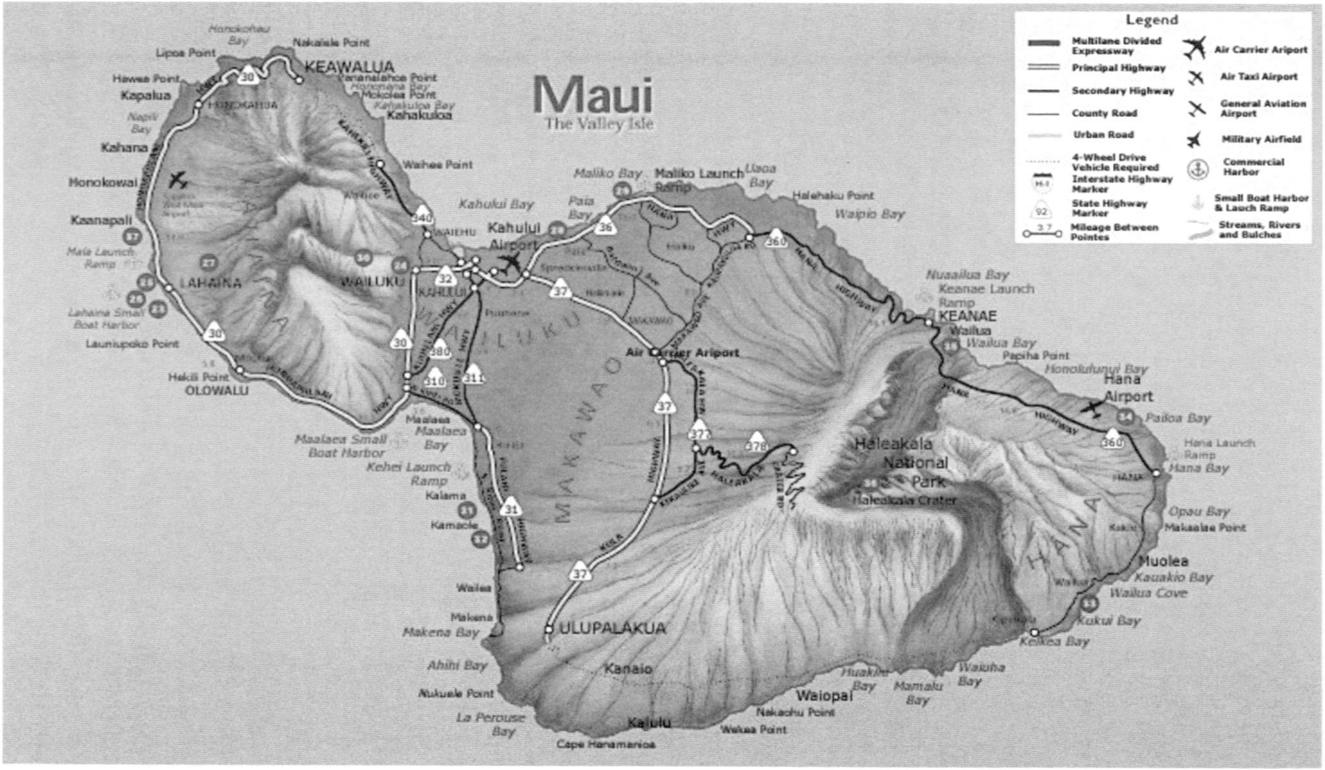

Figure 1.2. Roads Under State of Hawaii, Highways Division Jurisdiction, Maui District–Island of Maui (downloaded from http://hidot.hawaii.gov/highways/home/maui/maui-state-roads-and-highways/ on September 12, 2019)

at risk of erosion, and will eventually need to be replaced in certain locations (see Figure 1.3). For these reasons, pressure from Maui residents pining for a better commute are expected to build to a critical mass, and proponents for West Maui traffic alternatives should have enough political support to begin the conversation of a West Maui Mountains highway.

Initial Planning

A West Maui Mountains highway may take decades just to get the project started at the county, state, and federal levels. The present-day Maui County general plan, which replaced a prior general plan, is a term for a bundle of planning documents that guide future growth and policy direction in the county. The Countywide Policy Plan (CPP) acts as an overarching values statement and is an umbrella policy document for the county and community plans (see Figure 1.4).[10] The Maui Island Plan[11] functions as a regional plan and addresses the policies and issues that are not confined to just one community plan area, including regional systems such as transportation, utilities, and growth management for the Island of Maui. The Maui County Council adopted its first West Maui Community Plan in 1996[12] and its first Wailuku–Kahului Community

Figure 1.3. Sea-level rise will affect Honoapi'ilani Highway along the shoreline. Federal-Aid Highways 2035 Transportation Plan for the District of Maui, 2014:4-6

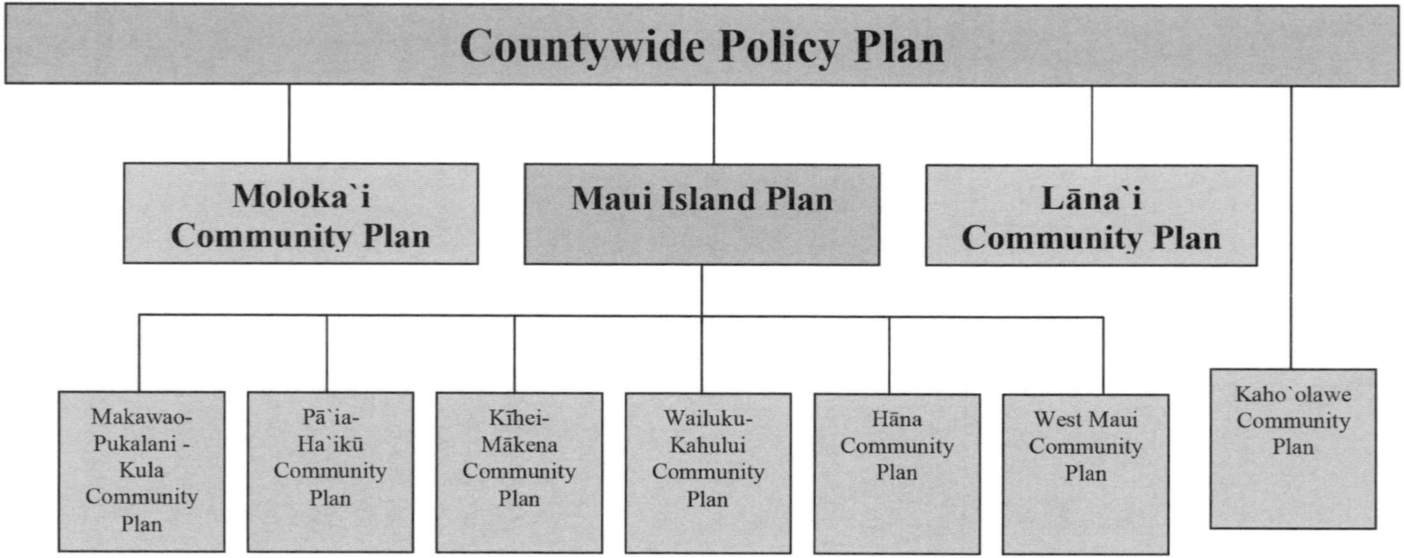

Figure 1.4. Relationship between Maui County community plans (Maui Island Plan, 2012: I–3)

Plan in 2002.[13] Presently, there is no direct mention of a West Maui Mountains highway in the aforementioned plans, and a West Maui Mountains highway is required to be consistent with its community development plans.[14]

A grassroots effort would be required to begin the conversation of a West Maui Mountains highway at the community level. The Maui County general plan and its community plans took years to complete and will take years to revise. The present-day CPP credited the Maui Economic Development Board with launching a broad-based public participation process to plan for the future of Maui County in 2003.[15] The effort brought together more than 1,700 participants into intensive, small-group participatory sessions to begin to define a vision for Maui County's future.[16] Because the Maui County general plan is a statement of residents' current needs and desires, the CPP largely incorporates the recommendations of Focus Maui Nui.[17] The CPP was eventually adopted in 2010. The Maui Island Plan was eventually adopted in 2012. A revision of the West Maui Community Plan, which was initially adopted in 1996, is expected in 2019.[18] The West Maui Community Plan will also be the first revised community plan in the county.[19] The other five Maui community plans will probably be revised before the Maui County general plan is updated. Assuming that it takes another few years to adopt all of its community plans and Maui County immediately begins revising its general plan and community plans, it will probably take on the order of fifteen years to incorporate a West Maui Mountains highway into the relevant plans.

A West Maui Mountains highway project, for funding and practical purposes, will also require federal support. The Statewide Federal-Aid Highways 2035 Transportation Plan and Federal-Aid Highways 2035 Transportation Plan for the District of Maui were both adopted in 2014 and have no mention of a West Maui Mountains highway. Both plans apply only to federal-aid highways on Maui.[20] Federal-aid highways are the National Highway System and all other public roads, except those federally classified as local roads or rural minor collectors. These roads are critical to providing for regional mobility; linking major sites such as airports, harbors, industrial areas, military facilities, major communities, and primary urban centers; and supporting commuter and freight travel. In addition to the connection between Kā'anapali/Lāhaina and Wailuku, a West Maui Mountains highway would also connect the Kapalua–West Maui Airport with the Kahului Maui International Airport (both of which are within the jurisdiction of the Federal Aviation Administration), and would almost certainly be considered a federal-aid highway.

Hawai'i's long-range transportation plan was developed with a minimum twenty-year forecast period.[21] Regional long-range transportation plans are developed in alignment with federal laws, thereby providing a link between statewide and regional planning efforts. The Federal-Aid Highways 2035 Transportation Plan for the District of Maui was an update of the Maui Long-Range Land Transportation Plan developed in 1997. Assuming that future federal plans follow a similar cycle, the next set of statewide and regional transportation plans that could include a West Maui Mountains highway would be drafted around 2030.

Assuming that Maui County general and community development plans, and state and regional long-range transportation plans, that are consistent with a future West Maui Mountains highway are drafted, project proponents will need to present the project for consideration as part of the State Transportation Improvement Program (STIP).[22] According to information provided by the State of Hawai'i Department of Transportation Highways Division's (HDOT-Highways), the STIP is a four-year program implementation plan that identifies federal, state, and county transportation projects that intend to be funded, in part, with federal highway and transit funds.[23] In addition to the four years of programmed funding under the most current version of the STIP, the Hawai'i STIP includes an additional two future illustrative years for information purposes only. The STIP must be fully updated at least every four years. Each update covers the next four-year period.[24]

The HDOT-Highways currently utilizes the following guideline to determine overall project selection. The HDOT-Highways notes that this overall method is not absolute and is subject to some intangible adjustments.[25]

First Priority

1. Mandated Projects, such as: (a) Americans with Disabilities Act (ADA), (b) Environmental Protection Agency (EPA) Compliance Projects;
2. Safety Projects, such as: (a) Hazard Elimination Program, (b) Guardrail Installation, (c) Rockfall/Slope Stabilization Mitigation; and
3. System Preservation Projects: (a) Bridge Program—Bridge Replacement, Bridge Rehabilitation/Widening, Seismic Retrofit, Bridge Lead Abatement, Bridge Repairs, Tunnel Repair, (b) Roadway Upgrades (no additional capacity), (c) Pavement Upgrades/Preservation.

Next Priority

1. Congestion Relief Projects, such as: (a) Traffic Signal Upgrades, (b) Operational Improvements (intersection improvements), (c) Intelligence Transportation System (ITS); and

2. Modernization Projects, such as: (a) Interim Capacity Improvement (road widening), (b) Regular or New Capacity Improvement (new roads or major widening).

Other Priority

1. Highway Planning and Research;
2. Non-highway Improvements (baseyards/maintenance facilities, buildings, etc.);
3. Bicycle/Pedestrian Facilities; and
4. Beautification/Landscaping.[26]

Planning and research for a West Maui Mountains highway would likely fall in the "Other Priority," item "1. Highway Planning and Research" category. Construction funding for a West Maui Mountains highway would likely fall within category "Next Priority," item "2. Modernization Projects such as [. . .] 2.b. Regular or New Capacity Improvement." Assuming that a West Maui Mountains highway project is approved and funded, it would take about a year to add the project-planning phase to the STIP, and additional years to add subsequent phases for the project.[27]

Assuming that contemporaneous efforts are made at the county, state, and federal levels, and said efforts are successful, it may take decades to include a West Maui Mountains highway project within the aforementioned plans. The first major task that would then require funding and approval is an environmental review.

Environmental Review—Generally

A West Maui Mountains highway would travel through the West Maui Forest Reserve, which lies within the State of Hawai'i Conservation District (see Figure 1.5). Because a West Maui Mountains highway would propose a use of land within the Conservation District, acceptance of an environmental impact statement (EIS) would be a condition precedent to approval of the request and commencement of the proposed project.[28] An EIS is an informational document that discloses the environmental effects of a proposed action, effects of a proposed action on the economic welfare, social welfare, and cultural practices of the community and state, effects of the economic activities arising out of the proposed action, measures proposed to minimize adverse effects, and alternatives to the action and their environmental effects.[29]

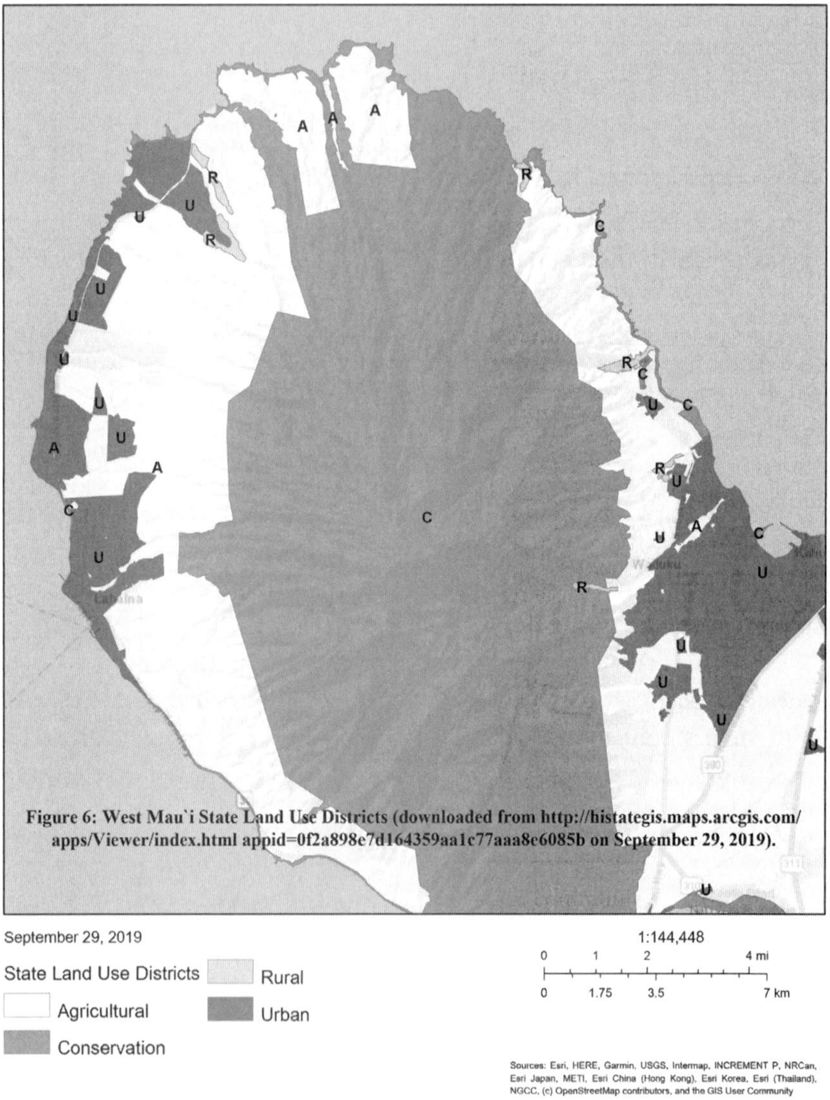

Figure 1.5. West Maui State Land Use Districts (downloaded from http://histategis .maps.arcgis.com/apps/Viewer/index.htmlappid=0f2a898e7d164359aa1c77aaa8e6085b on September 29, 2019)

H-3, a tunneled federal highway located on the island of Oʻahu that is comparable to a potential West Maui highway, was the first project in Hawaiʻi to require an EIS.[30] The environmental studies conducted for H-3 spanned twenty years and reached a height of four feet if stacked one on top of the other. During the construction of H-3, the DOT worked closely with numerous specialists in a variety of fields including archaeology, botany, ornithology, malacology, meteorology, history, folklore, Native Hawaiian culture, air/noise, bioelectromagnetics, water resources and hydrology. These studies added an enormous amount of information about Hawaiian history that would otherwise not have been available.[31] If funded, a similar effort would be needed for a West Maui Mountains highway.

Anticipated studies that would be required with an environmental review of a West Maui Mountains highway include, without limitation and in no particular order of importance, archaeological reports and surveys; cultural assessments; botanical, fauna, and invertebrate reports and surveys; and water quality studies. Archaeological reports and surveys as well as cultural assessments are required to ensure compliance with state historic preservation laws and protect the rights of Native Hawaiian practitioners. Botanical, fauna and invertebrate reports and surveys are required to address project impacts on plants, animals, and arthropods listed for protection by the State of Hawaiʻi Department of Land and Natural Resources or the U.S. Fish and Wildlife Service. Water quality studies will be required to assess whether the proposed project will adversely affect local water sources and coastal waters. These studies have a tremendous influence on projects like a West Maui Mountains highway because said projects are typically planned to avoid adversely affecting sensitive Native Hawaiian sites, protected species, and important island water sources. Depending on their results, they may halt a West Maui Mountains highway project.

Sensitive Native Hawaiian Sites

A West Maui Mountains highway should be planned to avoid Native Hawaiian sites that are considered sensitive. State historical preservation laws require the protection of certain sites identified or discovered during planning and construction.[32] Traditional and customary Native Hawaiian practices related to the West Maui Mountains are constitutionally protected.[33] *Kānaka Maoli,* which means full-blooded Hawaiian persons and is a distinction used to refer to present-day Native Hawaiians, have become more politically active in recent decades.[34] Once the majority of Hawaiʻi's population, Kānaka Maoli are now minorities in their own land.[35] During the late '60s and early '70s, a resurgence of the Hawaiian culture occurred and Kānaka Maoli started to realize that the perpetuation of their culture was important to restore the self-esteem of themselves and their children. Language, land issues, and identity have taken on greater importance to the Kānaka Maoli of today and, in their eyes, what was permissible to be built years ago on sacred grounds is now impermissible because of the importance of those sacred grounds to their culture.[36] The following addresses how a West Maui Mountains highway project may be planned to minimize adverse effects to sensitive Native Hawaiian sites.

Many prominent royals made their homes in Lāhainā, on the western slopes of Mauna Kahalawai, and the fertile lands in this region supported a vibrant population.[37] On the coastal lowlands, Kamehameha III made his home on an island in the fishpond called Moku'ula, which was fed by springs charged by mountain rain. Many of the lands to the south of Lāhainā contain remnants of ancient Hawaiian villages, agricultural terraces, petroglyphs and *heiau* (temple) sites, as well as many post-contact sites along the Lāhainā Pali Trail. To the north of Lāhainā are the six Hono-a-Pi'ilani, the bays of King Pi'ilani (from south to north), Honokōwai (bay drawing fresh water), Honokeana (cave bay), Honokahua (sites bay), Honolua (two bays), Honokōhau (bay drawing dew), and Hononana (animated bay), all of whose upper wet valleys contain vestiges of historic taro cultivation and many important sites including heiau, examples of historical agriculture and unknown burial sites.[38] For these reasons, excavation near lower portions of stream valleys or at the base of gulch walls or flat slopes in the present-day Lāhainā district are expected to yield evidence of historic Native Hawaiian habitation that may require preservation during the planning and construction phases of a West Maui Mountains highway.

In Wailuku, on the eastern slopes of Mauna Kahalawai, 'Īao Valley was considered one of the island's centers of civilization. Similar to Lāhaina, prominent ali'i, or chiefs, resided in this lush area, below which fertile soils and plentiful water supported a large resident population. 'Īao Stream is one of the Nā Wai 'Ehā, The Four Waters, which also included Waihe'e, Waiehu, and Waikapū Streams (see Figure 1.6).[39] With its abundance of fresh water, 'Īao Valley was a sacred place reserved for high chiefs, and for hundreds of years ali'i were laid to rest in secret burial sites along the valley's steep walls. The practice of burying ali'i in 'Īao Valley began in the eighth century and continued until 1736, with the burial of King Kekaulike.[40] Commoners were not permitted into 'Īao Valley, except during the annual Makahiki festival which was held on the grassy plateau above '*Īao* Needle. According to legend, Maui the demigod and Hina raised

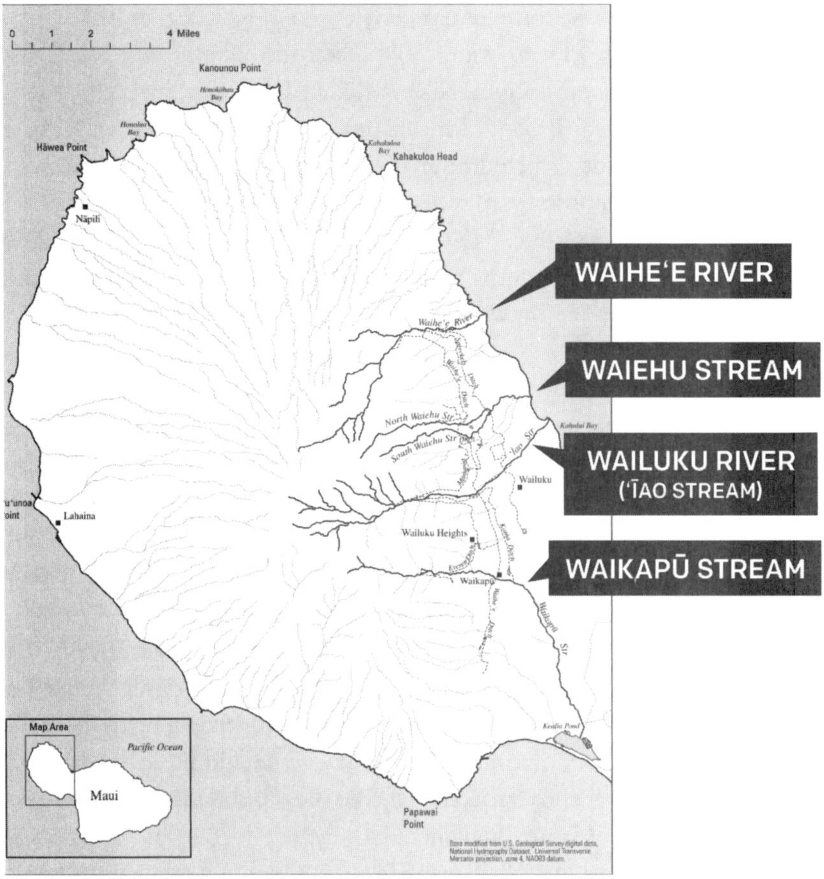

Figure 1.6. Map of the “Four Great Waters” of Maui (downloaded from https://earthjustice.org/sites/default/files/nwe-map-2792.jpg on September 12, 2019)

their daughter ‘Īao in the valley. ‘Īao became the lover of a half-man, half-fish god. This angered her father, who turned the man-fish into a pillar of stone that is now known as ‘Īao Needle.[41] Today, a 6.2-acre portion of ‘Īao Valley has also been designated as a state monument.[42] For these reasons, some may feel that ‘Īao Valley is too sensitive a site for a West Maui Mountains highway.

Shrouding the West Maui Mountains’ slopes, the native forest itself is of great cultural significance. Ancient Hawaiians believed they were direct kin of the plants and animals that shared their world and beings with great *mana*, spiritual power, could take on the form of other plants and animals. The upland forests were the sacred home of Ku, the god of war, governance, and leadership.

The forests were also the realm of Laka, goddess of hula and guardian of forest plants.[43]. In such a world, a person could talk directly to the winds and rains and expect a response, and animals like the ʻio, or Hawaiian hawk, could stand as a family's ancestral guardian.[44] The upland forest was *wao akua*, where entry required a strict protocol, including an offering and a statement of identity and purpose.[45] If the purpose were to collect trees, only a single specimen or species could be collected at a time.[46] For example, the taking of a large ʻōhiʻa was regarded as a sacred act, requiring a human sacrifice in return for the removal of the tree.[47] A highway project would be expected to address these issues during its planning phases.

Heiau indicate the presence of political power and the appropriate population to support the heiau. Early archaeological surveys identified seven heiau in the Kāʻanapali area.[48] Nā Wai ʻEhā was once home to 36 documented heiau—which was deemed the largest number of temples among all of Maui's communities.[49] At least eight heiau have been recorded in the vicinity of the ancient village of Lāhainā.[50] A West Maui Mountains highway would be expected to avoid heiau that are known or are discovered by the project.

Traditionally, Native Hawaiians often buried their dead in caves and lava tubes.[51] In order to protect the remains of loved ones from enemies who would desecrate them, Native Hawaiians searched for *lua meki* (deep pits) in the mountains, *lua huna* (hiding pits), and *ana huna* (hiding caves) along the deep ravines and sheer cliffs frequented by the *koaʻe* birds.[52] Because excavation is expected during construction of any highway, *iwi* (Native Hawaiian bones) may be uncovered during a West Maui Mountains highway project, and appropriate plans will be required to address these discoveries.

With respect to the upper regions of the West Maui Mountains, there are few if any known historical sites. At lower regions, however, specific locations may be important because of cultural significance.[53] Eleile Spring above Waiheʻe may not contain physical archeological remains, but is considered traditional cultural property because of its importance in story and song.[54] The lower reaches of the West Maui Mountains are visited periodically by Native Hawaiian practitioners for the gathering of plants for food preparation; hula costuming; medicine; scenting kapa, making spears, fishnets, feather capes, and heavy rope, and use of sticky fruits in capturing forest birds for feather work.[55] Native Hawaiians also gather freshwater animals that include, without limitation, mountain ʻōpae, ʻoʻopu, and hīhīwai.[56] These aquatic organisms thrive with abundant clean, cool stream flow and are dependent on healthy watersheds for their survival.[57] A West Maui Mountains highway would require years of archaeological and cultural assessments and surveys to identify sensitive Native Hawaiian sites and prepare plans to mitigate the project impact on said sites and existing Native Hawaiian traditional and customary practices.

Protected Native Hawaiian Species

A West Maui Mountains highway should also avoid native Hawaiian species that are protected by state and federal law. According to the State of Hawai'i Department of Land and Natural Resources, Hawai'i is referred to as the "Endangered Species Capital of the World." For example, more than 100 plant taxa have already gone extinct, and over 200 are considered to have 50 or fewer individuals remaining in the wild. While only comprising less than one percent of the United States' landmass, Hawai'i contains 44 percent of the nation's endangered and threatened plant species.[58] According to U.S. Fish and Wildlife Service figures, there are 79 animals and 424 plants that are listed as endangered species believed or known to occur in Hawai'i.[59]

The West Maui Mountains are home to thousands of species of native plants, birds, snails, insects and other arthropods. All native Hawaiian species are relatively rare in the world, and there are at least eighteen plant species that are endemic to West Maui in particular, making them especially extraordinary. The watershed encompasses an array of vegetation communities that are arranged across climatic and elevation zones. Studies in the West Maui Mountains watershed have already contributed to an improved understanding of evolution, unique genetic information transfer and other central biological concepts.[60] The broad range of native communities and rare species in the West Maui Mountains watershed are shown in Figure 1.7. The windward, northern regions host montane and lowland wet forests and shrublands, while the leeward, southern regions are home to montane and lowland dry and mesic forests and shrublands.[61] Arrays of rare species are found throughout the watersheds in varying environments.[62] The West Maui Mountains are home to a current count of approximately 146 rare plants, insects, birds, vegetation communities and one bat. As the forest continues to be explored, more unique species are found every year. As of 2013, the West Maui Mountains watershed contained 48 endangered species, one threatened, 13 candidate, and 84 species of concern tracked by state and federal agencies.[63]

Near the Pu'u Kukui summit at 5,788 feet, the landscape is dominated by montane bogs and wet, windswept shrublands that extend downward to more mesic forests and shrublands. Ki'owaiokihawahine represents a little-known

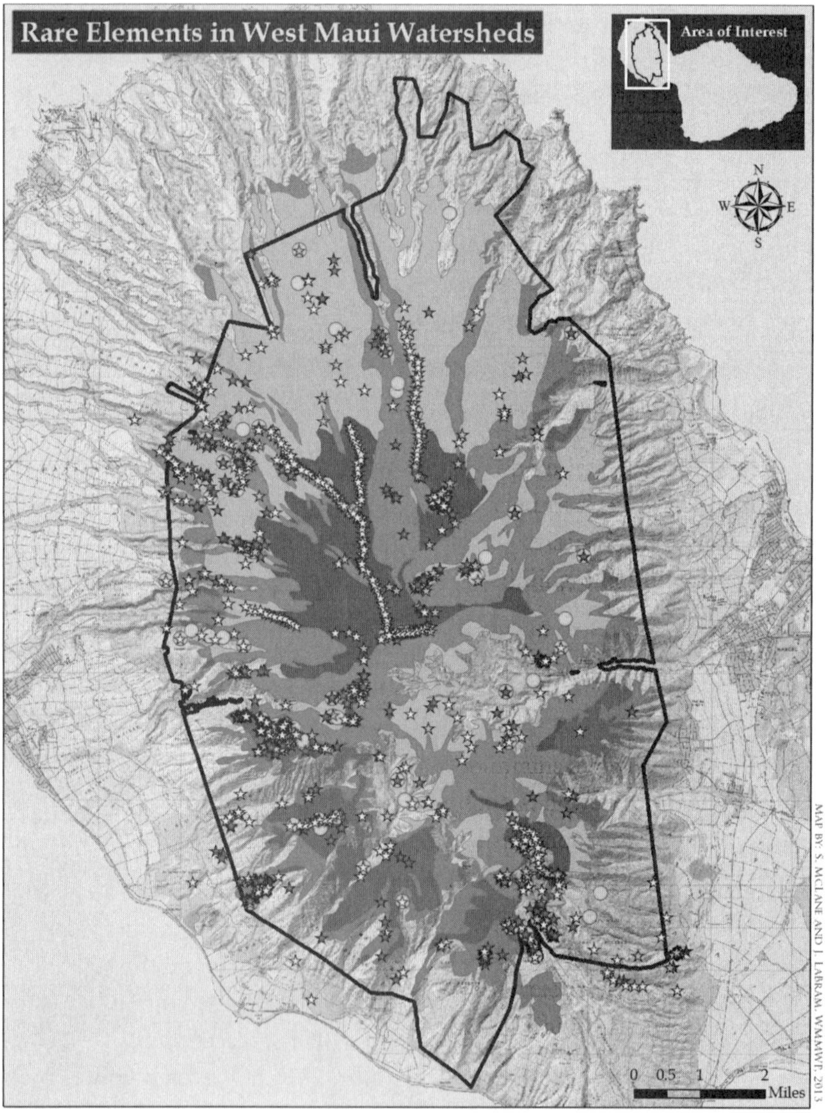

Figure 1.7. Map of rare species and native vegetation communities across the West Maui watersheds. West Maui Mountains Watershed Partnership, *West Maui Mountains Watershed Management Plan* 2013:13

ecosystem found only on Maui and Hawai'i.[64] Notable rare species that grow in this unique environment include 'ōhi'a, Hawaiian damselflies, and others. Other unusual ecosystems include Mauna 'Eke, a magmatic dome formed during the later years of the West Maui volcano. This plateau-like region is pocketed with deep sinkholes, bogs of standing water, and stunted yet pristine vegetation. These unique species include the 'Eke silversword, hinihina, and ko'oko'olau, as well as miniaturized giants like 'ōhi'a.[65]

Moving down the mountain slopes, other vegetation communities include koa forest, lama forest, diverse mesic forest with several dominant native tree species, and a variety of native shrubland types.[66] Uluhe ferns are common in these areas, and shrubs like pūkiawe and kanawao are frequently seen as well.[67] Below 3,000 feet elevation, there begins a transition from native-dominated into more alien-dominated vegetation types, with non-native trees and shrubs such as strawberry guava, ironwood, Koster's Curse, and others that grow increasingly prominent in a mixed native and alien canopy.[68] Below 2,000 feet, naturalized alien vegetation dominates, including varieties of guava forest and java plum, with the exception of small and sometime rare assemblages of native forest and shrubland stands such as wiliwili and naio. At the bottom edge of the watershed, plantings of introduced trees such as eucalyptus, Cook and Norfolk pines, silky oak, and naturalized alien vegetation occupy the lowest slopes.[69]

Maui is also home to a number of protected mammals. The West Maui Mountains watershed contains important habitat for at least three species of endangered birds: ua'u (Hawaiian dark-rumped petrel), nēnē (Hawaiian goose), and the koloa (Hawaiian duck). The ou is a forest bird once known in the area but is probably extinct. The U.S. Fish and Wildlife Service has proposed reintroducing the endangered forest bird akohekohe to West Maui. The ōpe'ape'a (Hawaiian hoary bat) has also been sighted on Maui.[70] The endangered ae'o or Hawaiian stilt has also been seen in West Maui.[71] Protected seabirds, including the Hawaiian petrel and the Newell's shearwater, may be adversely affected by this project.[72] These seabirds nest high in the mountains during the spring, summer and fall months. They fly over the lowlands during the late evening hours to reach their burrows and fly back to the ocean in the early dawn hours. These birds can be confused by bright lights and crash into poles, wires, and other structures and be injured or killed by the strike or by vehicles or animals such as cats, dogs, or mongoose. Young, inexperienced birds taking their inaugural fledgling flights in the late fall are particularly vulnerable.[73]

Once a potential highway path is identified, numerous endangered species studies will be required to locate protected native Hawaiian species, and plans will be necessary to avoid said species and mitigate the adverse effects caused by a West Maui Mountains highway. Due to the terrain of the area and the standard of care required to locate said species, numerous specialists will be required to perform the work, and these studies are expected to take years to complete.

Water Quality

Plans will be necessary to minimize the adverse effects of a highway project on the West Maui Mountains watershed. Water from the West Maui Mountains watershed is vitally important to the island—so important in fact, that public and private entities formed the West Maui Mountains Watershed Partnership (WMMWP) in 1998. The lands of the WMMWP encompass 47,319 acres of Mauna Kahalawai in the Lāhainā and Wailuku Districts of Maui Island.[74] Elevations on the Mauna Kahalawai range from near sea level on the southwest coast to 5,788 feet on the wet rainforest summit Puʻu Kukui.[75] On the summit and upper slopes of West Maui, cool air saturated with moisture sweeps across native forest and shrubland thickly clothed with foliage and epiphytic mosses. Even without rainfall, forest vegetation pulls moisture directly out of clouds and fog, and the condensed moisture falls upon a thick ground cover of native ferns and shrubs.[76] Studies have shown that a native Hawaiian forest can intercept fog drip to increase precipitation by as much as 30 percent, and as much as 10 to 15 percent of the recharge to our aquifers is thought to be from this fog drip alone.[77] West Maui's forests have a large area known as the "fog zone" where this type of condensation is a large part of the hydrologic cycle in the windward units. These areas are priority recharge areas for aquifers where healthy foliage and leaf litter buffer the release of stored water, delivering a more consistent and dependable source of water for eventual use long after the rain has ceased falling.[78]

The summit of Mauna Kahalawai experiences an average annual rainfall of 364 inches, making it one of the wettest places on the planet.[79] This rainfall contributes to 69 stream channels that originate from the watershed. Sixteen of these channels have sections that are continuous-perennial (flowing year-round), and the rest have reaches of intermittent and non-perennial flow (flowing year-round at upper elevations only, and intermittently at lower elevations). An estimated 25.55 billion gallons of fresh water can be provided each year by the West Maui Mountains watershed. This water is funneled to the communities of West Maui, Wailuku, Kahului, Pāʻia and Kīhei-Makena, providing water to approximately 77 percent of Maui County Department of Water Supply customers on Maui, in addition to many others on private systems (see Figure 1.8).[80]

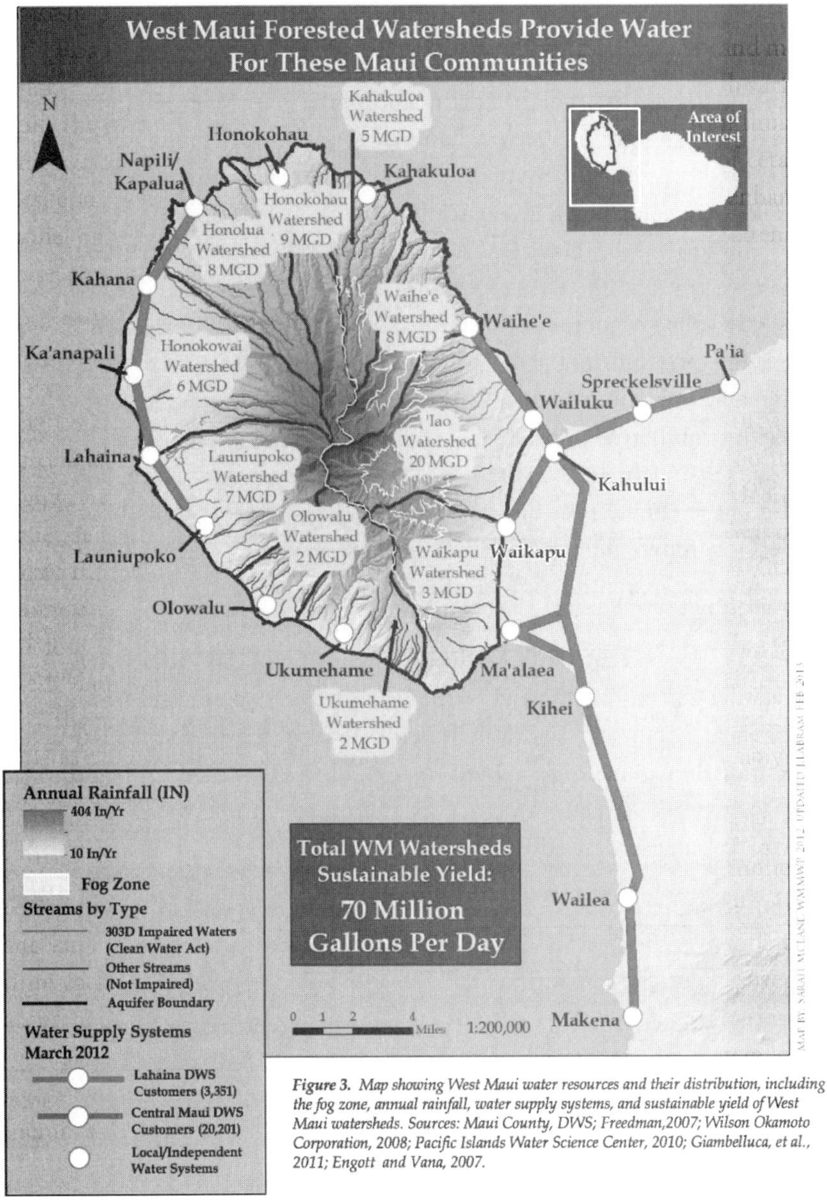

Figure 1.8. West Maui Forested Watersheds. West Maui Mountains Watershed Partnership, *West Maui Mountains Watershed Management Plan* 2013:15

Forested watersheds act as sponges, soaking up drip and precipitation that recharge both streams and aquifers. Native Hawaiian vegetation in particular has been shown to be more efficient at absorbing and collecting precipitation than a non-native forest, with almost twice the canopy water storage capacity of an invaded site. Indeed, the pristine core of the West Maui Mountains watershed is a key groundwater recharge area. Native forests are multilayer complexes of canopy trees, understory plants, shrubs, ferns, and mosses that absorb the kinetic energy of falling rain, reducing the rain's erosive capacity and increasing the infiltration of the rainwater into the ground. During photosynthesis, plants release water vapor into the atmosphere through evaporation and transpiration, a process called evapotranspiration. Evapotranspiration is increased in warm and sunny conditions. Open grasslands lose far more water to evapotranspiration than closed forest or shrubland. The cool ground-level shade provided by a healthy, multilayered forest will protect the water-holding layers from wind and harsh sunlight and suppress evapotranspirative loss of water. This allows much of the rainfall and condensed fog drip to percolate through the soil and collect in aquifers and streams as clean water.[81]

Another major function of a forested watershed is that of a soil anchor.[82] The roots of trees, shrubs, and associated understory plants grip the steep mountain slopes tenaciously, holding soils in place. In this way, forest trees and vegetation prevent erosion and maintain clear, clean water in streams that flow out to nearshore reefs and coastal waters.[83] Years of studies may be required to determine how a West Maui Mountains highway would affect the watershed and the quality of island water, and significant planning will be required to ensure that any adverse effects are minimized.

Other Issues

In addition to the issues described above, transportation-related EISes typically include studies that address how the project affects the environment's socioeconomics, traffic, climate and air quality, noise, geology, wildfire hazard, coastal zone, hazard materials risk, scenic character, and more. Briefly, a West Maui Mountains highway is expected to positively affect the island's socioeconomics and traffic, because people would move around the island more freely and quickly. But for those same reasons, the highway is expected to adversely affect climate and air quality, noise, geology, wildfire hazard, the coastal zone, hazardous materials risk, and scenic character. Site-specific issues are expected to include addressing areas used for recreation such as hiking, hunting, and dirt biking.[84] A West Maui Mountains highway would also need to avoid or replace existing infrastructure such as fencing, wells, and roads.

Cooperation by and between numerous property owners, governmental agencies, and private/public organizations would be required to pursue a West Maui Mountains highway project. For example, as of 2013, parties participating in the West Maui Mountains Watershed Program include the major landowners and land managers of the West Maui Mountains: the Hawai'i State Department of Land and Natural Resources; the Maui County Department of Water Supply; Ka'anapali Land Management Corp.; The Nature Conservancy of Hawai'i; Kahoma Land Company, LLC; Kamehameha Schools; Makila Land Co., LLC; Wailuku Water Company, Inc.; Maui Land & Pineapple Company, Inc.; the General Finance Group; the County of Maui; Tri-Isle Resource Conservation & Development Council, Inc.; and the U.S. Fish & Wildlife Service.[85] The West Maui Mountains Watershed Program manages the portion of the West Maui Mountains that are within the conservation district; therefore, this list excludes owners with properties that lie outside the district and would be affected by a highway route, and nonowner stakeholders with pro- and antidevelopment interests.

If an EIS is accepted, a West Maui Mountains highway would require permits or approvals (with decision-making governmental entities in parentheses) that include, without limitation:

- Conservation District Use Permit (State of Hawai'i Board of Land and Natural Resources)
- Coastal Zone Management Act Federal Consistency Review (State of Hawai'i Department of Business, Economic Development, and Tourism Office of Planning)
- Section 106 Consultation pursuant to the National Historic Preservation Act (State of Hawai'i Historic Preservation Officer)
- Section 7 Consultation pursuant to the Endangered Species Act (U.S. Fish and Wildlife Service)
- Department of the Army Approved Jurisdictional Determination Update pursuant to Section 404 of the Clean Water Act (U.S. Army Corps of Engineers)
- Section 4(f) of the U.S. Department of Transportation Act (Federal Highway Administration)

- National Pollutant Discharge Elimination System (NPDES) Permit (State of Hawaiʻi Department of Health)
- Historic Preservation Review pursuant to HRS Chapter 6E (State of Hawaiʻi Department of Land and Natural Resources, State Historic Preservation Division)
- Americans with Disabilities Act Review pursuant to HRS § 103-50 (State of Hawaiʻi Department of Health Disability and Communication Access Board)
- Occupancy and Use of State Highway Right-of-Way Permit (DOT)
- Community Noise Permit/Variance (State of Hawaiʻi Department of Health)
- Grading, grubbing, and stockpiling permit (County of Maui Department of Public Works)

Although many of the requirements related to the above approvals would have been addressed by an EIS (which would likely have been prepared prior to submitting applications for the above approvals) and some requests may be processed simultaneously, it may take years to apply for and receive said approvals. It is also possible that other approvals, for example, a special management area permit, may also be required.[86]

In the past, many parties have filed lawsuits successfully challenging the process or approval of the aforementioned permits for similar large-scale or transportation-related projects.[87] It is expected that similar efforts will be pursued if a West Maui Mountains highway project is initiated. For this reason, years of litigation should be added to the scheduling of a project like a West Maui Mountains highway.

Construction

The physical construction of a West Maui Mountains highway would probably take years to complete and cost billions of dollars; however, in comparison to the issues above and assuming that funding is provided, construction should be fairly straightforward. A West Maui Mountains highway would almost certainly have one or more tunnels to avoid adversely affecting sensitive Native Hawaiian sites, protected native Hawaiian species, and important watershed resources. Additionally, techniques have been developed by and through constructing H-3 to minimize the adverse effects that a highway may have through the West Maui Mountains (see Figure 1.9).

Figure 1.9. H-3 Freeway. Marilyn Kali, Hawaii's Interstate H-3 Freeway, Hawaii Department of Transportation, Public Affairs Office, 1997:2

Tunneling

Road tunnels are enclosed roadways with vehicle access that is restricted to portals regardless of type of structure or method of construction.[88] Road tunnels are feasible alternatives to traverse physical barriers such as mountains, existing roadways, railroads, or facilities; or to satisfy environmental or ecological requirements. In addition, road tunnels are visible means to minimize potential environmental impact such as traffic congestion, pedestrian movement, air quality, noise pollution, or visual intrusion; to protect areas of special cultural or historical value such as conservation of districts, buildings or private properties;

or for other sustainability reasons such as to avoid impact on natural habitat or reduce disturbance to surface land.[89] Here, a tunnel may provide the only feasible way to avoid sensitive Native Hawaiian sites, protected native Hawaiian species, and adversely affecting island water quality.

Planning for a road tunnel requires multidisciplinary involvement and assessments, and should generally adopt the same standards as for surface roads and bridge options, with some exceptions.[90] Certain considerations, such as lighting, ventilation, life safety, and operation and maintenance should be addressed specifically for tunnels. In addition to the capital construction cost, a life-cycle cost analysis should be performed, taking into account the life expectancy of a tunnel. It should be noted that the life expectancies of tunnels are significantly longer than those of other facilities such as bridges or roads.[91]

Successfully planning, designing and constructing a road tunnel project requires various types of investigative techniques to obtain a broad spectrum of pertinent topographic, geologic, subsurface, geo-hydrological, and structure information and data.[92] Generally, an investigation program for planning and design of a road tunnel project may include the following components:

- Existing Information Collection and Study
- Surveys and Site Reconnaissance
- Geologic Mapping
- Subsurface Investigations
- Environmental Studies
- Seismicity
- Geospatial Data Management

Similar investigations and monitoring are often needed during and after the construction to ensure the problems that occurred during construction are rectified or compensated, and short-term impacts are reversed.[93]

Road tunnels are often lined with concrete and internal finish surfaces.[94] Some rock tunnels are unlined except at portals and in certain areas where the rock is less competent. In this case, rock reinforcement is often needed. Rock reinforcement for initial support includes the use of rock bolts with internal metal straps and mine ties, untensioned steel dowels, or tensioned steel bolts. To prevent small fragments of rock from spalling, wire mesh, shotcrete, or a thin concrete lining may be used. Shotcrete can also be used as a final lining, or as a local solution to instabilities in a rock tunnel. It is typically placed in layers with welded wire fabric and/or steel fibers as reinforcement. The inside surface can be finished smooth and often without the fibers. Precast segmental lining is primarily used in conjunction with a tunnel-boring machine in soft ground and sometimes in rock. The segments are usually erected within the tail shield of the tunnel-boring machine. Segmental linings have been made of cast iron, steel, and concrete. Presently, however, all segmental linings are made of concrete. They are usually gasketed and bolted to prevent water penetration. Precast segmental linings are sometimes used as a temporary lining within which a cast-in-place final lining is placed, or as the final lining.[95]

Road tunnels are often finished with interior finishes for safety and maintenance requirements. The walls and the ceilings often receive a finish surface, while the roadway is often paved with asphalt pavement. The interior finishes, which usually are mounted or adhered to the final lining, consist of ceramic tiles, epoxy-coated metal panels, or various coatings. They provide enhanced tunnel lighting and visibility, provide fire protection for the lining, attenuate noise, and provide a surface easy to clean.[96]

Lessons from H-3

The DOT constructed H-3 in the latter half of the twentieth century, and lessons learned from H-3 would be applicable to a West Maui Mountains highway. H-3 was originally envisioned as a six-lane highway through Moanalua Valley at a cost of $250 million.[97] Thirty-seven years later, the highway was completed through H*ā*lawa Valley at a cost of $1.3 billion.[98] The H-3's Trans-Koʻolau Tunnels are the longest tunnels in Hawaiʻi.[99] The Hālawa-bound tunnel is 5,165 feet long and the K*ā*neʻohe-bound tunnel is 4,890 feet long.[100] Assuming that a West Maui Mountains highway is constructed at a similar cost and schedule as H-3, the project would take about ten years to construct, and assuming increased expenses due to inflation-driven labor and material costs, would probably cost billions of dollars.

The H-3 Trans-Koʻolau Tunnels were driven through both sides of the Koʻolau mountains through soil and volcanic rock using the latest tunneling techniques.[101] Holes were drilled in the rock, and explosives were set in place and later blasted. The tunnels were blasted approximately ten feet at a time from each side. When the two bores met, the laser survey techniques were so accurate that the two bores were only a fraction of an inch off in dimensions.[102]

When the excavation was complete, the tunnel was lined with a temporary layer of welded wire fabric and sprayed-on cement mortar. A plastic waterproof membrane was also placed at certain locations. Using tunnel lining forms, concrete was pumped into the forms in fifty-foot sections to create the walls and ceiling of the tunnel. The concrete lining is a minimum of 14 inches thick throughout the tunnel. A false ceiling was poured to create air plenums above it for the tunnel ventilation.[103]

Multistory portal buildings housing the ventilation, mechanical, electrical, and control systems support the tunnel operations. Each portal building houses four supply and four exhaust fans. Each fan is approximately 200 horsepower and capable of moving 210,000 cubic feet of air per minute when operated at high speed.[104] Supply air is delivered through a plenum above the tunnel ceiling and forced down to just above roadway level through precast wall panels.[105] The air is discharged into the tunnels through air ports spaced every five feet along the right shoulder of each tunnel.[106] Fresh air is swept across the roadway and then pulled up into the exhaust ports located in the ceiling above the left traffic turn lane. The carbon monoxide levels are monitored at 1,000-foot intervals and continually analyzed by sophisticated computers.[107]

Due to the sensitive location of the highways, the following innovative construction techniques were used to construct H-3:

- Instead of piledriving for piers, the DOT chose drilled shafts and cast-in-place concrete piers. This method reduced noise during construction, was suitable in a wide range of soil conditions, and was capable of carrying very large loads. The extensive use of drilled shafts for H-3 bridge foundations has advanced the knowledge and experience of engineers and contractors and has made the use of shafts a common practice in the islands.
- The concrete segmental viaducts on either side of the H-3 tunnel have long spans to reduce the number of piers, minimizing disruption of the land below. A color additive was used in the concrete mix to make the tunnel portals blend in with the mountainsides.
- Geotextiles were used extensively during clearing operations to prevent erosion.
- To maintain stream water quality, silt fences were installed along the stream alignment during construction to filter transported sediment.
- Using a lightweight fill of expanded polystyrene blocks, which are 80 times lighter than soil, for constructing a 70-foot-high embankment for the runaway truck ramp on soft ground avoided construction delays, reduced ground settlement and increased the stability of the embankment.

- Erosion control matting and hydromulching were used extensively to prevent erosion and to encourage quick regrowth of native vegetation.[108]

It is expected that the same construction practices developed to complete H-3 would be applied to a West Maui Mountains highway.

One of the most cost effective efforts made during the H-3 project was the construction of a mile-long exploratory tunnel through the Koʻolau Range.[109] This 13-foot-diameter tunnel was located beneath and between the main tunnels. Construction of the exploratory tunnel allowed engineers to determine the least expensive tunneling methods, water table and other data necessary to design the final tunnels. These data saved millions of dollars in construction costs by eliminating the need to budget for geological uncertainties. The exploratory tunnel also allowed the testing of various types of rock and ground support, including shotcrete and specially designed rock bolts. It now provides easy and safe access between the windward and leeward portals and to the main tunnels for maintenance.[110] A similar exploratory tunnel may be used for a West Maui Mountains highway and would be expected to provide comparable results.

Lastly, post-construction studies from H-3 may be useful for a West Maui Mountains highway. For example, from 1987 to 1997, the physical environments of North Hālawa Valley and Haiku Valley were disturbed by the construction of H-3.[111] However, in the short time since construction was completed, the valleys began recovering naturally as well as with the help of H-3 environmental mitigation measures such as replanting, best management practices, and terraced walls constructed on side slopes. During construction of H-3, several historical sites were discovered that were considered significant, and those sites were turned over to the Office of Hawaiian Affairs for restoration and protection.[112] Now that decades have passed since H-3 was opened, this environmental recovery and historical preservation may be confirmed, and said recovery and preservation techniques may be applied to a West Maui Mountains highway.

Potential Routes

The following assesses three potential West Maui Mountains highway routes: Kāʻanapali to Waiheʻe, Lāhainā to Waikapū, and ʻĪao Valley to Lāhainā. Of these routes, the ʻĪao Valley to Lāhainā route is the most natural path for a mountain highway; however, will probably be disqualified for cultural and water quality reasons. Additionally, the forested upper regions of the mountains are dominated by native tree species and are the most likely areas where endangered species may reside; therefore, each of these paths should begin, continue, and end below the 3,000 foot elevation mark where a transition from native-dominated vegetation to alien-dominated vegetation exists.

Kāʻanapali to Waiheʻe

The ancient Kāʻanapali district was noted for an *alaloa* (a long path or trail) that reportedly encircled the entire island.[113] "The north end of Maui also is traversed by a paved trail. Sections of it can be seen from Honolua to Honokohau to Kahukuloa. It is paved with beach rocks and has a width of four to six feet.... This trail is also spoken of as the Kihapiilani Trail."[114] A West Maui Mountains highway may run roughly parallel and *mauka* (toward the mountain) to this coastal trail to connect Kāʻanapali to Waiheʻe.

The northern portion of the West Maui Mountains contain numerous valleys that extend radially from Mount ʻEke. The rough terrain likely made these areas difficult to travel through and settle. Historically, relatively few Native Hawaiians occupied the northern portion of the West Maui Mountains, and those populations were concentrated along the coastline (see Figure 1.10). Even today, government roads along the coast require four-wheel drive, and relatively few people live in this area (see Figure 1.2). For these reasons, the likelihood that archaeological surveys will unearth historical sites worthy of preservation here is the lowest of the three routes. A Kāʻanapali–Waiheʻe route should also stay north of Na Wai ʻEha to minimize adverse effects to these West Maui Mountains watersheds. Additionally, since the existing roadways along the northern shore of West Maui are lightly travelled, a northern West Maui Mountains highway route would not be visible from most of the island, and would attract less attention than other potential routes. Conversely, multiple bridges and tunnels may be required to traverse the area, and a highway built along this route may be the most difficult to construct and the most expensive of the three potential routes discussed here.

The presence of protected and endangered species may provide the greatest challenge to a Kāʻanapali–Waiheʻe highway route. First, the ridges north of Mauna ʻEke may have the highest concentration of endangered species in the West Maui Mountains watershed (see Figure 1.7). One may reasonably assume that because so few people reside in or travel through the northern West Maui Mountains region, there may be rare native Hawaiian species that have not yet been discovered. One may also assume that because the region is so difficult to traverse, flora, fauna, and arthropod surveys of potential routes will be extremely costly and take years to complete. For these reasons, it is possible that the dis-

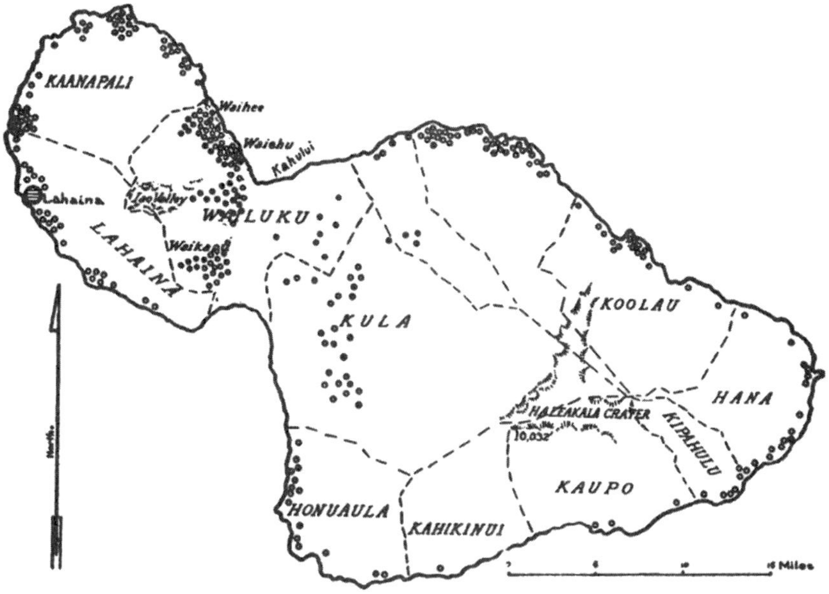

Figure 1.10. Map of Maui, area 728 square miles, showing distribution of population in 1853, o=50 persons, Lahaina, 2,750 people. Christopher Monahan, *Supplemental Archival Research on Cultural, Historical, and Archaeological Resources and Practices in Support of the Waihe'e Ridge Trail Environmental Assessment*, TCP Hawaii, LLC, 2016:9

covery of protected species in this area may be found in populations sufficient enough to prevent the construction of any highway through the northern West Maui Mountains.

Lāhainā to Waikapū

As in Kāʻanapali, trails from Lāhainā once extended from the coast to the mountains, linking regions for economic and social reasons.[115] The *ala nui* ("King's trail" built by Kihapiʻilani) extended along the coast, passing through all the major communities between Lāhainā and Mākena. A potential West Maui Mountains highway would be well mauka of this trail, through the southern West Maui Mountains, and connect Lāhainā and Waikapū.[116]

Potential Lāhainā-to-Waikapū highway routes may pass through dry cliffs or lowland dry shrubland and grassland; therefore, the likelihood of locating protected native Hawaiian species here is low. This conclusion is supported by flora and fauna surveys performed nearby.[117] For these reasons, if a highway tunnel through the southern West Maui Mountains is constructed below the

3,000-foot elevation line, endangered species are expected to be a nonissue through this route.

The potential presence of sensitive Native Hawaiian sites may prevent construction through a Lāhainā-to-Waikapū route. Many of the lands to the south of Lāhainā contain remnants of ancient Hawaiian villages, agricultural terraces, petroglyphs and heiau sites, as well as many post-contact sites along the Lāhainā Pali Trail.[118] Historically, many Native Hawaiians were spread throughout the Waikapū area (see Figure 1.10). The area is also replete with events of important Hawaiian history. For example, the Battle of Kakanilua, between *ali'i nui* (chief) Kahekili of Maui and Kalani'ōpu'u of Hawai'i, took place between Waikapū and Wailuku.[119] Kalani'ōpu'u planned to enter Wailuku via Kakanilua; however Kahekili's men occupied Kama'oma'o and the Waikapū area. Instead, Kalani'ōpu'u's men were ambushed by Kahekili's army, where scores of "spears, javelins, and other missiles poured like water." Kalani'ōpu'u's army was annihilated in what was called *Ahulau Ka Pi'ipi' i Kakanilua*, or *Slaughter-of-the Pi'ipi' i-at-Kakanilua*, one of the most legendary battles of pre-contact Hawai'i.[120] The guardian spirits of men, the 'aumakua spirits, were known to wander on the lower, sandy plains of Waikapū. This was a special place for the souls of the soldiers killed at Kakanilua.[121] An early missionary survey of this area mentioned thousands of human remains, which were most likely those from the Battle of Kakanilua.[122] Although the area had been under sugarcane production for years and iwi may have been destroyed or heavily disturbed, it is possible that earthwork on these lands may unearth human remains along this part of a proposed West Maui Mountains highway. For these reasons, years of archaeological surveys and cultural investigations may be required to locate an acceptable path that avoids sensitive Native Hawaiian sites along the Lāhainā-to-Waikapū mountain highway route.

'Īao Valley to Lāhainā

A walking path between Lāhainā and Wailuku through 'Īao Valley has been referenced historically on numerous occasions (see Figure 1.11). It is said that three roads connected Wailuku to Lāhainā.[123] One treacherous road that connected Lāhainā to Wailuku via 'Īao Valley is said to have been traversed by "adventurous residents" and "visitors" alike.[124] This passage has been described by the following.

> The tract leads right over the mountain, the ascent being made through a great gulch that lies close to Lahaina up to what is known as the Wailuku

Figure 1.11. West Maui Mountains and ʻĪao Valley. Maui Island Plan, 2012: 7–1

> Pass, and thence down the Iao Valley, of which I have already spoken. . . . It is perhaps the very best way of all by which to approach the wonder and beauties of the great gorge of the Iao.[125]

According to accounts of the Battle of ʻĪao, people fled Kamehameha to Kauwaʻupali ("precipice climbers" or "clawed of the cliff") and ʻĪao Needle, scrambling up the steep cliffs to escape.[126] Women, children, and the elderly fled up the gulch called Aʻi, and known as Black Gorge. Chief Kalanikupule and other Maui aliʻi are said to have escaped over the *pali* (cliff) to Lāhainā, where they secured canoes and fled to Oʻahu. Because it appears that one may reach Lāhainā from Wailuku through ʻĪao Valley by foot, ʻĪao Valley is probably the most direct route for a Wailuku-Lāhainā West Maui Mountains highway and would probably be the least costly of these three routes to construct.

Nevertheless, it is difficult to believe that ʻĪao Valley would ever be selected as the site of a highway project. As noted above, ʻĪao Valley was used for royal burials, was the location of one of the most famous battles in Hawaiian history, is the home of famous landmarks like the ʻĪao Needle, and is well represented in Native Hawaiian tales and folklore. Construction of highway columns or tunnels would require excavation that may uncover *royal* iwi and disturb or destroy historical landmarks, and therefore would likely raise significant opposition from the Kanaka Maoli and other similar stakeholders. An ʻĪao Valley–Lāhainā highway route would also travel through the Na Wai ʻEha, West Maui's largest watershed, and may adversely affect a significant portion of Maui's water supply (see Figures 1.5 and 1.8.) Any discussion regarding an ʻĪao Valley–Lāhainā highway route will probably be included in future West Maui Mountains highway plans for the purpose of specifically excluding this route from said plans.

Conclusion

A West Maui Mountains tunneled highway connecting Wailuku to Lāhainā/Kāʻanapali is feasible; however, it will take decades to plan and build, and probably cost billions of dollars to construct. Completion will largely depend on whether tunnels and bridges may be routed to minimize adverse effects to sensitive Native Hawaiian sites, protected species, and island water quality. If approved, construction of a tunneled highway is expected to be relatively straightforward because of lessons already learned by and through construction of H-3. Potential routes include, without limitation, Kāʻanapali to Waiheʻe, Lāhainā to Waikapū, or ʻĪao Valley to Lāhainā, with the ʻĪao Valley-to-Lāhainā route as the least likely selection of the three routes.

Notes

1. Dagan, Colleen, Robert Hill, Tanya L. Lee-Greig, and Hallett H. Hammatt, *Supplemental Cultural Impact Assessment for the Proposed Advanced Technology Solar Telescope (ATST) at Haleakalā High Altitude Observatories Papaʻanui Ahupuaʻa, Makawao District, Island of Maui TMK: (2) 2-2-2-07:008*, Cultural Surveys Hawaiʻi, Inc., 2007.
2. Ibid.
3. West Maui Mountains Watershed Partnership (WMMWP), *West Maui Mountains Watershed Management Plan*, 2013:18.
4. Ibid.
5. Perzinski, David and Michael Dega, *An Archaeological Assessment for the West Maui*

Well No. 2 Exploratory, DWS Job No. 11-06, Lahaina, Kahana Ahupuaʻa, Lahaina (Kaʻanapali) District, Maui, Hawaiʻi [TMK (2) 4-3-001:017], 2013:8.

6. Ibid. (citation omitted.)
7. Dagan, 2007:7.
8. Perzinski, David, and Michael Dega, *Archaeological Field Inspection and Literature Review for the Proposed Lāhainā No. 3 Force Main Replacement Project in Lāhainā, Wahikuli and Hanakāʻoʻo Ahupuaʻa, Lāhainā District, Island of Maui, Hawaiʻi [TMK (2) 4-4-13 (por), 4-5-21 (por)]*, 2009:12, citation omitted.
9. Federal Aid Highways 2035 Transportation Plan for the District of Maui at App. D at 52.
10. Countywide Policy Plan (CPP) as adopted by Maui County Council Ordinance No. 3732, effective date March 24, 2010 at 2.
11. Maui Island Plan, as adopted by Maui County Council Ordinance No. 4004, Effective date of Dec. 28, 2012.
12. West Maui Community Plan, as adopted by Maui County Council Ordinance No. 2476, 1996.
13. Wailuku-Kahului Community Plan, as adopted by Maui County Council Ordinance No. 3061, 2002.
14. See, *e.g.*, Maui County Code § 2.80B.070 ("Each community plan shall contain: [...] 10. A description of a projected multi-modal transportation system showing existing and proposed roadways, transit corridors, bikeways, and major thoroughfares."); *Gatri v. Blane*, 88 Hawaiʻi 108, 962 P.2d 367 (1998) (requiring that a development shall be consistent with the community plan).
15. CPP at 3.
16. Ibid.
17. Ibid.
18. www.mauicounty.gov/423/Community-Plans. *Accessed* September 11, 2019.
19. Ibid.
20. See ibid. at 1–2.
21. 23 United States Code 135.
22. 23 Code of Federal Regulations § 450.218(k).
23. http://hidot.hawaii.gov/highways/other/other-related-links/stip/. *Accessed* August 4, 2019.
24. Ibid.
25. Ibid.
26. Ibid.
27. Ibid.
28. Hawaiʻi Revised Statutes (HRS) § 343-5.
29. HRS § 343-2.
30. Kali, Marilyn. Hawaii's Interstate H-3 Freeway, Hawaii Department of Transportation, Public Affairs Office, 1997.

31. Ibid.
32. HRS Chapter 6E.
33. Hawai'i Constitution, Article XII, Section 7.
34. Maxwell, Kahu Charles Kauluwehi, and Adrian K. Kamali'i, *Cultural Resource Evaluation and Traditional Practices of the Proposed Advanced Technology Solar Telescope (ATST) at Haleakalā High Altitude Observatories*, CKM Cultural Resources, L.L.C., Pukalani, Hawai'i, 2006:iii.
35. Ibid. at iv.
36. Ibid.
37. WMMWP, 2013:19.
38. Ibid.
39. Ibid.
40. Ibid. (citation omitted).
41. Ibid.
42. https://dlnr.hawaii.gov/dsp/parks/maui/iao-valley-state-monument/. Downloaded on September 11, 2019.
43. Ibid.
44. Ibid. at 19–20 (citation omitted).
45. Ibid. at 20.
46. Ibid.
47. Ibid. (citation omitted).
48. Dagher, Cathleen, and Michael F. Dega, *Archaeological Inventory Survey for the Proposed West Maui Water Source Development Project Mahinahina Well (State Well No. 6-5638-004) (West Maui Well No. 1) and The Kahana Well (State Well No. 6-5738-002) (The West Maui Well No. 2)*, Scientific Consultant Services, Inc., 2019:23.
49. Monahan, Christopher, *Supplemental Archival Research on Cultural, Historical, and Archaeological Resources and Practices in Support of the Waihe'e Ridge Trail Environmental Assessment (EA)*, TCP Hawaii, LLC, 2016:8.
50. Perzinski, 2009:7.
51. Dagher, Cathleen, *A Cultural Impact Assessment for the Proposed West Maui Water Source Development Project Mahinahina Well (State Well No. 6-5638-004) (West Maui Well No. 1) and The Kahana Well (State Well No. 6-5738-002) (The West Maui Well No. 2)*, Scientific Consultant Services, Inc., 2019:59.
52. Ibid. (citation omitted).
53. *Final Environmental Assessment for the West Maui Mountains Watershed Protection Project*, The West Maui Mountains Watershed Partnership (WMMWP), 2001:9.
54. See Ibid.
55. See Ibid. at 10.
56. See Ibid. at 10–11.
57. See Ibid. at 11.

58. https://dlnr.hawaii.gov/ecosystems/rare-plants/. *Accessed on* August 23, 2019.
59. https://ecos.fws.gov/ecpo/reports/species-listed-by-state-report?state=HI &status=listed, *Accessed on* August 23, 2019.
60. WMMWP, 2013:11.
61. Ibid.
62. WMMWP, 2013:13.
63. Ibid. at 83.
64. Ibid. at 11.
65. Ibid.
66. Ibid.
67. Ibid. at 11–12.
68. Ibid. at 12.
69. Ibid.
70. WMMWP, 2001:9.
71. Hobdy, Robert W., *Biological Resources Survey for the Mahinahina Well & Transmission Line Project, Lahaina, Maui*, 2012:9.
72. Ibid. at 10.
73. Ibid.
74. WMMWP, 2013:8.
75. Ibid. at 14.
76. Ibid.
77. Ibid. (citation omitted).
78. Ibid.
79. Ibid. at 16 (citation omitted).
80. Ibid. (citation omitted).
81. Ibid. at 16–17 (citation omitted).
82. Ibid. at 21.
83. Ibid.
84. WWMWP, 2013:22–23.
85. WWMWP, 2013:7.
86. HRS Chapter 205A.
87. See, e.g., *Stop H-3 Assn. v. Coleman*, 533 F.2d 434 (9th Cir., 1976) (conservation district use permit voided because highway route planned through land that was entitled to protection as a historic site); *Sierra Club v. Dept. of Transp. of State*, 120 Hawai'i 181, 202 P.3d 1226 (2009) (holding that Act 2 of the Hawai'i Legislature's 2007 Special Session that allowed the Hawaii Superferry, Inc. to operate without environmental review was unconstitutional); *Kilakila 'O Haleakala v. Bd. of Land & Natural Res.*, 131 Hawai'i 193, 317 P.3d 27 (2013) (conservation district use permit for the construction of the Advanced Technology Solar Telescope on Haleakala voided for failure to hold a contested case hearing); and *Mauna Kea*

Anaina Hou v. Bd. of Land & Natural Res., 136 Hawai'i 376, 363 P.3d 224 (2015) (approval of the conservation district use permit for the Thirty Meter Telescope on Mauna Kea vacated for a violation of due process).

88. *Technical Manual for Design and Construction of Road Tunnels-Civil Elements*, U.S. Department of Transportation Federal Highway Administration (FHWA) Publication No. FHWA-NHI-10-034, 2009:1–1.
89. Ibid.
90. Ibid. at 1–2.
91. Ibid.
92. Ibid. at 3–1.
93. Ibid.
94. Ibid. at 1–4.
95. Ibid.
96. Ibid.
97. Kali, 1997:3.
98. Ibid.
99. Ibid. at 6.
100. Ibid.
101. Ibid.
102. Ibid.
103. Ibid.
104. Ibid.
105. Ibid. at 6–7.
106. Ibid. at 7.
107. Ibid.
108. Ibid. at 4–5.
109. Ibid. at 5.
110. Ibid.
111. State of Hawai'i Department of Transportation Highways Division (DOT), *Interstate Route H-3 Retention of Construction Access Roads: North Halawa Valley and Haiku Valley O'ahu, Hawai'i Final Environmental Assessment/Finding of No Significant Impact*, 1998:2–4.
112. Ibid. at 1-12.
113. Dagher, 2019:23, citations omitted.
114. Ibid. (citations omitted).
115. Perzinski, 2009:10.
116. Ibid.
117. See, e.g.: Char, Winona P., *Botanical Survey Lahaina HFDC Project, Lahaina District, Island of Maui*, 1989; Char, Winona P., *Supplemental Flora Assessment Lahaina Master Planned Project Off-Site Improvements Lahaina District, Island of Maui*, 1991; Hobdy, Robert W., *Biological Resources Survey for the Lahaina Bypass Corri-*

dor Project, Lahaina, Maui, Hawaii, 2012; Hobdy, Robert W., *Biological Resources Survey for the Mahinahina Well & Transmission Line Project Lahaina, Maui*, 2012; and Hobdy, Robert W., *Biological Resources Survey for the Central Maui Sanitary Landfill Facility Expansion Project*, 2016.

118. WMMWP, 2013:18.
119. Nielsen, Erika, Nicole Ishihara, Halett H. Hammat, *FINAL Cultural Impact Assessment for the Central Maui Landfill Facilities Project, Wailuku Ahupua'a, Wailuku District, Maui Island, TMK: (2) 3-8-003:019 (por.)*, Cultural Surveys Hawai'i, Inc., 2019:30.
120. Ibid. (citation omitted).
121. Ibid.
122. Ibid. at 99.
123. Nielson, 2019:36, citation omitted.
124. Ibid. (citation omitted).
125. Ibid. (citation omitted).
126. Ibid. at 32.

CHAPTER 2

MANAGED RETREAT OF COASTAL ROADS

Lauren Armstrong

The tension in the air was palpable as I stepped out of the car onto the shoulder of Honoapiʻilani Highway near Olowalu town on Maui's west side. To my right, residents were camped on the shoreline with signs painted "No Seawalls" and "Protect our Beaches." To my left, Maui's mayor was in a heated discussion with State Highways officials over plans to move the road inland and out of harm's way.

Days earlier, community and environmental advocacy groups filed a lawsuit to prevent further hardening of the West Maui coastline. Portions of the highway near Olowalu had been damaged by high surf and storms, triggering the State of Hawaiʻi Department of Transportation (HDOT) to announce that emergency seawall repairs were needed. Those in opposition to the repair project pointed out that Olowalu is home to a critical monk seal habitat, Maui's mother reef, and is a popular fishing and surfing spot. They also cited the fact that seawalls destroy beaches, limit public access, and threaten coral reefs.

After visiting the area and walking the coastline, HDOT decided that instead of constructing the emergency seawall, they would re-stripe the highway and move the lanes slightly mauka within the existing highway right-of-way, farther away from the pounding surf. The hope was that re-striping the road's lanes inland would buy transportation officials approximately three more years to try to obtain the funding needed to implement the long-term plan of highway realignment.

Three years later, funding for the realignment of the highway between Olowalu and the Pali has yet to be fully identified. In addition to the milepost 16 area of immediate concern near Olowalu, another section of the highway

Figure 2.1. Hawai'i Department of Transportation Director and Maui Tomorrow Executive Director inspect erosion threatening Honoapi'ilani Highway near Olowalu

just south at milepost 14 is critically undermined by waves. Following a site visit with state highways officials and concerned community groups, it was decided to protect the road with temporary erosion control bags to delay the need for another permanent coastal hardening project. Meanwhile, erosion in the area is critical and worsening.

Near-term approaches to resiliency face the fact that major construction funding hasn't yet been secured, yet safety concerns are immediate. HDOT is conducting a feasibility study to look at coastal highway protection alternatives for this area, including the possibility of moving a section of the road inland within the existing right-of-way to buy time for a long-term solution.

A comprehensive study to update the Pali-to-Puamana Parkway Master Plan and move forward with realignment alternatives for the eight-mile stretch between Olowalu and the Pali is needed as soon as possible. A Planning and Environmental Linkages (PEL) study is being initiated to address safety and resilience issues for Honoapi'ilani Highway. The study can move the project closer to fulfilling environmental review requirements—a critical early step in any new road project. Potential impacts of constructing a new road inland on the cultural and natural resources in the area must be carefully considered. Once an Environmental Impact Statement (EIS) is approved, design and construction of the new road can move forward.

For any major project like building a new road, government agencies must include community members in the planning process early and often. Sitting down together to review maps and consider data like sea level rise projections and cultural site locations, the project team can find a path forward that meets the needs of present and future generations.

While Honoapiʻilani Highway is the ideal candidate for managed retreat, it's not the only road in West Maui that will require adaptive management. Lower Honoapiʻilani Road and Front Street are also threatened by erosion and sea level rise. Difficult decisions will need to be made about whether to continue protecting these roads in place, elevating them, or moving them inland. Retreat of coastal roads in highly developed areas may require planning tools such as transfer of development rights, and will involve many property owners. The relatively undeveloped status of lands mauka of Honoapiʻilani Highway means there is space to move the road inland. As land uses change over time, the opportunity to realign the highway will become even more complex and costly as more landowners are involved.

The aim of this chapter is to inform readers about ongoing efforts to implement managed retreat for West Maui's critically threatened roadways, and to identify paths forward for near and long-term solutions. First, this chapter will consider the historical, social and geographic context of transportation in West Maui. Then, it will look at current impacts of coastal hazards to roadways and the anticipated future impacts as hazards worsen over time with climate change and sea level rise. Finally, the chapter will present thoughts on implementation: how to pull together funding and community support to realize the vision of a realigned Honoapiʻilani Highway with open space along the oceanfront for the benefit of present and future generations.

Historic Perspective

Cultural and historical information about how people lived and traveled in West Maui provides insight about the significance of Honoapiʻilani Highway and can help inform efforts to move the road inland. In ancient Hawaiʻi, outrigger canoes were used for coastal travel between villages and for interisland travel, while trails within each ahupuaʻa provided access between the uplands and the coast. Most permanent villages were near sheltered beaches, which provided access to good fishing grounds as well as facilitating canoe travel between settlements.[1]

In ancient times the Island of Maui was divided into three territories with different rulers. Around 1550, King Pi'ilani unified East and West Maui and commissioned many significant public works projects including fishponds, lo'i kalo and segments of a paved stone trail, called "Alaloa" or the long trail, which eventually connected villages across Maui.[2]

Pi'ilani died at Lahaina, and the Kingdom of Maui passed to his son Lono-a-Pi'ilani. Ultimately, Lono's younger brother Kiha-a-Pi'ilani came to rule Maui and resumed the work his father had started in West Maui of connecting the entire island with a network of trails including the East Maui sections of the Alaloa. The Alaloa trail was the only ancient pathway to encircle any Hawaiian island, measuring four to six feet wide and 138 miles long. It ran not only along the coast, but also up the Kaupō Gap and through the summit area and crater of Haleakalā.[3]

The Alaloa simplified local and regional travel and communication, and allowed the chief's messengers to quickly get from one part of the island to another. The trail was used for the annual harvest festival of Makahiki and to collect taxes, promote production, enforce order, and move armies.

By the 1820s major changes were happening in the Hawaiian Kingdom. Protestant missionaries built stations in the same locations as the traditional Hawaiian royal centers, which were also developing as trade points with foreign vessels. Eventually wider, straighter trails were built to accommodate horse-drawn carts. Unlike the earlier trails, these later trails could not conform to the natural, sometimes steep terrain. They often bypassed the traditional trails as more remote coastal villages became depopulated due to introduced diseases and the changing economic and social systems.

Sometimes new corridors were constructed over the alignments of the ancient trails, or totally realigned, thus abandoning the older Alaloa for general public use. In addition to these modifications in trail location and type due to changing uses, trails were also relocated as a result of natural occurrences such as lava flows, tsunami, and other events.

By the early 1850s, specific criteria were developed for realigning trails and roadways, including the straightening of alignments and construction of causeways and bridges. The emerging roadwork system was supervised by district overseers and funded through government appropriations using labor by prisoners. With the passing of time, emphasis was given to areas of substantial population. Because of the ongoing decline of the Hawaiian population and the near abandonment of isolated communities formerly accessed by the Alaloa, segments of the trail were abandoned.

In the later years of the Hawaiian monarchy, the need to define and protect Hawaiian trails and roadways was recognized, particularly in support of native tenants living in remote locations. Often these native tenants' lands were surrounded by tracts of land held by large landowners who challenged rights of access.

In 1892, Queen Liliʻuokalani and the Legislature of the Kingdom of Hawaiʻi signed into law the Highways Act of 1892. All roads, trails and bridges in the Hawaiian Islands built by the government or by private parties, and dedicated or abandoned to the public as a highway, were declared by the Highways Act to be public highways.[4] The Highways Act has taken new significance in recent years as community advocates push for more public access to roads and routes beyond the typical sphere of county- and state-maintained roads.

Portions of modern day Honoapiʻilani Highway were likely built on top of or near the ancient Alaloa trail, passing through areas traditionally inhabited by Native Hawaiians. West Maui's storied coastline is the site of rich fishing grounds, villages, heiau, and burial sites. In 1790, hundreds of Native Hawaiians were shot in their canoes by sailors on an American trading ship in an event known as the Olowalu Massacre. This tragic event expanded the use of Western warfare technology by aliʻi to unify the Hawaiian Islands.[5]

Lahaina was capital of the Kingdom of Hawaiʻi from 1820 to 1845 and was an important whaling port. Preferring Lahaina to Honolulu, King Kamehameha III lived on Mokuʻula, a tiny island now buried beneath an abandoned baseball field at a county park. The island is considered sacred to many Hawaiians as a *piko*, or symbolic center of energy and power, and is the burial site of several Hawaiian royals. Mokuʻula was surrounded by a spring-fed wetland pond where Hawaiians cultivated loʻi kalo and fishponds. Around this time the Pacific whaling fleet began to visit Lahaina and play a significant role in the Hawaiian economy. Sailors from the whaling ships brought diseases that contributed to the decline of the Native Hawaiian population and sparked conflict with the missionaries. By the 1850s whaling was in decline as oil was discovered in America.

Established in 1860, Pioneer Mill Company was the first plantation to grow sugar commercially in Lahaina, and the company built one of Hawaiʻi's first sugar mills. For 139 years, the Pioneer Mill was a mainstay of West Maui's economy. Almost every resident of Lahaina had some connection to the mill. By 1935 the Pioneer Mill company cultivated over 10,000 acres of sugar cane. At its peak in the 1960s, the mill processed 60,000 tons of sugar annually. Sugar cane was first transported from the fields to the mill by flumes and cattle carts. Beginning in the 1880s, it was transported by train over miles of narrow-gauge railroad track along the West Maui mountain slopes. By 1953, trucks had replaced the trains.[6]

In the late 1950s, Pioneer Mill's parent company, American Factors, began building a resort community in the north most ahupua'a of Lahaina and named after Lahaina's neighboring district, Kā'anapali. Visitors began flocking to the resorts, beaches, golf courses, and tennis courts. Ka'anapali Airport was built in the sugar fields along the "North Beach" portion of the Ka'anapali Resort planned development area. The Kā'anapali area is acknowledged as one of the first master-planned resort communities in the world, and has become a model for resorts around the globe. Five hotels and six condominium villages face Kā'anapali Beach. Further north, additional residential, resort and commercial development in Honokōwai, Nāpili, and Kahana has drawn many residents and visitors to this formerly remote area of Maui.

West Maui today is a busy and beautiful area, impacted substantially by the tourism industry that is its primary economic engine. Fundamental to resident and visitor quality of experience are the beaches and coral reefs along the West Maui shoreline. Despite its normally tranquil appearance, the shoreline is a dynamic and hazardous place. A highway right on the coastline is scenic but extremely vulnerable.

The Threat of Isolation

Like many of Hawai'i's communities, West Maui is linked to the island's primary urban center of Central Maui by a single belt roadway owned and maintained by the State of Hawai'i Department of Transportation (HDOT). Honoapi'ilani Highway (Route 30) begins at Main Street in Wailuku and continues for 42 miles, ending at Kahekili Highway near Līpoa Point. The route transitions to the county portion of Kahekili Highway: a narrow, winding, single-lane road, which mainly services the local traffic in Kahakuloa. The county road eventually connects to the state portion of Kahekili Highway (Route 340), which continues for four miles until it ties into Waiehu Beach Road and Market Street.

Honoapi'ilani Highway operates as a two-lane principal arterial on the National Highway System and Freight Network System with posted speeds between 35 and 55 miles per hour. The highway cross-section is an undivided highway of two 12-foot lanes with four- to eight-foot paved shoulders. The alignment of the highway generally follows the shoreline for most of its route, and the majority of the terrain is flat, with the exception of the Pali section, which winds around sea cliffs.

Residents and visitors depend on Honoapiʻilani Highway for commuting, commerce and recreation. The development of Kāʻanapali as a resort destination in the 1970s created many local jobs but also created traffic strain on the highway as it winds around the Pali cliffs and along the shoreline. About half of West Maui employees commute in from other communities, and half of West Maui residents commute out to work in other parts of Maui. Together, inbound and outbound commuters make up a significant portion of the 25,000-plus daily vehicle trips over the Pali. The remainder of trips are residents traveling for non-work purposes and visitors traveling to and from West Maui.

West Maui's high number of visitor accommodations makes it unique among communities on coastal belt roads, like those of West Oʻahu and North Shore Kauaʻi. Over 40 percent of Maui's 2.6 million annual visitors stay in hotels, timeshares, and vacation rentals in West Maui.[7] Every day thousands of visitors rent cars in Kahului and drive to West Maui, causing traffic to back up to Māʻalaea and extend travel times between West and Central Maui.

Reducing dependence on assets located in other parts of Maui is a goal to strive for, but having reliable road access is imperative for the foreseeable future. Closures of Honoapiʻilani Highway, which occur more frequently than other arterials, are traumatic. Families of commuters are separated, visitors miss flights, and businesses suffer. Traffic accidents, high ocean surges crossing portions of the roadway, and fire and smoke hazards along the route have resulted in disruptions to the traffic flow and sometimes complete road closures. Without a hospital, and with limited grocery stores and supplies, West Maui relies on the road connection to Central Maui. Due to Honoapiʻilani Highway's proximity to the ocean, West Maui is one storm away from being cut off from the rest of the island.

The portion of Honoapiʻilani Highway from Pāpalaua Park to the southern terminus of Lahaina bypass near Olowalu landfill (between mileposts 11 and 18) is of special concern due to coastal hazards like erosion and flooding. Waves regularly splash up and over seawalls at Ukumehame, damaging cars with corrosive saltwater and causing drivers to swerve dangerously into the oncoming lane.

The West Maui Transportation Access Plan was developed to address the vulnerability of Honoapiʻilani Highway to road closures, which "severely complicate and restrict travel to and from West Maui."[8] One topic addressed in the plan is alternative routes. Due to the legacy of sugar cultivation in West Maui, areas between Olowalu and Kāʻanapali are laced with cane haul roads to access the former croplands mauka of the highway. These cane haul roads can serve as emergency alternate routes in the event of road closures.

West Maui's traffic problems can also be mitigated by improvements to an Intelligent Transportation System (ITS). ITS is the application of advanced detection, computing, and communication technology to the transportation system to achieve increases in efficiency, safety, and environmental quality. Some examples are modernized traffic signals, dynamic message signs, and real-time information about traffic conditions. As of September 2019, images from traffic cameras at ten signal locations around Maui are available for the public to view on the HDOT website.

Government agencies have developed communication strategies to disseminate public notifications of closure to help reduce the number of vehicles stuck on Honoapiʻilani Highway during extended closures. Many agencies are involved in closures, including the Maui County Departments of Fire, Parks, Police, Public Works, Transportation, and Water; the Maui Visitors Bureau, HDOT Airports, Harbors, and Highways Divisions, and State Department of Land and Natural Resources (DLNR) Division of Boating and Ocean Recreation. All of these agencies have to coordinate in the case of emergencies.

Public notifications via radio, phone, and Internet provide details on the nature of the closure, its estimated duration, alternate routes and modes of transportation services available, procedures for parking or return of rental cars, emergency medical services, shelter locations, and child and pet care service providers. The alternate surface transportation route via Kahakuloa can be activated and controlled at the discretion of the County of Maui Police Chief. This alternate route is not recommended for visitor use. Lahaina Small Boat Harbor, Māʻalaea Small Boat Harbor and Kapalua Airport are links for marine and aviation alternatives.

Emergency closures on Honoapiʻilani Highway will only become more prevalent with climate change-induced droughts and storms. As the county and Maui Electric Company refine fire mitigation and management plans, there is also a need to mitigate coastal hazards like flooding, erosion, and wave run-up.

Climate Science and the Changing Shoreline

Flooding, caused by hurricanes, tropical storms, tsunami, or heavy rain, is the most common natural hazard in Hawaiʻi. High waves and coastal erosion are also serious threats to people and infrastructure statewide and especially in West Maui. Development along the shoreline and in low-lying areas increases vulnerability to these natural hazards. Climate change and sea level rise will increase the frequency and severity of impacts from storm waves and erosion.

West Maui's coastline is impacted by waves from wrapping northwest swells in the winter, south swells in the summer, Kona storms that approach from the south, and occasional hurricanes. The coast along Honoapiʻilani Highway is partially shielded from the full energy of northwest swells by the islands of Molokaʻi and Lānaʻi and partially from south swells by Kahoʻolawe. Sand migrates to different areas of the beaches seasonally.

Around 14 percent of the total length of beaches in West Maui has been completely lost to erosion since the early 1900s.[9] This is the highest percentage of beach loss of any region on Maui, Kauaʻi, and Oʻahu. Many beaches have eroded to expose beach rock formations parallel to the shoreline, backshore deposits that can degrade water quality, and seawalls that were once fronted by sand. Seawall failure has been common in this area over the past decade, and there have been at least 18 permit requests for major seawall repair since 2007.

In Hawaiʻi and elsewhere, the historical response to erosion has been to armor the shoreline with seawalls, rock revetments, and other hard structures. We now know that armoring eroding shorelines leads to beach loss and accelerates erosion in neighboring areas. Most cases on Maui where a beach has been completely lost are adjacent to shoreline armoring. State and county coastal zone management officials consider shoreline armoring a last-resort solution and prefer to identify alternative responses.

Adapting to climate change and sea level rise can make West Maui communities more resilient to present and future coastal hazards. It is important to consider the potential exposure to existing coastal hazards as well as future scenarios that include climate change and sea level rise exposure. Beach nourishment is an interim adaptation strategy in the face of continuing sea level rise. Retreating from vulnerable areas eliminates risk rather than just temporarily reducing it, and also preserves coastal ecosystems, making retreat the only long-term option.[10]

Between 2012 and 2015, roughly $13 million was spent on two highway protection projects at Ukumehame and Launiupoko, and others were planned. As mentioned in the beginning of this chapter, community concerns relating to construction and cumulative impacts of those armoring projects caused HDOT to at least temporarily defer additional armoring projects. There has also been renewed conversation within the community toward highway realignment strategies. If the armoring approach returns, it will carry an increasing price tag and be less effective at keeping the road safe in the face of sea level rise. Regardless of existing armoring, the highway is still affected regularly by wave overtopping and remains susceptible to substantial damage or destruction from chronic erosion, or a major coastal storm or tsunami.

Climate change and sea level rise aren't new ideas, but we are still grappling with how best to address their consequences. When I was a college student in Vermont, a group of us formed an organization to strategize about ways to get our campus to be carbon neutral by using renewable energy and sourcing food locally. Our advisor was Bill McKibben, a scholar-in-residence who had authored *The End of Nature* in 1989, warning of global climate change due to human burning of fossil fuels. By 2007, McKibben's worst fears were beginning to come true as droughts, floods, major storms, and rising sea levels threatened many of the world's most vulnerable communities.

To run vehicles and power plants, humans have burned enough coal, gas, and oil to raise the concentration of carbon dioxide in the atmosphere from 275 parts per million to 400 parts per million over the past 200 years. Carbon dioxide traps heat that would have otherwise radiated back out to space. By changing the amount of the sun's heat that returns to space, we've changed the earth's energy balance and the basic way the planet operates. Extreme drought and rainfall, massive wildfires and coastal flooding have become the new norm. We're now in uncharted territory for weather, with the earth's warming accelerating faster than expected.[11]

Sea level rise is caused by melting ice caps and glaciers, and by thermal expansion of ocean water due to higher global temperatures. Many towns and cities in Hawai'i and around the world developed near the ocean due to rich ecosystems and access to trade. Now, living near the ocean also means vulnerability to rising water levels.

The Intergovernmental Panel on Climate Change (IPCC) has predicted up to 3.2 feet of global sea level rise by the year 2100 if greenhouse gas emissions continue at the current rate of increase.[12] However, recent observations and updated projections suggest that sea level will increase at a much more rapid rate. The most up-to-date scientific literature points to eight-plus feet of sea level rise as a worst-case scenario by the end of this century.[13] Further, sea level rise is projected to be higher than global averages around tropical regions, including Hawai'i. Flooding events during seasonal or extreme high tides will be experienced decades before the projected global sea levels are reached.

Exact amounts of sea level rise depend on amounts of carbon emissions and the earth's response to human-caused changes. Due to uncertainties about timing of impacts and the need for action now, the Hawaii Sea Level Rise Vulnerability and Adaptation Report[14] recommends planning for 3.2 feet of sea level rise now, and being ready to track changes and adjust that projection upward.

Vulnerability to sea level rise is based on modeling coastal hazards from passive flooding, annual high-wave flooding, and coastal erosion in the sea level rise exposure area (SLR-XA). The DLNR report provides a range of sea level rise projections and vulnerability scenarios. The exposure area with 3.2 feet of sea level rise represents hazards that may occur by 2050. Vulnerability to 1.1 feet of sea level rise is expected for current or near-term exposure to coastal hazards and sea level rise.

Over 38 miles of major roads would be chronically flooded across Hawai'i with 3.2 feet of sea level rise, encompassing 11 miles of roads on Maui including sections of Honoapi'ilani Highway.[15] Of the 11 miles of State Highway on Maui within the 3.2 SLR-XA, approximately 6.6 miles, or 60 percent, are in West Maui along Honoapi'ilani Highway. Since the highway was built directly behind low-lying beaches, it is prone to erosion and wave overwash during seasonal high tides and high waves. These seasonal events are already causing traffic disruptions and safety concerns, and will become more frequent and serious long before flooding conditions from sea level rise become permanent. An additional 4.7 miles of county and private roads are also within the 3.2 SLR-XA.

Utilities like water, wastewater, and electrical systems that run parallel and underneath roadways would also be impacted and ultimately destroyed. This chronically flooded infrastructure would have significant impacts on local communities and major effects around each island through loss of commerce, loss of access to emergency services, and increased traffic on other roads and highways. Repair, protection, or relocation of vulnerable roadways are already expensive efforts that will only worsen with rising sea levels.

With 3.2 feet of sea level rise, Lahaina's historic district would be exposed to chronic flooding, along with portions of the town itself, which is West Maui's visitor, service, commercial and residential center. Over 100 acres of public beaches and parks on Maui are within the SLR-XA with 3.2 feet of sea level rise. Many parks are located on the seaward side of major roads, and demonstrate how lightly developed parks can act as a buffer between eroding shorelines and development for many decades. Sea level rise will lead to extensive beach loss if widespread shoreline hardening is permitted and beach systems are not allowed to migrate landward.

Many beaches on Maui are backed by deposits of older beach and dune sand, which are crucial sources of sediment along eroding coasts. In a natural state, a beach can be maintained as it migrates landward if there is sufficient sand available in the backshore to nourish the beach as it erodes. Shoreline hardening locks up this backshore sediment source, leading to narrowing and loss of chronically eroding beaches.

Maui's beaches are important recreational and cultural gathering places, and drive the visitor economy. Maui has lost more than four miles of beaches to coastal erosion-fronting seawalls and other shoreline armoring. Many more miles of beach could be lost with sea level rise if widespread armoring is allowed.[16]

While specific responses to sea level rise need to be place-based, broader regional issues should also be considered, like whether to armor in place or to relocate roads and other critical infrastructure inland. The discussion around how to adapt Honoapi'ilani Highway to climate change is not happening in a vacuum, but there are considerations specific to the area that make it a unique challenge requiring a unique solution. This road is one of the few opportunities for managed retreat inland where there is ample vacant land immediately mauka and outside of the SLR-XA.

The DLNR report offers several recommendations for adapting to sea level rise. Moving Honoapi'ilani Highway inland from the SLR-XA with 3.2 feet of sea level rise would be consistent with four of the key recommendations: enable legacy beaches to persist with sea level rise, preserve Native Hawaiian culture and communities with sea level rise, protect nearshore water quality from sea level rise impacts, and promote collaboration and accountability for adapting to sea level rise.

Sea level rise threatens many State highways throughout Hawai'i with periodic wave run-up, erosion and eventually, permanent inundation. What can we do to plan ahead and take the appropriate steps to mitigate climate change and adapt to impacts like sea level rise?

Another recommendation of the report is that all major new developments and capital improvement projects should be subjected to an in-depth analysis of sea level rise impacts based on elevation, tolerance for risk, and lifetime of the structure. There is a need for in-depth assessment of vulnerability and evaluation of adaptation strategies for all critical infrastructure through the state, including Honoapi'ilani Highway.

While a number of agencies are responsible for various aspects of coastal management, HDOT maintains highways that provide the primary access to communities. The recently completed Statewide Coastal Highway Program Report[17] assesses and ranks the susceptibility of State of Hawai'i coastal roads to erosion and structural degradation due to ocean hazards such as waves, currents, tides and sea level rise. The study, led by the University of Hawai'i Department of Civil and Environmental Engineering, established a Coastal Road Erosion Susceptibility Index (CRESI) based on the concept that the width of land between the road and the ocean acts as a buffer to erosion and therefore controls how vulnerable a particular location is to structural road damage and collapse. Figure 2.2 shows the CRESI susceptibility index for Māʻalaea to Olowalu, which includes some of the state's most vulnerable stretches of roadway.

The report includes a cost-benefit analysis of the various adaptation alternatives on a scale from one to five according to level of support and/or benefit based on social, technical, administrative, political, economic, and environmental considerations. There are several types of adaptation options that fall under five general categories: protect; accommodate; relocate; monitor (no action); and a combination of relocate, protect, and/or accommodate.

"Protect" is a strategy to keep water out with artificial armoring or natural protection. A hard structure, such as a seawall or revetment, may be built, or protection may involve a soft approach such as a dune or beach nourishment. Two popular soft protection alternatives are beach nourishment and living

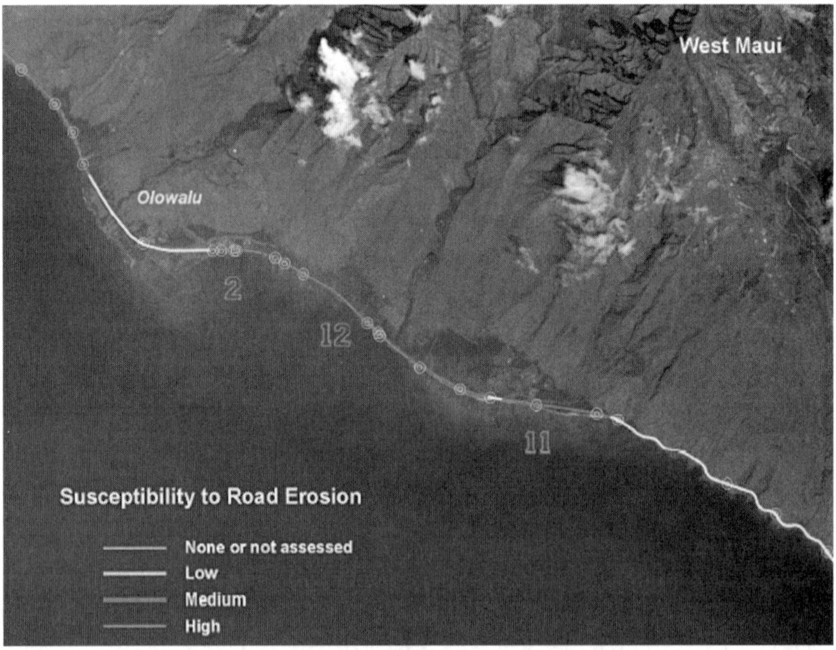

Figure 2.2. Coastal Road Erosion Susceptibility Index for Māʻalaea to Olowalu

dunes. The cost is relatively low to protect the shoreline and highway from storm surge. However, they typically require replenishment after each storm. Protection provides a buffer between the ocean and road, but armoring can make coastal erosion on adjacent stretches of shoreline worse.

"Accommodate" is the ability to live with water. Roads can be elevated, flood control is improved, and wetlands and natural environment are enhanced. Costs associated with elevating the road are high, and hard protection would also likely be needed.

"No action/monitor" has little to no cost and is used where there is no road susceptibility or where little to no ocean hazard exists.

"Relocate" is abandoning a vulnerable coastal road and building a new road away from the water. Road relocation is an expensive option, but a permanent one, and can be considered when a road needs to be abandoned due to permanent inundation, such as sea level rise. Open space or wetlands can be restored to establish or maintain freshwater buffer areas that provide ecosystem services like flood protection and habitat. Adding a beach park or multi-use path can greatly enhance the usability of the area. The road is also protected against long-term climate change impacts like sea level rise. Obtaining development rights to privately owned land can be a challenge to implementing relocation or realignment as a managed retreat strategy.

A "Combination" approach brings together the alternatives from Relocate, Protect, and/or Accommodate. There are three combinations of treatments for susceptible coastal roads: Hard Protection/Elevated Road; Hard/Soft Protection; and Relocate/Add Green Space.

Natural adaptation strategies enhance the resilience of shorelines by allowing natural processes to buffer storm waves and sea level rise impacts while maintaining the safety of human infrastructure outside the hazard zone. Wetlands are natural, desirable, and allow water to be accommodated, but are anticipated to have a high initial cost. However, once wetlands are in place, they need little maintenance. Wetlands can adapt to SLR and storm surge, and can mitigate erosion.

Another green alternative includes adding a green space, such as a park or vegetation, near beach areas where wind and water erosion are issues. Vegetative cover is popular on Hawaiʻi's beaches and provides a buffer between the road and the beach as well as shade from the sun. Many indigenous Hawaiian plants grow naturally by the beach and need little maintenance.

The criteria used in the study to consider state highways for relocation were projected to be affected by sea level rise and storm surge inundation as early as 2050, and with land available to move the road inland. Statewide, the only recommended areas for road relocation are half a mile in East O'ahu and two miles of North Kihei Road along Keālia Pond.

For West Maui, the State Coastal Highway Program Report recommended adaptation measures include "M: Monitor/No Action" along the majority of Honoapi'ilani Highway; "P-SD: Living Dunes Protection" near milepost 11.6 in Ukumehame; and "P-H: Hard Protection" near mileposts 13 and 14 near Olowalu.

The report is not entirely clear as to why "Relocate" was not identified as the recommended adaptation for Honoapi'ilani Highway between Ukumehame and Olowalu, but the State DOT is moving forward with plans to relocate the highway inland. High upfront costs for relocation compared to hard protection and lack of political will may be among the reasons relocation/realignment of the highway has faltered in the past. What becomes clear is how important it is for community members and other agencies to support the State DOT in finding alternatives to hard protection. Truly considering the environmental and social costs of seawalls and revetments in addition to the financial costs makes them a less attractive option than relocation and living shorelines.

The cost of dealing with climate change is very high, but will only increase with time. Climate scientists in 2017 testified in federal court that if we don't take much stronger action now, future citizens would have to pay $535 trillion to cope with global warming.[18] The state and counties should consider potential benefits in terms of long-term cost savings from implementing sea level rise adaption measures now (e.g., major flood proofing or relocation) compared to the cost of maintaining and repairing chronically threatened public infrastructure over the next 30 to 70 years.[19]

Why Managed Retreat?

The decisions we make now will determine whether future generations can enjoy a living shoreline. Adaptation options are to protect, elevate, or retreat. Assets can be protected in place, elevated above the flood zone, or moved inland away from the threat. Each of these approaches must be carefully considered in a place-specific context, but in general managed retreat allows shorelines to evolve naturally, and beaches to persist without shoreline armoring.

Lahaina resident Mariah Gill described the situation that had led her to create a website called *Save our West Maui Coastline*. Over the past several years, our reefs and beaches have been degraded by coastal armoring meant to protect the road from waves. The walls only cause the waves to splash up and over the road, and scour sand away from adjacent beaches. Having the road so close to the ocean is dangerous for people driving to and from West Maui and for people at the beaches. It's only a matter of time before more lives are lost to traffic accidents.

This sentiment is echoed by many Maui residents. Recently at Launiupoko, I ran into a friend with deep family ties in West Maui. I commented on the loveliness of the park, with its shade trees and rippling waves framed by coconut palms. My friend immediately replied, "Yeah, I wish we had more parks like this! Let's move the road mauka already." As her kids played in the surf, we talked about how dangerous it is for people to access the coastline via Honoapi'ilani Highway with cars whizzing by at 60 miles an hour. "You know, I'm also worried about the seawalls making our beaches disappear. What if the West Maui we left for our kids looked nothing like the coastline we grew up with?"

One of the Hawaiian cultural perspectives on the importance of managed retreat came from a panelist at a community forum on adaptation who stated, "Kanaloa is coming, and we have to make way." If human beings can't adapt to sea level rise in a manner that allows shorelines to migrate inland, we will face irretrievable loss as a society.

Ocean Beach Master Plan

We can learn from the successes and challenges of coastal adaptation efforts in other places. One model for planning managed retreat and public open space is the Ocean Beach Master Plan in San Francisco. Ocean Beach is a 3.5-mile sandy beach that attracts 300,000 visitors each year and is also home to major elements of the city's wastewater and stormwater infrastructure. Storm waves erode the coastal bluffs and move sand seasonally. With sea level rise, erosion is worsening and threatens wastewater systems and roads including the Great Highway. Since 2010, city, state, and federal agencies have been working together with beach users and community members to adapt to coastal changes.

Due to the complex nature of managed retreat, several agencies have come together to form the Ocean Beach Coordination Team. Members include the City Departments of Planning, Recreation and Parks, Public Works, and Transportation; the Public Utilities Commission; San Francisco Bay Area Planning and Urban Research (SPUR); the San Francisco Zoo; the California State Coastal Conservancy; and elected officials. The Planning Department maintains a web portal to updated information about Ocean Beach adaptation efforts.

The Ocean Beach Master Plan[20] is a comprehensive vision to address sea level rise, protect infrastructure, restore coastal ecosystems, and improve public access. The Plan includes over 40 recommendations grouped into six "key moves" by area:

South Reach

- Key Move 1: Reroute the Great Highway
- Key Move 2: Introduce a multipurpose coastal protection/restoration/access system

Middle Reach

- Key Move 3: Reduce the width of the Great Highway to provide amenities and facilitate managed retreat (later removed from the Plan)
- Key Move 4: Restore the dunes along the middle reach

North Reach

- Key Move 5: Create better connection between Golden Gate Park and Ocean Beach
- Key Move 6: Introduce bicycle and pedestrian improvements north of Balboa Street

Key Move 1, rerouting the Great Highway inland, would offer a recreational resource for cyclists, pedestrians and beach users while allowing for a healthier ecosystem. The current landscape of asphalt, rubble, and boulders can be gradually transformed into a coastal trail linking recreational areas. Infrastructure would remain, but the structures used to protect it would be designed with access, aesthetics, and natural resources in mind. While emphasizing improved non-auto access, this proposal would actually yield more coastal access parking. In place of the existing parking lot, which is vulnerable to erosion, new lots would be provided.

As a result of these planning efforts, a number of projects are currently underway to implement aspects of the Ocean Beach Master Plan and prepare Ocean Beach for a changing climate. These projects, implemented by members of the Ocean Beach Coordination Team, are designed to address sea level rise and coastal erosion by making changes to roadways and implementing coastal improvements.

What would a comprehensive coastal adaptation plan along the lines of the Ocean Beach Master Plan look like for West Maui? Maui County could consider updating the Pali to Puamana Parkway Master Plan or similar efforts as a land use complement to the HDOT Honoapiʻilani Highway Resiliency Study and the County Parks planning efforts. Such a plan could provide an updated comprehensive vision for highway realignment, coastal ecosystem restoration and access systems, and nature-based protection.

The planning process would bring together key stakeholders to address some of the challenges and concerns about realigning the highway, such as access and management of the coastal area makai of the new road. Within the County of Maui, the Departments of Parks and Recreation, Planning, and Public Works are key players, but other departments must also be consulted. The State Department of Land and Natural Resources would also need to be consulted, because they have jurisdiction over areas makai of the highway.

Nature-based protection strategies like dune or wetland restoration help buffer roads from flooding and storm waves. A key aspect of the Ocean Beach Master Plan and many other coastal restoration projects is dune revegetation to hold sand in place. While these "soft" protection measures may need to be replenished from year to year or following storm events, they provide a holistic approach to managing coastal areas.

Planning Efforts on Maui

In 2005 the "Pali to Puamana Parkway Master Plan" was led by the Maui County Planning Department to recommend a proposed realignment of Honoapiʻilani Highway from Papalaua Park to Puamana Park, to recommend a proposed open space preserve and to protect the shoreline environment, to increase roadway capacity, to protect public health and safety by getting the highway out of the tsunami inundation zone, and to recommend methods of accommodating new land uses for the area through the implementation of the West Maui Community Plan.[21]

The plan was developed with input from key stakeholders from West Maui Taxpayers Association, Goodfellow Brothers, Makila Properties, Lahaina Town Action Committee, Lahaina Restoration Society, Maui Tomorrow, Puamana Homeowners' Association, American Institute of Architects, REALTORS® Association of Maui, Lahaina Town Action Committee, Rotary Club of Lahaina, and the Maui Coastal Land Trust Board of Directors. Other groups may also be included moving forward.

The plan considers three possible alignments for a new route to West Maui: Mauka Alignment, an inland alignment that creates development parcels makai of the proposed alignment; Makai Alignment, an alignment that requires minimum land acquisition and avoids natural hazards; and Alternative 3: Mid-Level Alignment, an alignment that shares features from the other alternatives that requires moderate land acquisition and avoids natural hazards. Natural hazards mapped for the study include tsunami zone, flood zone, and erosion zone. Sea level rise projections were not yet available at the time of the plan.

The technical advisory committee and stakeholders went through an iterative process to determine which alignment best met the goals of the project to avoid coastal hazards, to create a vision for new park lands makai of the highway, and to provide a road acquisition strategy. Ultimately the plan recommended the Mid-Level Alignment. Following that alignment, 390 acres of land would be required for the new highway and park. Of this total, 153 acres are within the proposed highway right-of-way and include private and government lands. The remaining 238 acres is land available for recreation use and open space. An additional 74 acres of the existing highway right-of-way is also available for use as pedestrian or bicycle facilities.

The Plan recommends county actions to protect the planned highway corridor from unplanned and incompatible activities:

- Designate the highway corridor within the West Maui Community Plan as a future transportation corridor.
- Designate lands makai of the proposed highway corridor as open space in the West Maui Community Plan and rezone the lands to Open Space and Park.
- Prepare legislation to set aside funds for the acquisition of lands within the open-space corridor.
- Implement land dedication requirements during the land entitlement phases of land planning.
- Identify easements to be protected (such as views, shoreline access, stream setbacks, and pedestrian access).
- Encourage the State Department of Transportation to minimize the number of locations where access can be gained along the new highway corridor.
- Construction of a four-lane highway through this area should be added to state and county lists of highway projects.

Honoapiʻilani Highway's current alignment fosters ocean activities because of its proximity to the shore. In certain locations, such as in Ukumehame and Olowalu, the ocean is nearly at the shoulder of the highway. Alignment of the new roadway should balance the need to connect with the ocean with the need to move the road away from coastal hazards. Even with a minimum alignment mauka, the opportunity to create a linear shoreline park is greatly enhanced. Multimodal connections to bicycle and walking paths, bus service and the new road would improve residents' quality of life and visitor experience. The old highway could be initially used as a local road to access the beach parks, and eventually be abandoned to allow beaches to migrate inland. Figure. 2.3 illustrates a draft vision of a multimodal transportation network connecting a series of open spaces and parks.

What has hindered this vision from becoming a reality? Efforts to complete an environmental review for the highway realignment project, most recently in 2009, were delayed and ultimately deferred by failure to gain rights of entry to the necessary land, and the project scope is so large that funding has been difficult to secure. The realigned highway will require a public-private sector partnership to succeed.

For years the project has been identified as a four-lane highway from Māʻalaea to Launiupoko, which came in at a cost estimate of $650 million in

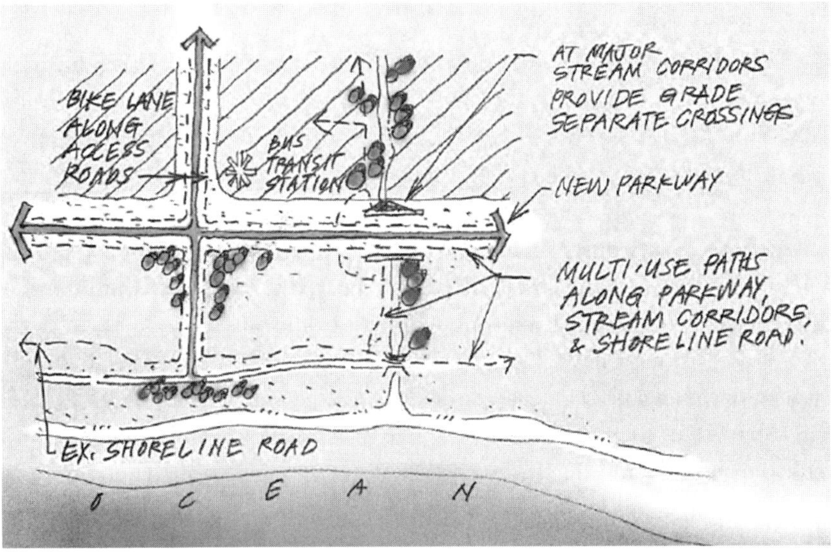

Figure 2.3. Pali to Puamana Parkway conceptual drawing

the 2035 Regional Federal-Aid Transportation Plan for the District of Maui (HDOT, 2014). The price tag for a project of that magnitude is likely closer to $1 billion in today's dollars, due in large part to the cost of developing a four-lane highway around the Pali. The Pali will continue to be problematic for access to West Maui, especially during wildfires. However, separating the project scope of Honoapi'ilani Highway realignment to address safety and resilience concerns for the coastal segment between the tunnel and Olowalu will facilitate moving the project forward sooner—before irreversible damage is done with coastal armoring.

In 2018 the Maui Metropolitan Planning Organization (MPO) added "Honoapi'ilani Highway Realignment, Olowalu to Pali" as a project to the Maui Transportation Improvement Program (TIP). The TIP authorizes the use of federal funds for highway, bus, bicycle, and pedestrian projects. The four-year program is approved every three years by the Maui MPO Policy Board, whose membership includes directors from the county departments of Planning, Public Works and Transportation, the HDOT director, three county councilmembers and two state legislators.

But, the $2,000,000 for the project's planning phase in 2020 is just a starting place. Ideally that number will increase to include design and construction, and move into a closer year as funding is identified. Maui MPO, the county, and HDOT are coordinating efforts to complete the necessary studies and identify funding for the realignment, and public support is key to establishing the priority of this project.

Land ownership along the existing highway is a mix of public and privately owned lands. Previous county administrations have made significant efforts to realize the vision of the Pali to Puamana Parkway. The county has acquired oceanfront land to preserve as parks and open space. In 2006 the County of Maui purchased 100 acres of land near Ukumehame from private owners, and in 2013 the county purchased an additional 148 acres near Launiupoko. Management of these coastal lands will be coordinated through the county, and in partnership with state agencies and members of the public.

To consider a new alignment for the Honoapi'ilani Highway, several aspects of the area need to be accounted for. Pre-contact sites and features identified by archaeological studies such as heiau, petroglyphs, habitation sites, agricultural features, and burial sites need to be carefully identified and potential impacts mitigated. Post-contact agricultural features such as waterways, mill sites, and villages created to house the workers should be preserved and integrated into park plans where possible.

Traditions should also be taken into account, such as the Alaloa trail to connect to Lahaina and Mā'alaea, mauka-makai trails within each ahupua'a, and the traditional land division markers that identified ahupua'a. Interpretation of the historic and cultural features of the area should acknowledge and perpetuate these features and provide points of interest in the area. This can be accomplished through placement of ahupua'a district boundary markers, historic site signs indicating a historic site, and interpretive signs at lookouts.

The new highway project should consider the incorporation of additional monkeypod trees as a defining element in the Olowalu area. Natural open spaces provide a strong connection with nature. Where parks are not developed, an open-space system should include large sections of natural landscapes along with parks and recreational-use areas. Streams provide a mauka-makai connection that can be developed as a pedestrian pathway.

The potential impact to public safety for the highway to support evacuation and to facilitate the movement of goods and people during a tsunami is an important consideration, so the new highway alignment should be outside the tsunami run-up zone.

The new roadway alignment should provide sequences of views that provide visual interest and display the beauty of the natural and cultural landscapes. Planning for a new highway alignment must place viewpoints and lookouts in areas that allow for safe access and protected observation points.

Community Participation

Broad community support for realigning the highway is essential. The planning process needs to make it clear that land makai of the highway will be preserved for open space and public access. A 2013 *Lahaina News* article highlights some of the community concerns that highway realignment advocates need to be aware of.

"To many West Siders, Highway 30 is much more than an asphalt roadway; it's a cherished connection of the people to the land and the ocean beyond definition, designation, study, ownership, acreage or price tag. It's the gateway to the soul of Lahaina. It's one of the only places left where you can just pull off the road and watch the sunset without having to find a parking space in a hotel parking lot first," one passionate local told the *Lahaina News*. The fear, real or not, is that the proposed highway will be realigned mauka. Developers would then have the opportunity to sell the land along the shoreline for the development of "rich man estates," thereby blocking traditional access for fishing, surfing, camping, and communing.[22]

Concerns about potential impacts of moving the highway inland persist. At a 2018 West Maui community meeting on transportation, a resident stated concerns about the West Maui coastline becoming completely walled off by private development if the road were to be moved inland. "We'd rather have higher seawalls than lose access to the coastline." Sadly, there is no simple solution. Seawalls would eventually diminish the shoreline to the point where public access would be to just a seawall, no beach. This has happened in so many places around the world, but fortunately there are planning and engineering techniques to avoid losing West Maui's unique shoreline.

Land-use planning tools include zoning, special management area (SMA) permits, and community plans. The national Coastal Zone Management (CZM) Act of 1972 established that the state, rather than the federal government, was in the best position to manage the zone connecting land and sea. In 1973, the Hawai'i State Legislature mandated a statewide CZM program, which in 1977 was codified in Hawai'i Revised Statutes, Chapter 205A. The regulatory reach of HRS 205A is the entire state, including coastal waters out to the limit of the state's police and management authority.

HRS 205A grants individual counties with regulatory authority over designated areas of concern that are termed the Special Management Area (SMA). The SMA generally extends from the shoreline inland to the nearest highway, generally the most sensitive coastal areas. Within the SMA, the counties have established rules that govern the immediate shoreline area, such as shoreline setbacks and procedures for variances. Today the SMA permit has become the most recognized component of the CZM program. In the County of Maui, the Special Management Area is regulated by the Maui Planning Commission according to a set of rules that should be evaluated and updated to provide improved coastal management and community resilience as our knowledge of the impacts of coastal hazards, climate change, and sea level rise continues to improve.

The County Planning Department is currently updating the West Maui Community Plan. During the last update to the West Maui Community Plan in 1996, the county was only just beginning to learn about climate change and how it could affect Maui County in the future. Since then, the Islands have started experiencing the effects of climate change in the form of rising sea levels with higher tides, roadway overwash and erosion, more frequent and higher intensity storms, and many other issues. West Maui is particularly vulnerable to the effects of climate change due to the amount of development and infrastructure immediately adjacent to the shoreline. The West Maui Community Plan update considers the current and expected future impacts of climate change, key challenges for residents and businesses in West Maui, and potential strategies to consider implementing. One consideration is the designation of "Parks and open space" as a land use along the oceanfront.

Other departments have a role to play as well. The County Parks Department is engaged in a systemwide planning process as well as individual park master plans. The county-owned area south of Launiupoko is on the list of parks slated for a master plan. Issues to be addressed in the planning process are access, parking, trail networks, stormwater management, sea level rise, wildfire mitigation, public safety and cultural preservation, among many more.

For other areas that may become part of a coastal park network, the county can work with nonprofits like Hawaiian Islands Land Trust (HILT) to place conservation easements on land. There are wonderful opportunities to partner with community groups to manage a living shoreline with native vegetation, habitat and space for people to gather and relax.

A Call to Action

A key question that needs to be addressed for the Honoapi'ilani Highway realignment project to move forward is: how are we going to pay for it? The estimated cost of $75 million to $100 million is beyond what can be funded with annual Federal Highway Administration (FHWA) allocations to Maui, unless the Maui Metropolitan Planning Organization (MPO) and HDOT decide to postpone all other transportation projects for at least four years. This is an unlikely scenario given the critical maintenance needs and federal mandate to preserve the existing transportation system.

In 2019 the Hawai'i State legislature passed an additional rental motor vehicle surcharge of $2 per vehicle per day, generating around $10.5 million annually for Maui. The legislation specifies that revenues are to be used for state highway capacity projects. HDOT estimates that the state could float a $200 million revenue bond to cover the cost to design and construct a few major highway capacity projects on Maui: Lahaina bypass north, Pu'unene Avenue Improvements, and Pa'ia Relief Route. The state legislature could consider an additional rental car surcharge to cover the cost to rebuild Honoapi'ilani Highway inland.

Other funding mechanisms under discussion are tolling, or a bond funded by a percent of property taxes, such as Community Facilities Districts. Making Honoapi'ilani Highway a toll road would require changing the State law, and is not likely to generate enough revenue to finance a revenue bond. Property taxes are decided by the County Council, and a Community Facilities District or Special Improvement District would need to be approved by the affected residents and businesses.

Although Honoapiʻilani Highway is a state road, the County of Maui could also look to identify funding sources. The county could consider passing an ordinance to enact a 0.5% General Excise Tax (GET) surcharge, as Kauaʻi County, Hawaiʻi County and the City and County of Honolulu have done to raise funds for transportation improvements. It is estimated that nearly half of GET is paid by visitors, based on the amount spent on taxable goods. Potential regressive impacts of the GET surcharge to low income residents could be offset by a rebate program, or by the state's earned income tax credit.

While decisionmakers wrangle with funding mechanisms, community members give elected leaders their input. The West Maui Community Plan, Maui MPO meetings and county budget hearings are good venues to share information and opinions about how to address the critical situation of sea level rise. Creating an online portal for data and efforts related to Honoapiʻilani Highway realignment would enable government agencies and the public to share information. This resource would serve as a foundation for sound decision-making and accountability throughout the project. Such an effort could be led by the community with support from county, state and federal agencies.

The time to act is now. The County of Maui owns significant portions of land mauka of the highway, and other landowners in the area are amenable to realigning the highway inland. Open space and public parks along the coastline, without a major highway only a few feet away, would be a gift to current and future generations of Maui residents and visitors. Moving the highway inland is the right thing to do, and we should do it before it gets even more difficult and expensive.

Now more than ever, with protests and lawsuits more the norm than the exception, the only way for a new road to be built in the name of climate adaptation is with thoughtful and collaborative approaches. The public should have opportunities to engage early and often with the planning process, to share their knowledge about the cultural and natural resources of the area. Robust and inclusive engagement will help us all move forward together.

Notes

1. Young, Peter T. 2014. "Maui Alaloa." *Accessed online at*: www.totakeresponsibility.com/2014/03/maui-alaloa.html.
2. Kamakau, Samuel. 1838. *Ka Mo'olelo Hawai'i*. Accessed online at: www.ulukau.org/.
3. Young, Peter T. 2014. "Maui Alaloa." *Accessed online at*: www.totakeresponsibility.com/2014/03/maui-alaloa.html.
4. Ibid.
5. Pignataro, Anthony. 2016. "Hawaii's 'Wounded Knee': Remembering the Olowalu Massacre." *Maui Time. Accessed at*: www.mauitime.com.
6. Lahaina Restoration Foundation. 2019. "Pioneer Mill Co. Locomotives and Smokestack Exhibit." *Accessed at*: http://lahainarestoration.org/pioneer-mill-smokestack-locomotives/.
7. State of Hawaii Department of Business, Economic Development and Tourism (DBEDT). 2018. "Monthly Visitor Statistics." *Accessed at*: https://dbedt.hawaii.gov/visitor/tourism/.
8. State of Hawai'i Department of Transportation. 2009, "West Maui Transportation Access Plan."
9. U.S. Global Change Research Program. 2014. "National Climate Assessment: Hawai'i Highlights." *Accessed at*: https://nca2014.globalchange.gov/highlights/regions/hawaii#intro-section-2.
10. County of Maui Department of Planning, Long Range Division. 2018. "West Maui Community Plan Climate Change and Sea Level Rise Technical Resource Paper." December 2018. *Accessed at*: https://wearemaui.org/technical-resource-papers-climate-change-and-sea-level-rise.
11. McKibben, Bill. 2019. *Falter: Has the Human Game Begun to Play Itself Out?* Henry Holt and Company.
12. U.S. Global Change Research Program. 2014. "National Climate Assessment: Hawai'i Highlights." *Accessed at*: https://nca2014.globalchange.gov/highlights/regions/hawaii#intro-section-2.
13. Sweet, et al. 2017. *Global and Regional Sea Level Rise Scenarios for the United States*. NOAA Technical Report NOS CO-OPS 083. NOAA/NOS Center for Operational Oceanographic Products and Services.
14. State of Hawai'i Department of Land and Natural Resources, Office of Conservation and Coastal Lands. 2017. "Hawai'i Sea Level Rise Vulnerability and Adaptation Report." December 2017. *Accessed at*: https://climateadaptation.hawaii.gov/wp-content/uploads/2017/12/SLR-Report_Dec2017.pdf.
15. Ibid.
16. Ibid.

17. Francis, O., H. Brandes, G. Zhang, D. Ma, L. Yang, O. Doygun, H. Togia, C. Rossi, G. Costanzo. 2019. "State of Hawaii Statewide Coastal Highway Program Report." Prepared for the State of Hawaiʻi Department of Transportation, Project Number HWY-06-16, August 21, 2019. *Accessed online at*: https://hidot.hawaii.gov/highways/files/2019/09/State-of-Hawaii-Statewide-Coastal-Highway-Program-Report_Final_2019.pdf.
18. Radford. 2017.
19. State of Hawaiʻi Department of Land and Natural Resources, Office of Conservation and Coastal Lands. 2017. "Hawaiʻi Sea Level Rise Vulnerability and Adaptation Report." December 2017. *Accessed at*: https://climateadaptation.hawaii.gov/wp-content/uploads/2017/12/SLR-Report_Dec2017.pdf.
20. San Francisco Bay Area Planning and Urban Research Association (SPUR). 2012. "Ocean Beach Master Plan." June 2012. *Accessed at*: www.spur.org/publications/spur-report/2012-05-21/ocean-beach-master-plan.
21. R.M. Towill for Maui County Planning Department. 2005. "Pali to Puamana Parkway Master Plan."
22. Rockett, Louise. 2013. "County Interested in Buying Launiupoko Tracts for Pali to Puamana Parkway." *Lahaina News*, March 28, 2013. *Accessed at*: www.lahainanews.com.

Chapter 3

CONGESTION, COMMUTING, AND CARPOOLING

Dawn Hegger-Nordblom

We all love the Island of Maui. Maui offers a unique island lifestyle that varies from town to town, from Makawao's paniolo rodeos and famous Komoda Bakery to Pāʻia Town's surfing and windsurfing activities, Kīhei's beaches, historic Wailuku and Lahaina's Front Street—from the spectacular road to Hāna that leads us on a beautiful adventure on the backbone of Haleakalā to the rugged communities of Kaupō and Keʻanae.

The Maui lifestyle is coveted and envied throughout the world. Visitors flock to Maui for its natural beauty, adventure, and weather to make memories of a lifetime. Maui has more return visitors than those visiting Maui for the first time.

For those who live on Maui, we know the island's resources are finite. I ask the question: is it possible to put a price tag on the beaches and ocean resources that give us joy in being one with nature? The spectacular waterfalls invigorate and excite the soul, as do those cool mountain hikes and trails that let us so enjoy being ourselves at our very best. No talking—just walking, breathing, using mental energy on how to best traverse a slalom course through the trees, grass and nature that surrounds us. What is the intrinsic value of this lifestyle?

How do we protect Maui from overuse? Where are the checks and balances to regulate land use, yet balance the economy that supports Maui? Who determines which issues are prioritized over the things that are prized and loved and representative of Maui? How can we as a society help ourselves? What can we learn from the past to guide our future? What can culture and past island history teach us today?

Maui's Generation Z/iGeneration (seven to 22 years old), Millennials or Generation Y (23 to 38 years old), Generation X (39 to 54 years old), Baby Boomers (55 to 73 years old), and the Silent Generation (74 to 91 years old) will make choices that shape the future regarding our socioeconomic, environmental, and land use needs.[1]

Smart decisions are needed to carry Maui into the next century with regard to current and proposed infrastructure; water resources; cultural, historical, and archeological resources; food sustainability; and current and proposed land use. Let us address the necessary changes to ensure our community can grow and address the future of climate change.

This chapter will identify factors that contribute to West Maui's congestion as well as possible solutions, such as carpooling and ride sharing to and from West Maui to alleviate congestion. Can Transportation Network Companies (TNCs) or a TNC-like app help alleviate traffic congestion to help commuters traveling to and from the West Side?

Commuting to and from West Maui reminds me of the David Bowie/Queen song "Under Pressure":[2]

> Pressure
>   Pushing down on me
> Pressing down on you,
> No man asks for
>   Under pressure
>   That burns a building down
> Splits a family in two
> Puts people on streets

Maui Island is known as the "Valley Isle." Maui is the second-largest island in the State of Hawai'i and has an area of 727.2 square miles.[3] Maui County consists of the Islands of Maui, Molokai, Lāna'i, and the two smaller uninhabited islands of Kaho'olawe and Molokini. Maui County has a total area of 2,398 square miles: 1,162 square miles of land and 1,237 square miles of water.[4]

Whale season, fire season, hurricane season, daily commuting, and regular daily activities add pressure on commuters and visitors to get to and from West Maui. Traffic congestion is created by several factors: (1) limited highway options, (2) small boat facilities, (3) an influx of visitors, (4) the number of people employed in West Maui but living outside of West Maui, and (5) the number of people living in West Maui but employed outside of West Maui.

Most Maui travelers arrive via air transportation to Kahului Airport (OGG). Commuter airports are also located at Kapalua Airport (JHM) and

Hana Airport (HNM).[5] Ports of call for cruise ships are located at Kahului Harbor and the Lahaina Small Boat Harbor, where cruise ships' tender boats dock. Honoapi'ilani Highway (30), Kahekili Highway (340), Haleakala Highway (37), Hana Highway (360), Mokulele Highway (311), Kula Highway (377), Kuihelani Highway (380) and county roadways allow residents, commuters and visitors to access Central Maui (Wailuku, Kahului), South Maui (Wailea, Kīhei), East Maui (Ha'ikū, Hāna), Upcountry (Pukalani, Makawao, Kula), and West Maui (Lahaina).[6]

West Maui's traffic congestion is exacerbated by limited transportation options. Honoapi'ilani Highway is a two-lane highway that travels from Mā'alaea to Lahaina to Honokōhau Valley. The highway crosses the scenic view plane corridor of the West Maui Mountains, known as Mauna Kahalawai. From Honokōhau Valley the freeway becomes Kahekili Highway, which alternates between a two- to one-lane highway. Widening the latter highway to alleviate traffic would require major funding in the form of capital improvement project (CIP) funds from the State of Hawai'i, the Department of Transportation (DOT), and Maui County.

There is no ferry service to transport passengers from central Maui's Kahului Harbor, Mā'alaea Small Boat Harbor, or the Kihei Launch to the West Side's Lahaina Small Boat Harbor. A ferry service departs and arrives to and from Lahaina Small Boat Harbor for Lāna'i Island commuters and visitors. Mala Wharf serves only as a launch ramp for commercial and noncommercial boaters.[7] Most of the boating facilities are recreational in nature (sport fishing, scuba diving, dinner cruises or sailing, whale-watching[8]).

The JHM commuter airport is located adjacent to the Kā'anapali and Nāpili–Honokōwai neighborhoods. The State DOT Airports Division's report titled "Airport Activity Statistics by Calendar Year," noted in 2016 that JHM received 75,295 passengers.[9] An email from the State DOT Airports Division Engineering Branch, Planning Section (AIR-EP) notes that in 2018, JHM received 100,624 passengers.[10]

Data is not available from the State Department of Business and Economic Development (DBEDT), Hawai'i Tourism Agency (HTA) for the Annual Visitor Research Reports for 2018. However, the State HTA 2017 Annual Visitor Research Report Maui Island Visitor Characteristics 2017 vs. 2016 data indicated the following statistics:

- 2,744,994 annual visitors came to Maui County in 2017 versus the 2,634,237 annual visitors that came to Maui County in 2016 (a 4.2 percent change).

- 1,747,039 annual visitors came to only Maui in 2017 versus the 1,683,204 annual visitors that came to only Maui in 2016 (a 3.8 percent change).
- The average daily census on Maui increased 3.3 percent to 60,506 visitors in 2017.
- The average length of stay in Hawai'i was 8.05 days.
- The proportion of people visiting Maui for the first time in comparison to travelers returning to Maui was 32.4 percent to 67.6 percent.
- Six out of ten Maui visitors (63.6 percent) stayed exclusively on Maui while the rest visited other islands.
- Over half the number of Maui visitors (56.1 percent) stayed in hotels, 27.3 percent of visitors stayed in condominiums, 11 percent stayed in timeshares, 7.3 percent stayed in rental homes, and 6.2 percent stayed with friends and/or relatives.
- Most Maui visitors (84.9 percent) came to the state for a vacation; 5.5 percent came for pleasure (honeymoon/wedding, pleasure/vacation); 5.2 percent came to visit friends and/or relatives; and 4.8 percent of visitors came for meetings, conventions, and incentives.
- The largest share of Maui visitors in 2017 were from the U.S. West (49.6 percent), U.S. East 27.3 percent, Canada (9.6 percent), Asia (excepting Japan) (3.0 percent), Oceania (2.7 percent), Europe (2.2 percent), and Japan (2.1 percent).[11]

The State DBEDT HTA Monthly Visitor Statistics Island Highlights Report indicated in April 2019 there were 249,076 visitor arrivals. In January 2019 there were 233,320 visitors, in February 2019 there were 220,801 visitors, and in March 2019 there were 273,846 visitors. Most visitors stayed in hotels, condos, timeshares, cruise ships, with friends/relatives, bed and breakfasts, rental houses, hostels, campsites/beaches, private rooms in homes, and/or shared rooms/spaces in private homes.[12]

Past population counts from the 2000 census indicate a population of 128,241 Maui residents. According to the U.S. Census Bureau of 2017 County and MSA population, there were 166,348 Maui residents. The population increased 30 percent from 2000 to 2017.[13]

The County of Maui Department of Planning's "We Are West Maui" website noted West Maui's population grew from 22,000 people in 2010 to approximately 25,000 people in 2017. The resident population between the years 2004 and 2016 grew due to a 59 percent natural increase rate, a six percent net domestic migration rate, and a 35 percent net international migration rate.

In 2017, West Maui's daytime population totaled 63,706 people, which consisted of 10,287 residents, 33,551 visitors (53 percent), and 19,868 workers (31 percent).[14]

The area of West Maui comprises a 96-square-mile area that covers approximately nine percent of the island's west side. As noted, Mauna Kahalawai is a prominent feature of West Maui.[15] West Maui has four distinct geographical neighborhoods: Kapalua, Kāʻanapali, Lahaina, and Ukumehame.[16]

Although West Maui had 25,000 residents in comparison to the island's overall population of 166,348, West Maui had a higher concentration of jobs than the rest of Maui County and the state overall. The top ten 2017 west side business categories by sales and number of firms fell into the following categories: Accommodations/Food Services, Retail Trade, Real Estate/Rental/Leasing, Manufacturing, Wholesale Trade, Admin/Support/Waste Management & Remediation, Arts/Entertainment/Recreation, Construction, Health Care/Social Assistance, and Transportation/Warehouse.[17]

How many people commuted in and out of West Maui daily? A 2014 West Maui Jobs diagram notes there were 14,449 primary jobs in West Maui.

The West Maui Jobs Inflow and Outflow diagram indicates 7,444 people who lived outside of West Maui were employed in West Maui. Conversely, there were 4,938 people who lived in West Maui but were employed outside of West Maui. The total number of commuters that came in and out of West Maui daily was 12,382.[18] Areas located outside of West Maui related to these statistics included Wailuku-Kahului, Makawao-Pukalani-Kula, Pāʻia-Haʻikū, Kīhei-Mākena, and Hāna. There were 7,005 people who were both employed and lived in West Maui.

We have discussed the factors of traffic congestion to and from West Maui and the competing factors due to infrastructure, monthly visitors, and the number of employed residents. Other factors that increased traffic congestion to and from West Maui included income, job-to-housing ratio, housing availability, median home values, and lack of housing.

Currently, the federal minimum wage is $7.25 per hour. In January 2018, the minimum wage in Hawaiʻi was raised $0.85 from $9.25 to $10.10 by the state legislature. The DBEDT estimated: "The basic minimum living wage for a single person, without children, living in Hawaiʻi was approximately $17.00 per hour."[19] This number was based on the premise that every person working forty hours a week earned a wage that provided basic shelter, food, and medical care. During the 2019 legislative session, the legislature discussed raising the minimum wage to $15 per hour. However, no legislation was enacted.

According to the We Are West Maui Community Profile for Housing, the jobs-to-housing availability ratio is 2.06 for West Maui. West Maui statistics show there are 8,742 occupied dwelling units to 18,018 jobs. West Maui households have two jobs for every one occupied household, thus increasing the number of commuters to and from West Maui. In comparison, Maui County's jobs-to-housing ratio was 1.37, and the state's overall jobs-to-housing ratio was 1.29.[20]

If additional housing options were available, traffic and congestion to and from West Maui could potentially decrease. Data indicated the 2017 median owner-occupied home was valued at $754,808. The number of homes valued at less than $500,000 was 29 percent, and the number of homes valued at more than $1 million dollars was 33 percent.[21]

The 2017 data indicated West Maui residents housing units increased by 12 percent in 2010 to 13,318 housing units. The remaining units were either owner-occupied units in West Maui (31 percent), were renter-occupied (35 percent), or were vacant (34 percent). Vacant units consisted of vacant for-sale properties, vacant for-rent properties, and second and/or occasional-use homes.[22] It is unclear from the data presented if the vacant for-rent properties were short- or long-term rental properties. If the number of vacant properties were made available to West Maui commuters and/or residents, traffic congestion could lessen.

Currently, 7.5 percent of households live below the poverty line in West Maui versus the 11 percent of households that live below the poverty line in Maui County overall. West Maui does have low-income housing units such as the Lahaina Surf, Hale Mahaolu Eono 5, Sunset Terrace Apartments, Hale Lahaina, Weinberg Court (Lahaina Affordables), Honokowai Villa Apartments, Front Street Apartments, and the West Maui Community Resource Center.[23]

The 2017 household income indicated West Maui's median income was $76,817. The 2017 Household Income Net Worth Distribution graph indicated 23 percent of West Maui residents had a net worth of less than $15,000, 22 percent had a net worth over $500,000, and 20 percent fell within the $50,000 to $149,999 range.[24]

Traffic congestion to and from West Maui increased exponentially due to the lack of available housing, limited highway infrastructure options, a high influx of Maui visitors, and the sheer number of daily commuters. This has had a negative effect on lifestyle and local enjoyment.

The County of Maui's Bus Public Transit System provides residents with bus transit options within West Maui and the Central, South, East, and Upcountry Maui communities.[25] The We Are West Maui Community Profile Technical Resource paper indicated in the 2016 Maui Short Range Transit Plan (MSRTP) that within West Maui, Route #25 (known as the Kaanapali Islander) was the best performing route in the system. Improvements regarding route alignments, later evening service, earlier starts, and added bus stops are envisioned by the county. Other West Maui bus routes are Route #20 (The Lahaina Islander), Route #28 (West Maui Islander—formally known as Route #30 Napili Islander), and Route #23 (The Lahaina Villager).

Commuter bus service serves the major employment areas in West Maui. Bus commuters can board the bus at designated locations to access the Kīhei-Kapalua, Makawao-Kapalua, and Wailuku-Kapalua routes. The fare is $2 for each one-way commuter route, and monthly passes are available for $45.[26]

2018 data from the Maui County Bus Public Transit System indicated the following commuter data:

- The Kīhei-Kapalua route had an average daily boarding number of 28 riders and an annual boarding number of 10,038 riders.
- The Makawao-Kapalua route had an average daily boarding number of 102 riders and an annual boarding number of 37,210 riders.
- The Wailuku-Kapalua route had an average daily boarding number of 344 riders and an annual boarding number of 125,449 riders.

Data from Maui County indicated the 2014 West Maui Ridership totals for the combined Islander, Village, and Commuter routes had an average daily boarding of 3,273 riders and annual boarding of 1,194,392 riders.

What other transportation options were available for West Side commuters? I asked the State DOT for data regarding commuter statistics; however, they referred me to the We Are West Maui website for information.

The Community Profile, Transportation Page ESRI 2017 data indicates in the 2010–2014 ACS Workers Commute Mode that commuter travel modes for West Maui broke down as follows:

- Drove (alone): West Maui 65% versus Maui County 71%
- Carpooled: West Maui 12% versus Maui County 14%
- Walked: West Maui 8% versus Maui County 4%
- Work at home: West Maui and Maui County 6%
- Bicycled: West Maui 4% versus 1.5%

- Took public transportation: West Maui and Maui County 4%
- Took a bus or trolley bus: West Maui and Maui County 4%
- Took other means of transportation: West Maui and Maui County 3%
- Motorcycled: West Maui 2% versus Maui County 1%
- Took a taxicab, streetcar, trolley, subway, elevated train, or railroad: West Maui and Maui County 0%

The We Are West Maui Workers Commute to Work Duration data indicated time spent commuting for Maui County workers. West Maui residents spent less time driving to work than workers located in other parts of Maui County. Residents commuted less than ten miles to work (59 percent), and 74 percent either worked at home or drove for fewer than twenty minutes to work.[27]

Are there possible solutions that can be utilized to ease West Maui traffic congestion to and from the West Side? Commuters currently have several options to travel via driving their own personal vehicles, carpooling, and utilizing the Maui County Bus Public Transit System. Can TNCs or a TNC-like app help alleviate traffic congestion with carpool and rideshare options to help commuters?

A TNC is also known as a mobility service provider (MSP). A TNC matches riders with vehicles through a website and mobile app via smartphone. It is a "digital application that matches potential riders with drivers in real time."[28] TNCs are also referred to as ride-hailing services. TNCs are examples of the terms "sharing economy" and "shared mobility."[29] In a sharing economy, individuals "rent" or "share" their cars, homes, and personal time to other individuals. Shared mobility is the shared use of a vehicle, bicycle, or other transportation mode on an as-needed basis.

When TNCs first started around 2009, the marketplace for rideshare services was limited. The more TNCs evolved, and the more normalized the app-based ride sharing trend became, the more TNCs appeared in tech sectors.[30]

Both of Lyft's founders had used ridesharing in their pasts. Lyft's chief executive officer, Logan Green, used to share rides from the University of California, Santa Barbara to visit his girlfriend in Los Angeles via Craigslist's ride boards. He had no information about the identity of the other passengers or the drivers, which led to anxiety.

Lyft's president, John Zimmer, used to take transportation classes at Cornell University. He was inspired by the number of empty seats while commuting to and from New York City. He noted ridesharing "is a huge opportunity to create efficiency to save a lot of money and reduce our environmental footprint." Ridesharing is the next step towards efficiency.[31]

When Facebook opened its Artificial Programming Interface (API) to third parties, Green and Zimmer used Facebook Connect to enable Zimride (the TNC precursor to Lyft) to link drivers and passengers through their profile information.[32]

In 2012, based on the success of Zimride, Green and Zimmer launched Lyft at Cornell. Within six months, 20 percent of the campus had signed up to utilize Lyft.[33] Both realized Lyft's potential impact within the TNC industry and focused Lyft as a TNC for shorter trips within cities. In 2013, the company name changed from Zimride to Lyft. Zimride was sold to Enterprise Holdings (the parent company of Enterprise Rent-A-Car) to enable the company to focus on Lyft's growth.

It goes without saying that without the use of technology and smartphones, TNC companies would not exist. The digital application ("app") helps match potential riders with drivers in real time. Let's discuss how TNCs work and why ridesharing is so popular.

While Lyft was capitalizing on utilizing the Facebook Connect API, the first ridesharing company, Uber Technologies, Inc. (Uber) was being developed. To be the first TNC and rideshare company helped Uber's brand. Uber has used this branding to capitalize on Uber's other services.[34]

Lyft and Uber are popular because they are convenient and they give riders transportation choices other than carpooling, taking the bus, or hailing a taxicab.[35] However, psychology and social behavior do play a significant role along with technology.

One of the reasons Uber and Lyft are popular is not just the technology that allows the apps to connect potential passengers to drivers, but that when the ride is over, the rider's satisfaction is immediate. Through the rideshare app platform, technology has enabled the rider to both express satisfaction and vent frustration after a ride. With a taxicab, if the ride is not up to par, there is no one to complain to in real time. Thus, the psychological benefits of a rider being able to get results quickly and to communicate feelings plays a powerful role in using a TNC.

The blog article "Five lessons from BuzzFeed and Uber on Building Closed-Loop Growth Systems" noted one of the reasons Uber is effective is that it "uses data to fuel production adoption and deliver customer value." Companies such as Uber, BuzzFeed, Airbnb, Amazon, GitHub, and Netflix have created "powerful closed-loop feedback systems."

A closed-loop system operates when a customer uses a product and takes an "action." In this case, the Uber rider opens the app and orders a ride to and from a location. All this data from the interaction is captured and fed into the system to improve the next customer's experience. With a closed-loop system, Uber "takes the input action, measures your activity and behavior, tracks the output, and uses all that information to inform the rest of the system" in the form of feedback. In this way, when a rider is in Lahaina and asks for a ride from Whalers Village to Front Street, Uber can optimize pricing for rides and match demand (ride requests) with supply (cars).[36]

An open-loop system occurs when an action is taken but there is no feedback. Input is processed like output, but data is not captured. For example, the *Lahaina News* has varied reader content in the form of entertainment, ads, stories about Lahaina and local activity, event calendars, and tech news. However, the newspaper gets no feedback but for opinion letters, which may be printed in a later edition.

Both Uber and Lyft contain similar features through the rideshare app platform:

- Both have online ride-sharing applications that connect riders with drivers in their community.
- Potential riders must download the Lyft or Uber mobile app to their iOS- or Android-based phone, sign up, enter a valid phone number, and enter a valid form of payment (credit card, Apple Pay, Google Wallet, or PayPal).
- Riders request a ride by entering their starting and ending destination through the app, which locates the nearest driver.
- All rides are cashless.
- Once a driver is located, the app shows the driver's name, ratings by past riders, and photos of the driver and car.
- Riders can monitor the driver's arrival.
- Riders and drivers can contact each other (via the app platform).
- Once the trip is complete, funds are debited from the rider's account.
- Tipping is allowed and is billed to the rider's payment method.
- No ride is anonymous.
- The name, make, and model of the car is available to the rider.
- Drivers are 21 years old or older.
- Riders and (Lyft) drivers can rate their experience.

The main difference between Uber and Lyft is name recognition. Uber was the first TNC and ridesharing company. Uber was started in 2009–2010 by Garrett Camp and Travis Kalanick as they tried to address San Francisco's taxi problem. They developed the Uber app to help connect riders and local drivers. The "app provided a convenient alternative to taxis and poorly-funded transportation systems." The Uber platform recognized that by providing rides at a lower cost and a higher level of service than taxis, it met and satisfied potential customers' budgets.[37]

Marketing agency Single Grain's article "Ten Lessons Startups Can Learn from Uber's Growth" noted Uber's vision was to offer to riders "a better ride experience." Their original business model and plan was more complicated than the current model. Uber tried to achieve their initial goal by offering luxury car(s), but realized the company just needed to offer a "better experience"; luxury cars were just one way to offer this option.[38]

Based in San Francisco, California, Uber operates in 785 metropolitan areas in the United States, and worldwide in 77 countries.[39] On Maui, Uber offers UberX, UberXL, and Select car service. An UberX is a 2006 car or newer, allowing for four-person seating with bag storage. The cars have air conditioning and heat, and must be four-doors with five seat belts. An Uber XL car has similar features to UberX; the main difference is the car is bigger to carry additional luggage and passengers. An Uber Select is a luxury car (BMW, Porsche, Acura, Cadillac, Audi, Tesla, Infiniti, Lincoln, Mercedes Benz, Lexus). The fares are higher due to the expected luxurious experience and highly rated drivers.[40]

Uber has been plagued by criticism regarding deceptive pricing known as "surge pricing." The 2014 Slate article "Uber's Surge Pricing Honesty Problem" noted that when Uber raised their prices during major events, inclement weather, and other unusual events, negative publicity ensued. Uber's poor communication regarding their rationale of the higher prices drew criticism. Uber addressed the disparity by noting the Uber app would warn future riders about price increases and when they would end.[41]

An article from the blog Percolate, "5 Lessons from BuzzFeed and Uber on Building Closed-Loop Growth Systems," noted the right answer for pricing "isn't to maximize fares per trip . . . it's to optimize for drivers' earnings per hour while efficiently matching supply and demand within their market." Uber's controversial dynamic surge pricing is "closely underpinned by market economics with all the transaction's participants in mind." Uber's dynamic pricing passed the surge-pricing earnings on to the drivers during periods of demand imbalances, thereby attracting more drivers to drive to balance driver supply and ride requests. "The transportation market is more efficient, so drivers maximize their revenue and more people get rides." It noted Uber started out small, refined their respective closed-loop growth systems, and then identified the inflection points (people and technology) to make it to scale.[42]

Uber has been faced with riders being sexually assaulted, drivers cheating passengers out of money, and safety issues. Uber hired a PR team and placed internal controls to address public relations issues.

Uber also offers rideshare options, such as UberPool and UberGO; Uber Eats (food delivery); Uber Freight; and Uber Jump (bikeshare). With UberPool, a rider can share the ride with other riders traveling to the same area and pay less than a normal Uber ride. UberX can only take four riders at a time. They cannot share the ride and must pay the full fare. UberGO is a less expensive option available in India.

Lyft is based in San Francisco, California. Lyft operates in 640 cities in the United States and in nine cities in Canada.[43] Lyft is the second-largest TNC, behind Uber, with a 30 percent market share in the U.S.[44]

Lyft's brand was known by the large, furry pink mustaches that drivers attached to the front of their cars, and the drivers' and passengers' fist-bumping tradition.[45] The pink furry mustache was eventually replaced by the "glowstache"—a small, glowing plastic dashboard mustache. In December 2016, Lyft introduced a color-changing dashboard indicator called the "Amp."

According to business statistics blog DMR's June 2019 article, "50 Interesting Lyft Statistics and Facts (2019)/By the Numbers," Lyft has:

- 20.5 million active riders
- 1.4 million drivers
- Has given one billion rides
- Gives over one million rides per day
- Gives an average of 178.4 million Lyft rides quarterly
- Gave 375.5 million rides in 2017
- Gave 160 million rides in 2016
- Made $2.16 billion in revenue in 2018 versus $1.05 billion in 2017
- Lyft's revenue per active rider: $37.86
- Lyft's reported value: $15.1 billion
- Percentage of U.S. covered by Lyft service: 95%
- Reported average that Lyft drivers earn before expenses: $29.47
- Number of Lyft gift card rides: 630,000
- Amount Lyft raised in their IPO: $2 billion
- Number of self-driving miles Lyft and Aptiv have covered: 50,000
- Amount Lyft drivers have earned in tips to date: $500 million

- Number of Lyft rides to the airport: 76 million
- Percentage of Lyft rides that occur in winter: 47%
- Number of Lyft rides during Happy Hour: 88 million.[46]

Lyft notes their primary concern is safety. Rides are tracked via global positioning system (GPS). Riders receive the driver's picture and license plate number before the car arrives and can send real-time GPS data and estimated time of arrival to family or friends. The riders and drivers rate each other on a scale of one to five stars when the ride is complete; the ratings establish the reputations of the drivers and riders within the app platform. Rides with low ratings or concerning feedback are flagged by Lyft's Trust & Safety Team. Drivers or riders may be removed from the platform and reinstated once the complaint has been investigated. Drivers averaging low ratings will not be matched with riders. Lyft deactivates the driver from further rides if a safety-related complaint is lodged.[47]

Lyft drivers undergo mandatory local, state, and national background checks conducted by Checkr.[48] Lyft checks the national sex offender registries in the US. Lyft has a zero tolerance drug and alcohol policy. Lyft drivers are insured with a million-dollar commercial liability policy that is primary to a driver's personal policy. Additional coverages include contingent comprehensive and collision coverage, contingent liability coverage, and uninsured/underinsured motorist coverage.[49]

On Maui, Lyft offers Lyft and Lyft XL car services. Lyft is the basic and most popular service that matches riders with nearby drivers. Lyft XL matches riders with a vehicle that can seat at least six passengers.[50]

The author contacted Lyft regarding the company's overall vision via LinkedIn email on June 6, 2019. Ms. Lauren Alexander, Lyft's Policy Communications Manager, responded via a June 17, 2019 email:

> Lyft was founded in 2012 by Green and Zimmer to improve people's lives with the world's best transportation and is available to approximately 95 percent of the United States population as well as select cities in Canada. Lyft is committed to effecting positive change for our cities by offsetting carbon emissions from all rides, and by promoting transportation equity through shared rides, bikeshare systems, electric scooters, and public transit partnerships.
>
> We started Lyft with a vision for a world we want to live in—one where we spend less time in traffic and more time with each other. That

translates into the kind of company we are working to build. Lyft is making car ownership optional. Lyft is making cities better through a network of shared rides, bikes (including electric bikes), e-scooters, and self-driving vehicles that better connect you to public transit. In 2018, almost half of our riders reported that they use their cars less because of Lyft, and 22 percent reported that owning a car has become less important.

In Hawai'i specifically, 40 percent of Lyft users report exploring more areas in their city as a result of Lyft. Nationally, spending in local economies increased by $3 billion due to the availability of Lyft. Lyft provides a flexible earning opportunity for drivers. The moms, students, seniors and veterans that drive for Lyft are able to earn additional income for their families while having the freedom of working where, when, and how much they want. Lyft also provides a reliable ride home on late nights out. Seventy-six percent of riders are less likely to drive substance impaired due to the availability of Lyft.[51]

Lyft's Economic Impact Report for 2019 indicated the following Hawai'i statistics:[52]

Drivers:

- 95% drove fewer than 20 hours per week.
- 25% were veterans.
- 26% were over the age of 50.
- 30% were female.
- 98% said schedule is important.

Car Ownership:

- 27% said they do not own or lease a personal vehicle.
- 44% would purchase a vehicle if Lyft became unavailable.
- 63% non-car owners say Lyft impacted their decision not to own or lease a personal vehicle.
- 44% of vehicle owners used their cars less because of Lyft.
- 49% of riders used Lyft to get to the airport.
- 31% of riders spent more at local business as result of Lyft.
- 36% of riders were more likely to attend community events as a result of using Lyft.

Multimodal:

- Ridesharing increased public transit ridership by 5% in two years for the average transit agency.
- 45% of riders took public transit at least once a week.
- 21% used Lyft to get around when public transit did not operate.
- 26% of Lyft rideshare users have used bike share or scooter share.
- Late night rides account for 11% of the rides on the platform.

Public Health:

- 76% of riders were less likely to drive impaired due to the availability of Lyft.
- 31% of riders used Lyft to access healthcare services.
- 24% of healthcare riders stated that without Lyft they were less likely to make it to their regular appointments.

Ride for Everyone:

- 56% of rides started in low-income areas.

Lyft's CEO's vision is to create a network of self-driving cars. Lyft has partnered with General Motors (2016), NuTonomy (2017), Ford Motor Company (2017), GoMentum Station (2018),[53] Magna International (2018), and Blue Vision Labs (2018) to create this vision. Beyond the concept of self-driving cars, Lyft's projects are wide-ranging and include:

- One million guests/riders transported by the "Minnie Van" at the Walt Disney World Resort.
- Lyft is the official rideshare of Walt Disney World Resort and Disneyland Resort.[54]
- The Allscripts platform app allowed healthcare providers to arrange rides for patients who lacked transportation to appointments—the service was available to 2,500 hospitals, 180,000 physicians, and approximately 7 million patients.
- The acquisition of Motivate: the bicycle sharing system operator of Capital Bikeshare and Citi Bike.
- The addition of 28,000 Citi Bikes.

- The launch of scooter fleets in Colorado, Virginia, Georgia, Texas, California, Tennessee, and Washington, D.C.
- The completion of 5,000 rides using self-driving cars in Las Vegas.
- The production of 10 Waymo self-driving cars in Phoenix, Arizona.

There are other TNCs besides Lyft and Uber worth mentioning, such as Gett and Via. Via shares rides for $5 in premium vehicles and gives a 5–20 percent boost in pay to drivers for accepting riders along the route. If a driver picks up extra riders that match the route, this lessens the driver's demand, puts fewer miles on the vehicle, and eliminates double long-distance trips. Most of the trips are during commuting hours.

Gett is dedicated to reducing harmful emissions in the atmosphere while minimizing wasted time between rides. Gett acquired Juno, which was a ride-hailing app in New York with a "driver-friendly culture that gave Uber and Lyft a run for their money."[55]

Many states wrestled with categorizing TNCs—are they technology companies, transportation companies, or both? In the March 21, 2019 ITDP article titled "A Salvation or a Pestilence for Cities? A New Guide for Regulating Uber, Lyft, and other TNC," the authors noted:

> One of the preliminary challenges in regulating TNCs is that of categorization. Should TNCs be regulated like transportation companies or technology companies? Now that many TNCs are moving into other forms of transportation like bike and scooter sharing, automobile-based categorization may not be sufficient. It is important to remember that the category chosen for TNCs will determine which government body or department oversees their regulation.
>
> Cities should consider opportunities to regulate TNCs on a regional scale, given the tendency of TNC trips to cross municipal, county, or even state lines. Transport for London oversees the management of TNCs and other private hire vehicles for the City of London, and the surrounding 32 boroughs. Regional coordination helps minimize administrative costs of regulation and provides consistency in enforcement. Even if coordination is not officially placed under the purview of a regional body, standardizing regulations across neighboring municipalities can achieve similar results. Cities have struggled to adequately regulate TNCs due to a number of structural barriers including a lack of political will, resistance from existing transportation modes like taxis, or a lack of government capacity.[56]

The 2016 Mercatus Center article "Rethinking Taxi Regulations: The Case for Fundamental Reform" recommends a "fundamental reform of the entire regulatory regime in order to create a fair, open, and competitive transportation market." The article notes:

> Taxi regulations limit competition, thereby yielding higher prices, lower quality, and antiquated technologies and practices. Now is an opportune time to rethink the entire structure of taxi regulations. Policymakers should start with a blank slate, identifying the systemic market failure that the regulations aim to address and then proposing alternative solutions with their expected benefits and costs. These alternatives should include the option of no regulation. Only then can ride sharing regulatory policies best serve consumers.[57]

Since 2015, the Hawai'i State Legislature, lawmakers, and the City and County of Honolulu have considered separate legislation regarding Uber's operations in Honolulu. The May 2016 Legislature session closed with no enacted legislation.[58]

Since December 2017, the State DOT tested the efficiency of TNCs (Uber, Lyft) in a pilot program at the Daniel K. Inouye International Airport (HNL). The program proved the "operational feasibility of the services" as well as finding a demand for them. The DOT noted TNCs were received well by the public at HNL, and "we are pleased to offer the option to neighbor island travelers."[59] The pilot program and the public hearings found significant support and interest in TNC services.

On August 2018, the Legislature amended the State DOT Airport Division, Hawai'i Administrative Rules (HAR), Chapter 19–20.1, Commercial Services at Public Airport, Subchapter 9, Prearranged Ground Transportation. The rules defined a TNC and set annual administrative fees as well as a required percentage of monthly gross receipts[60] to allow TNCs to operate at HNL on a permanent basis. Governor Ige approved the rule following statewide public hearings.[61]

On February 1, 2019, the State DOT approved TNCs for passenger pickup at OGG, JHM, Lihue Airport (LIH) on Kaua'i, Ellison Onizuka Kona International Airport at Keahole (KOA), and Hilo International Airport (ITO).[62]

The DOT's HARs were amended in 2018 to allow TNCs to operate at HNL and the neighbor island airports. However, there are no current overall statewide regulations regarding TNCs. Hawai'i revised statutes (HRSs) and

HARs need to be enacted to minimize administrative costs of regulation, have consistent rules, address the safety of residents and passengers, enhance transportation options for the state, and ensure TNCs are operating within a consistent statewide regulatory framework.

In January 2019, Chair of the Senate Committee on Transportation Lorraine Inouye introduced Senate Bill 1161, relating to transportation network companies, to the Hawai'i Senate's 30th Legislature. The bill was to enact statewide rules to ensure a level playing field for prearranged ground transportation companies.[63] In January 2019, House Committee Bill HB1093 (companion bill to Senate Bill 1161 SD2) was introduced by Senator Henry J. C. Aquino, chair of the House Committee on Transportation.[64] Both bills have similar language regarding the need for statewide TNC regulations. The latest version of House Bill 1093 SD1 appropriated funds to the DOT.[65] Both bills allow the State DOT to permit and regulate TNCs. Senate Bill 1161 SD2 sought to amend the HRS by adding a Chapter titled "TRANSPORTATION NETWORK COMPANIES," complete with definitions for TNCs and TNC drivers; permits and annual permit fees; fare transparency; requirements for a state agent, an identification process for drivers and vehicles, electronic receipts; insurance and driver requirements, discrimination; auditing procedures; and uniform statewide regulation.

Testifiers in support of Senate Bill 1161 consisted of the State DOT, City and County of Honolulu Department of Customer Services (DCS), Uber, and Lyft. The State DOT provided testimony in support of the bill but didn't understand the program's requirements; further discussion was required to determine how much it would cost to fund the staff and program. They noted transportation options were good for the community, demand was apparent, and the bill contained language to protect the public's safety.[66]

The City and County of Honolulu Department of Transportation Services (DTS) provided testimony in support of the bill, but noted they have the right to oversee and charge appropriate fees to TNCs within the single statewide regulatory framework. The City's DCS had issues with the oversight and accountability of TNCs, permit and annual fees, funding, the potential loophole regarding oversight of motor vehicle agency(s) and moving violations, and vehicle inspections. They wanted to ensure the bill gave the local jurisdiction the appropriate tools to identify who, what, where, when, and why as it relates to TNC operations.[67]

Traci Lee, Senior Public Policy Manager at Lyft, provided testimony in support of Senate Bill 1161:

> As of 2019, 45 states across the country have passed statewide legislation like Senate Bill 1161 that regulates Lyft in a safe and comprehensive manner. Lyft hopes Hawai'i can join that effort and allow consumers to have the ability of choosing Lyft in Hawai'i. Lyft enhanced local transportation options for locals and tourists, and acts as a complement to existing transportation infrastructure investments. Throughout the US, Lyft has partnered with different transportation agencies and municipalities to make it easier for people to use public transit by serving as first-mile and last-mile connectors, or by being a guaranteed ride home from work (incentivizing carpooling and the use of public transit in at least one direction).
>
> Since June 2014, Lyft has been a transportation option on Oahu. Since March 2017, Lyft has been available on the Big Island, Maui, and Kauai. Lyft provided a transportation option for communities that are traditionally underserved by other forms of transit. Riders like the service because they know are going to get seamless, affordable, and reliable transportation that is regulated statewide.
>
> Lyft is more than just a ridesharing application. It is a unique and flexible economic opportunity that turns anyone with a car into an entrepreneur, who can set a schedule according to their terms.
>
> Lyft is contributing to a more sustainable Hawai'i. Over 80 percent of cars on the road have only one occupant. By getting a Lyft instead of driving their cars, people in Hawai'i are saving time, reducing congestion, freeing up parking, making efficient use of existing roads, and supporting sustainable transportation infrastructure.
>
> Senate Bill 1161 is a path towards providing consumers, drivers and visitors a consistent experience with Lyft. We urge this committee to support establishing a clear, workable regulatory framework that can be applied to all ridesharing companies regardless of size and cities of operation to ensure that safe, reliable and affordable rides are available for all in Hawai'i.

Lyft also suggested technical edits to the bill's language in testimony. Lyft noted the proposed Express Drive program language would prohibit a TNC from owning a TNC vehicle in Hawai'i.[68] Other edits included: (1) that any vehicle may qualify as a TNC vehicle, (2) how to display the TNC driver and TNC vehicle's license plate number to a passenger; (4) amended the bill's language regarding the HRS, Chapter 431, INSURANCE, Insurance Code, Section 431:10C-703 to be concise;[69] (5) inserted language to amend the driver application to include correct language to align with the U.S. Department of Justice national sex offender registry; and (6) replaced the word "proof" with "valid."

Tabatha Chow, Uber's senior operations manager, wrote testimony in support of the bills and noted they "would provide uniform regulations for TNC operations throughout all of Hawai'i." The company's driver screening and other operating requirements are currently mandated for Honolulu under the City's Revised Ordinances of Honolulu (ROH), Chapter 12. Uber's technology platform app connects local, independent drivers with Hawai'i residents and visitors. The author reached out to Ms. Chow for a statement via a LinkedIn email on June 6, 2019 but did not receive a response.

The State Office of Information Practices (OIP), Hawai'i Insurers Council, and City's DTS took no position on the bills.[70]

Testimony in opposition to the bills were from Charley's Taxi, individual taxicab owners, Island Limo, the Hawaii Transportation Association, Roberts Hawaii, and the Hawaii Passenger and Property Carriers Association.

Charley's Taxi noted "the Legislature should not be picking winners and losers in the transportation industry in Hawai'i."[71] "TNCs should not be allowed to come into the state to upset the market and jeopardize the viability of our local transportation business . . . they (TNCs) must play by the same rules as everyone else."[72] Charley's Taxi noted TNCs should follow the same county ordinances for taxicab operators and the Public Utilities Commission's (PUC) HRS Chapter 271, Regarding Motor Carrier Law.[73]

Charley's Taxi, AllWays Charley's (a licensed TNC)[74], Roberts Hawaii, Island Limo Hawaii Transportation Association, Island Limo, and multiple taxi drivers had similar concerns:

- The bills are flawed—they give TNCs (Uber, Lyft) special treatment and economic advantages over local certified PUC motor carriers and operators.
- Taxicab operators and motor carriers are regulated by the PUC, and they cannot discriminate against riders.
- The bills are discriminatory and are biased against taxi drivers.
- The consumer is at risk, as TNCs are not bound by the counties' ordinances to transport riders in the most direct and shortest route possible.
- Surge pricing is allowed under the bill and does not protect unsophisticated consumers (kupuna) or visitors.
- Not everyone has a credit card or Internet access; this is a form of discrimination.

- TNCs can pick and choose their riders and choose not to accept a trip.
- The bill's proposed audit of TNCs is not transparent.
- TNCs can conduct their own background checks or have them administered by a third party of their choice, but taxicab companies cannot, pursuant to county ordinances.
- Additional comments are reserved for convicted felons and misdemeanors relating to driving, violent or sexual offenses.
- The PUC should allow the counties to regulate TNCs, as the DOT does not have the staff or funds to implement regulatory requirements and/or a permit system.
- Lyft and Uber are monopolizing the taxi and TNC market and are operating outside the Motor Carrier Act.
- TNC drivers fall into the legal definition of a contract carrier.
- Uber and Lyft will monopolize pricing and profits as Hawai'i considers passing legislation designed to unfairly benefit TNCs at the expense of the local regulated companies.
- TNCs operate with fewer insurance coverage standards, but comparable public coverage standards and comparable liability coverages, than taxis and PUC operators.
- TNCs can change rates and fares based on rider demand as opposed to the set fare structures that taxis and other PUC operators must follow (and seek approval to change).
- There is no need to reinvent a regulatory structure.
- Regulations need to cover enforcement inspections by the PUC and the DOT, not the whim of the TNCs.[75]

Local taxicab drivers noted they're being put at an unfair disadvantage due to the rules they have to adhere to and believe that they are being run out of business by competitors. As journalist Cameron Miculka notes, "It's an issue communities have faced throughout the country as ridesharing has upended traditional transportation companies, and between a local fare schedule that hasn't changed in a decade and a lack of regulations specifically aimed at Uber and Lyft (which are considered transportation network companies and not taxi companies), long-time taxicab drivers are feeling the pressure."[76] Full-time jobs are being replaced with part-time positions as taxi fleets have been cut in half. Airport revenue is down 86 percent. The state's transportation industry is being destroyed.

Testimony noted that in Hawai'i County Codes, Chapter 18, PUBLIC

TRANSPORTATION, Common Carrier[77] taxi drivers have to charge rates fixed in statute: $3 for the start of a ride and first eighth of a mile or minute of waiting/elapsed time, and $0.40 for each additional eighth of a mile and additional minute of waiting or elapsed time. Taxicab drivers may charge $1 for luggage. TNC drivers are not restricted to these fixed fare rates. The fees were last set in 2008 when the county council raised rates. A taxi driver noted they must charge the same amount—if a different amount is charged then its fraud or tax evasion. This lack of regulatory rules for TNCs gives them an unfair advantage over taxicab drivers.

Taxicab drivers make upfront investments and pay for the cab's meter, top light, and lettering. Taxicab companies and drivers must navigate more paperwork and applications. Vehicles require inspection and a certificate if they are operating on the Big Island from the Hawai'i County Transportation Commission.[78] Taxicab owners must get a license for the vehicle and a personal license. Taxicab drivers must submit a ten-year background check from the courthouse, a seven-year driver's abstract, a doctor's clearance, and pass a test. It can cost $10,000 to get a vehicle up to taxicab standard requirements.

Hawai'i is the only state that does not have a centralized motor vehicle agency; each county separately regulates the DMV. The Hawai'i State Judiciary assesses moving violations. If a TNC driver gets a ticket, it is reflected on their driver's license record, but it does not indicate the number of moving violations. Critics have identified this loophole in both bills.

Critics also noted the language needs to be worked out. The annual permit fee should be moved to a per-volume approach based on the number of independent contractors and/or employees. The independent contractor and/or employee count should be the total registered number with the vendors, and not defined as off-peak or part time. The price of the permit should be based on the number of employees regardless of status (full time or part time). Fees should be used to fund staff, enforcement, and recordkeeping. The proposed audit procedures language should change to a full audit versus the proposed "samples" given by the TNC. The confidentiality clause needs to be revised. Section 11 of the bill pertaining to the recordkeeping requirement is inconsistent with current law, pursuant to HRS, Chapter 431, INSURANCE, Insurance Code Section, 431:10C-704(a)(1), and (a)(2).[79]

People love the island of Maui. Tourists come to Maui to experience a unique lifestyle, adventure, beautiful weather, and to experience a trip of a lifetime. What can we learn from the current facts regarding the number of Maui visitors, numbers of commuters to and from West Maui, lack of housing, home ownership that is out of reach for residents, current public transportation options, and how residents commute to work? What smart decisions can be made? What improvements regarding the current infrastructure (highways, harbors, airports) and resources are being addressed to meet climate change?

The We Are West Maui Climate Change and Sea Level Rise Technical Resource Paper indicated the West Side is vulnerable to tsunamis, flooding, high waves, and coastal erosion. Since the early 1900s, West Maui has lost approximately 14 percent of beach length to erosion—more than Maui, Kaua'i, and O'ahu. Long-term planning and approval is needed to guide developers about maintaining current development and constructing future development outside of the sea sea-level rise exposure area.[80]

The author acknowledges the State's initiative to meet climate change. The state's Climate Commission[81] report to the State Legislature, 2019 Regular Session, titled, "Hawai'i Climate Change Mitigation and Adaptation Commission," and the Hawai'i Sea Level Rise and Vulnerability and Adaptation Report both indicated places and locations vulnerable to sea level rise and possible scenarios for adaptation.[82]

Maui County's Mayor Arakawa Sea Level Proclamation, dated February 22, 2018, accepted the "2017 Hawai'i Sea Level Rise Vulnerability and Adaptation Report," Hawai'i Sea Level Rise Data Viewer, and Sea Level Rise Exposure Area (SLR-XA); it directs county Departments to use the appropriate sources to address sea level rise in Maui's communities, and addresses climate change and the need to adapt to climate change to protect Maui County's future.[83]

The author acknowledges the State's strides to meet the 2045 Renewable Energy Goal. In 2015, Governor Ige signed into law bills to strengthen Hawai'i's commitment to clean energy by directing the PUC to oversee the state's utilities to generate 100 percent of their electricity sales from renewable energy resources by 2045.[84]

Commuters to and from West Maui could use help in the form of a rideshare app platform/TNC to reduce daily traffic congestion. An "Uber/Lyft"-type rideshare platform app will have positive benefits, as there will be a reduction in the use of personal vehicles, reduction to use of infrastructure, decreased traffic congestion, creation of jobs, contribution to the economy and reduction in carbon emissions.

Whoever runs the proposed rideshare app platform, whether it is Maui County, a non-governmental entity, a non-profit, or a public-private partnership (P3), needs to address the type of app platform to be utilized. The rideshare app platform will likely require up-to-date technology, programming and funds—

requirements this chapter has not touched upon. The app platform is probably expensive and would require funds, but the cost is unclear.

To fund the idea of alternative transportation, perhaps Maui County may look at enacting an empty-homes tax like Vancouver, Canada, pursuant to the Vacancy Tax Bylaw No. 11674. An empty-homes tax stems from a residential property owner declaration regarding the status of their property. If an unoccupied residential property is vacant more than six months out of the year, the owners will be subject to a tax of one percent of the property's annually assessed taxable value. The tax does not apply to principal residences or homes rented for six months of the year. Maui County could use the net revenues from the tax to reinvest in affordable housing initiatives, or in this case alternative transportation options like ridesharing.[85]

Senate Bill 1161 SD2 and House Bill 1039 SD1 SD2 tried to attach TNCs administratively to the State DOT, but they didn't understand how the program would run and how much the program would cost. *The State DOT was talking about running a proposed program for a TNC app platform that is already being utilized effectively by TNCs.*

If a P3 rideshare were started, who would run it? The general public needs transparency, and the current lack of an HRS and HAR regulatory framework is a major deterrent. The P3 would have to be attached administratively to a state and/or county agency. The HRS, HARs and/or county ordinances or codes would need to be created by an appropriate governing body and approved with public input. Funding, staffing and logistics would need to be generated and approved by the appropriate parties. And last but not least, if the P3 employees were not considered employees, then union classifications would need to be created—which can be a headache.

Multiple factors would go into the P3 that the county or state does not have, such as: the current resources to meet cost and pricing to match current supply and demand, driver accountability, driver flexibility, insurance and liability coverage, compensation, a TNC app platform and adequate technology, and an app platform integrated with an online map program.

TNCs create a liaison between riders who need transportation to drivers who need to work—this is a win-win scenario. Further, riders that use TNCs use psychology and alter their social behavior. One of the strongest reasons that Uber and Lyft succeeded is not just the technology that allows the app to connect potential passengers to drivers, but that when the ride is over, the customer's satisfaction is immediate. Technology has enabled the passenger to show happiness and vent frustration or anger through the app platform. Thus, the psychological benefits of being able to get results quickly and communicate feelings plays a powerful role in the use of a TNC.

The state PUC is authorized to inspect TNCs, but they have given the responsibility over to local jurisdictions. The PUC does not regulate TNCs. However, this is the complete opposite of what taxicab companies believed the PUC does regulate when they provided testimony for Senate Bill 1161 SD2 and House Bill 1039 SD1 SD2.

Taxicab companies noted, "long-established and well thought-out regulations already exist for the transportation of passengers for the safety and security of those passengers and the general public. The action is still transporting passengers. TNCs fall into the definition of the PUC's Common Carrier and the definition of a Federal and the State DOT's motor carrier."[86]

The PUC notes that the misinterpretation stems from the wording and "type" of activity that the PUC regulates. The PUC's authority comes from HRS, Chapter 271, and HAR, Chapter 6-62. The language in both chapters refers to the PUC's oversight and regulation of the transportation of people and/or property over public highways for compensation. TNC activities and businesses are "considered" a "similar" activity akin to taxis. The PUC exempts taxicabs under HRS, Chapter 269, TRANSPORTATION AND UTILITIES, PUBLIC UTILITIES COMMISSION, Section 269-1(2)(B), "an owner or operator of a taxicab as defined in this section,"[87] and therefore does not regulate TNCs. The PUC noted taxis should be regulated by specific county codes.[88]

Maui County's Code of Ordinances, Title 5, "Business Licenses and Regulations, Chapter 5.16. Taxicabs," regulates taxis and taxicab operations. Critics of TNCs say they may or may not fall under this code. Maui taxicabs are heavily regulated by Maui County and pay fees and taxes, yet TNCs have yet to be addressed.[89]

The author emailed Maui County's Department of Transportation Director Marc Takamori[90] as well as Deputy Director Michael Du Pont regarding TNCs. In a phone conversation with them they noted Maui County's Department of Finance, Division of Motor Vehicle Registration (DMV) and Licensing Division was in charge of regulating taxicabs. The DMV does not regulate taxicabs; however, the Maui County Council may be addressing TNCs in the future.[91]

The author called Maui County Councilmember Yuki Lei Sugimura, who is the chair of the Multimodal Transportation Committee. Her office affirmed that TNCs would be addressed during the upcoming 2019–2021 committee assignments.[92]

The County of Hawai'i's Code 1983 does not identify TNCs in Chapter

18, PUBLIC TRANSPORTATION: the chapter that regulates taxicabs, school buses and the public transit system.[93]

In December 2016, Honolulu's City Council passed Bill 55 (ROH 16-38) relating to Private Transportation Companies (PTCs) and drivers. A PTC is either a taxi or TNC. The ROH defined TNCs, set the number of standards for operators, limited passengers to the number of seat belts in the vehicle, and restricted drivers from smoking in their vehicle with passengers. The City's Customer Service Division, DMV, Licensing and Permits, maintains oversight and accountability of TNCs on O'ahu. The agency ensures the safe operations and standard assurances to the public regarding TNCs.[94]

However, it seems that TNCs, like Airbnb and other Internet-based companies, have a "new business model" the state has not seen before. Maybe these companies should be placed into a different category or new division entirely before placing them into an existing state entity or division, where the rules have to be streamlined or amended to make them fit. TNCs seem to be a round piece of luggage being placed into a square luggage bin, and the passenger wrestling with the luggage is the legislature.

TNCs do need to be regulated statewide. The bill was carried over to the 2020 Legislative session scheduled to convene in January 15, 2020. However, on March 17, 2020, due to the coronavirus pandemic, the Hawai'i State Legislature suspended its session, and on June 19, 2020, both Senate and House conferees were discharged. When the State Legislature reconvenes, House Bill 1093 SD1 SD2 will require a team of senators and representatives to meet in conference committee meetings to determine whether a final form of the bill (conference draft CD1) can be agreed upon.[95] Senate Bill 1161 has a lot further to go.

Counties may want to revisit their codes and ordinances governing taxicabs so they are on a fair and equitable footing with TNCs. In February 2019, Senator Inouye remarked, "By enshrining businesses such as Uber and Lyft into state law, the ride-sharing apps will be even harder for traditional cabs to compete against."[96]

Taxicabs can utilize rideshare app platforms as well. For instance, Curb and zTrip are two TNC rideshare app platforms aimed at taxicab companies. Curb allows passengers to hail yellow cabs in advance through an app, which can also track the car. The taxicab fare is based on how long the meter is running and allows for detours, which Uber does not. However, the fares are higher and there is an up-front service fee.

ZTrip is a rideshare app platform-based taxi service that lets pre-existing taxicab drivers work through online ride-hailing. Customizable pickup options and up-front pricing are available. Drivers can either use their own car or lease a zTrip car to prevent using their own automobiles.

Ultimately, we should not to try to duplicate a "rideshare-like app." As both Uber and Lyft have already created advanced ridesharing apps, and considering the cost of technology development, why waste time and funds trying to reinvent the wheel?

The author reached out to Lyft and Uber via LinkedIn messaging on June 5, 2019. Uber did not respond. An immediate response via email and phone came from Ms. Alexander and Ms. Lee[97] from Lyft. They provided the following answers to questions via email on June 17, 2019:

> *Q: You mentioned that Lyft is looking at transportation holistically. Are there cities where Lyft has stepped in to help with their transportation requirements that have shortcomings in their modal system? Can you explain how Lyft stepped in to help? I think you mentioned Seattle and Louisiana as cities that had issues such as bus shortages.*
>
> A: Lyft is committed to effecting positive change for our cities by promoting transportation equity through shared rides, bikeshare systems, electric scooters, and public transit partnerships. We recognize the critical role public transit plays in the communities we serve as many of our most popular pick-up/drop-off spots are adjacent to public transit stations. We look forward to continued partnerships with transit agencies around the country, as we explore how Lyft can help support local transportation needs.
>
> Lyft works with transportation partners to design programs that help the agencies address the specific gaps in service and/or transportation access barriers the agency is working to solve.
>
> Our partnership development process is a service planning exercise that revolves around questions of geographical coverage, service hours, passenger fares, etc.
>
> We recently partnered with various transit agencies in Seattle to help them navigate a huge infrastructure project that closed the major highway artery in the city, the Alaskan Viaduct. We provided shared ride discounts to various transit stops to help ease congestion during this constrained period.

The author was referred to a link regarding Shared Ride Discounts.[98] Lyft partnered with the City of Seattle, King County Metro, and Sound Transit to provide affordable and reliable transportation to get riders through the viaduct closure. Shared rides were offered at a $2.75 discount to match the cost of the public transit to and from select transit hubs, and to encourage the public's use of transit. Lyft installed a "Nearby Transit" feature in the app so Seattle riders could view public transit information.

Lyft saw a nine-percent spike in shared rides to and from light rail stations and transit hubs between January 14 and 16, 2019, at the start of the Viaduct closure, at three stations.[99]

In January 2019, Lyft partnered with Valley Regional Transit, located in Boise, Idaho, to get riders between 14 pre-approved bus stops and their homes for a $2 flat fee.[100] "We're behind our peers in terms of transit," VRT Principal Planner Stephen Hunt told *BW* last July. "And we're not talking about spectacular cities of transit Nirvana. We're talking about Reno, Nevada, and Spokane, Washington, which invest four to five times more than what we do on per-capita transportation." The VRT announced the program to combat the city's transit woes. "There is often considerable distance a commuter must travel to or from their final destination when taking the bus," wrote VRT Mobility Collaborative Program Director Kaite. "This distance, referred to as first and last mile, can be an inconvenience or even a deterrent to using public transportation." Lyft noted the program will improve access to public transportation and help decouple access to convenient regional mobility from auto ownership."[101]

Lyft partnerships are "envisioned in a world in which cities are not built around parking lots and roads, but are reimagined to center around our communities. And we believe that partnering with public transit agencies is critical to this vision." Lyft is working with agency partners to develop new approaches to first-last mile programs, suburban mobility, and on-demand transportation. Lyft's municipal partners have included:

- The City of Monrovia, California to enable residents and visitors to access a Lyft ride in the GoMonrovia service area for $0.50 to connect to the Los Angeles Metro Gold Line. The P3 provided the community with an enhanced and affordable transportation option.
- The Regional Transportation Commission (RTC) of Southern Nevada, to provide an on-demand transportation pilot program to the paratransit community. Customers noted the life-transforming impact the RTC and Lyft provided them by enabling same-day, on-demand travel versus booking rides days out in advance.
- Pierce County Transit, Washington to bridge first-last-mile gaps to bus and rail stations in Pierce County, adding mobility and new multimodal

options. This program was made available via the 2016 Federal Transit Administration's Mobility on Demand Sandbox Grant Program, Limited Access Connections.[102]

- Transportation Authority of Marin County, California, to provide passenger discounts to expand access to use the Lyft Line to and from the region's new SMART rail line.
- Charlotte Area Transit System, North Carolina, to provide discounted first-last-mile trips to Charlotte's new light rail extension.

Lyft is working with public transportation agencies to reshape the way communities move and make it easier for communities across the country to access transit solutions. Lyft is open to working with a city, county or transportation agency to increase mobility.[103]

Q: Can you provide a statement how Lyft might benefit communities in the future?

A: We envision a world in which cities are not built around parking lots and roads but are reimagined to center around our communities. And we believe that partnering with public transit agencies is critical to this vision. You can read more about our commitment to cities and specifically our City Works program.[104]

Lyft's City Works program serves cities and those who have dedicated themselves to shaping them. Lyft committed a minimum of $50 million a year (or one percent of profits, whichever is greater) to continue to improve city life through grassroots transportation initiatives, such as: providing transportation options, developing transportation infrastructure, creating clean energy, Lyft City works LA, helping with disaster recovery efforts, access to healthy food, environmental sustainability, civic engagement, and an ongoing commitment to LGBTQ+ equality and inclusion.

Lyft provides free and reduced rider prices for medical patients, low-income seniors, veterans in transition, and victims of natural disasters. Lyft notes increasing mobility is a proven way to boost economic opportunity for lower-income residents lacking in transportation options. In partnership with local governments, transit agencies, and nonprofit organizations Lyft is helping cities quickly and efficiently expand their transportation infrastructure with bikes, scooters, transit, and shared rides.

Lyft invests heavily in products minimizing single-occupancy rides (Shared Saver rides, Lyft Bikes, and Scooters). Lyft collaborates with local and national advocacy groups to fight for climate action, and more green spaces within cities. Lyft is working with local civic and nonprofit leaders to provide transportation, develop infrastructure, and to reduce emissions in Los Angeles.

Lyft offers nonprofits seeking transportation grants to support their communities. The Wheels for All program during disasters helped people travel safely to shelters, hospitals, evacuation centers, and blood donation centers. Lyft's Grocery Access Program (DC metro area) partnered with Martha's Table to give residents living in food deserts access to fresh and healthy foods. Lyft is a fully carbon-neutral company and has committed to offsetting over a million metric tons of carbon annually. Lyft helped with voter registration (2018 midterms) by providing discounted and free rides to people who lack transportation options.[105]

Q: You mentioned Lyft has stepped in to replace first- and last-mile connectors.

A: First and last mile connections simply refer to the literal first and last mile individuals might have to travel on foot or otherwise to reach their final destination when using public transit.

Q: Does Lyft have a transportation-focused department... may I get a short summary about their goal(s)?

A: Lyft defines itself as a transportation network, so I think just speaking to the company, in general, is fine.

Q: I mentioned to you that I was located in West Maui and that the book is exploring the option for a type of ride sharing app. I was wondering what type of factors Lyft's transportation department or focus group would consider.

A: Lyft is available in West Maui to my knowledge, and so we would always encourage folks to use our app accordingly. As I mentioned above, we are excited about our transit partnerships and continuing to integrate transit into our app. We would certainly be open to more conversations with local leadership on how best to assist with transit needs there.

Q: You mentioned sustainable plan and also climate change. What is Lyft's position on the future of ownership of cars and how best to help with climate change?

A: A Year of Carbon Neutral Rides:

A year ago, we became one of the world's largest purchasers of carbon offsets and made all Lyft rides carbon neutral. Last September, we took it a step further and committed to full carbon neutrality. Since April 2018, we've effectively eliminated the amount of carbon that it would take 2.4 million acres of trees to remove in a single year by purchasing 2,062,500 metric tons of carbon offsets.

While making all Lyft rides carbon neutral doesn't solve climate change, it's a big step forward. We've also made other efforts to lessen our environmental impact, including minimizing single-occupancy rides by adding shared saver rides and bikes and scooters to the Lyft app, expanding the number of electric vehicles on the road, and working with local advocacy groups to bring more green space to our cities.[106]

Earth Day—One Day, One Butt, One Seat:[107]

To make a difference on Earth Day, Lyft is looking to the OG carbon-free form of transport: the bicycle. Lyft is constantly thinking about butt-math: a car has five seats; a person has one butt. The more people share the ride, the more cars are off the road. Although Lyft rides are carbon neutral and we're working to introduce thousands of electric vehicles to the Lyft app this year, we are not there yet. The benefits of bike riding are evident: It's healthier. It can be faster. And it's better for our planet. That's why we now operate one of the largest bikeshare networks in the country. On April 22, all participating bikeshare rides are free. Ride a bike—your bike, a buddy's bike, a neighbor's bike, any bike—and do your part for the Earth.

Share a Seat in a Shared (Ride): Request a shared ride and we'll match you with riders heading the same direction, and you'll save a few bucks in the process. Less congestion is a sweet way to help save the earth. By becoming America's largest bikeshare service as well as launching Lyft scooters and integrating public transit into the Lyft app, we're working to create a better future for the communities we serve and build on our promise to offer transportation options that are better for the environment.

My final thoughts are: if we continue to move in the direction of trying to change or amend laws for the state or the counties for TNCs—technology is going to outpace us.

In 2015, the cost of owning a car was $33,560. By 2020, car ownership will cost $7,517 due to depreciation.[108] If car ownership is optional due to the availability of multiple transportation options, this is to our advantage. We can say goodbye to car ownership, reduce traffic congestion, free up parking areas, make efficient use of existing roads, support sustainable transportation infrastructure, and promote transportation equity.

Maui is addressing climate change as we are exploring all available transportation options for our future generations. By focusing on reducing our carbon footprint we can offset carbon emissions. Ridesharing is one step towards a sustainable Maui. We should look to TNCs to help enhance transportation for residents, commuters and tourists. TNCs can step in and act as a complement to existing transportation infrastructure investments on Maui. TNCs allow people to be efficient, save time, save money, and reduce their environmental footprint.

Notes

1. www.pewresearch.org/fact-tank/2019/01/17/where-millennials-end-and-generation-z-begins/.
2. https://genius.com/Queen-and-david-bowie-under-pressure-lyrics.
3. https://en.wikipedia.org/wiki/Maui.
4. https://en.wikipedia.org/wiki/Maui_County,_Hawaii.
5. http://airports.hawaii.gov/ogg/.
6. https://hidot.hawaii.gov/highways/home/maui/maui-state-roads-and-highways/.
7. https://dlnr.hawaii.gov/dobor/maui-island-facilities/.
8. Maui, Lanai, Molokai, and Kahoolawe are located in the Hawaiian Islands Humpback Whale National Marine Sanctuary (HIHWNMS). Visitors come to Maui for whale watching season. The industry makes approximately $20 million in revenue per year from the annual migration from November through May (or peak season from January through March) of approximately 10,000 humpback whales every year.
9. http://airports.hawaii.gov/jhm/; http://hidot.hawaii.gov/airports/files/2013/01/annual-air-traffic-statistics.pdf; https://hidot.hawaii.gov/airports/files/2012/12/annual-air-traffic-statistics_20170607.pdf.
10. Email from HDOT AIR EP Iris Fujii on June 19, 2019.
11. www.hawaiitourismauthority.org/research/annual-visitor-research-reports/ and https://dbedt.hawaii.gov/visitor/visitor-research/.
12. www.hawaiitourismauthority.org/research/monthly-visitor-statistics/.
13. https://mauinow.com/2018/04/09/report-maui-population-continues-to-increase-as-honolulus-declines/.
14. www.mauicounty.gov/DocumentCenter/View/110172/InfoBoard_CommProfile_POP_20170826.

15. https://en.wikipedia.org/wiki/West_Maui_Mountains.
16. We Are West Maui, West Maui Community Plan, Community Profile, January 2018. https://wearemaui.org/technical-resource-papers-community-profile.
17. www.mauicounty.gov/DocumentCenter/View/110169/InfoBoard_CommProfile_ECON_20170826 & We Are West Maui's 2017 Community profile: Economy.
18. www.mauicounty.gov/DocumentCenter/View/110169/InfoBoard_CommProfile_ECON_201708.
19. https://squareup.com/townsquare/guide-to-hawaii-minimum-wage.
20. Maui County jobs-to-housing ratio was 1.37 (58,761 occupied dwelling units to 80,686 jobs). For the state, the jobs-to-housing ratio was 1.29 (482,729 occupied dwelling units/624,579 jobs), www.mauicounty.gov/DocumentCenter/View/110170/InfoBoard_CommProfile_HOUSING_20170826.
21. Ibid.
22. www.mauicounty.gov/DocumentCenter/View/110170/InfoBoard_CommProfile_HOUSING_20170826.
23. https://affordablehousingonline.com/housing-search/Hawaii/Lahaina.
24. www.mauicounty.gov/DocumentCenter/View/110171/InfoBoard_CommProfile_INCOME_20170826.
25. www.mauicounty.gov/605/Bus-Service-Information.
26. www.mauicounty.gov/608/Maui-Bus-Commuter-Service.
27. www.mauicounty.gov/DocumentCenter/View/110196/InfoBoard_CommProfile_TRANSP3_20170912.
28. www.itdp.org/2019/03/21/ridesharing-tnc-guidelines/.
29. https://en.wikipedia.org/wiki/Shared_mobility.
30. "Top 6 Rideshare Services that Drivers are Using (and Why)." https://gridwise.io/rideshare/top-6-rideshare-services/.
31. https://en.wikipedia.org/wiki/Zimride.
32. www.businessinsider.com/how-john-zimmer-and-logan-green-started-lyft-2017-10.
33. The name Zimride comes from Logan Green's 2005 trip to Zimbabwe, where he observed the local residents sharing minivan taxis.
34. www.singlegrain.com/blog-posts/business/10-lessons-startups-can-learn-ubers-growth/.
35. Ibid.
36. https://blog.percolate.com/2015/01/5-lessons-buzzfeed-uber-building-closed-loop-growth-systems/#.
37. www.singlegrain.com/blog-posts/business/10-lessons-startups-can-learn-ubers-growth.
38. Ibid.
39. www.uberguide.net/difference-between-ubergo-and-uberx/.
40. www.uberguide.net/what-is-uber-select/.

41. https://slate.com/business/2014/01/uber-surge-pricing-more-transparency-than-people-want.html.
42. https://blog.percolate.com/2015/01/5-lessons-buzzfeed-uber-building-closed-loop-growth-systems/#.
43. https://en.wikipedia.org/wiki/Lyft.
44. https://secondmeasure.com/datapoints/rideshare-industry-overview/.
45. The fist-bumping was dropped in 2014.
46. https://expandedramblings.com/index.php/lyft-statistics/2/.
47. Lyft does not allow passengers to know their rating.
48. It is the leading provider of background checks across the country and is accredited by the National Association of Professional Background Screeners, which requires a rigorous audit of its procedures and policies by an independent auditor appointed by the Background Screen Credentialing Council.
49. Contingent comprehensive and collision coverage (up to $50,000 with a $2,500 deductible) which is applied from the time a driver accepts a ride request, until the time the ride is ended in the app. Contingent Liability Coverage (up to $50,000 per person/$100,000 per accident/$25,000 property damage) which applies from the time when a driver flips into driver mode until the driver accepts a ride request. Uninsured/underinsured Motorist Coverage (to comply with local regulations and/or state laws) and applies from the time a driver accepts a ride request in the app until the time the ride is ended in the app.
50. Lyft is the basic and most popular offering that matches passengers with nearby drivers. Lyft XL matches passengers with a vehicle that can seat at least 6 passengers. Lux matches passengers with a luxury vehicle that seats at least 4 passengers. Lux Black matches passengers with a luxury black exterior vehicle ride that seats at least four passengers. Lux Black XL matches passengers with a black exterior luxury car that seats up to 6. The Shared Ride option, which is not available in all cities, is the cheapest option and will match passengers with other riders if they are going in the same direction.
51. Information via email from Lauren Alexander, Lyft, June 7, 2019 and June 17, 2019. Direct communication from Traci Lee, Senior Public Policy Manager at Lyft, June 6, 2019.
52. www.lyftimpact.com/stats/states/hawaii.
53. GoMentum Station is located at the former Naval Weapons Station in Concord, California. It is owned by Contra Costa Transportation.
54. https://disneyparks.disney.go.com/blog/2019/06/disney-minnie-van-service-celebrates-milestone-new-enhancements-coming-as-lyft-becomes-official-rideshare-at-disney-parks/.
55. https://gridwise.io/rideshare/top-6-rideshare-services/.
56. www.itdp.org/2019/03/21/ridesharing-tnc-guidelines/.

57. Rethinking Taxi Regulations: The Case for Fundamental Reform/. www.mercatus.org/system/files/Farren_Taxi_FINAL.pdf.
58. https://mauinow.com/2016/05/27/the-maui-uber-experience/.
59. Deputy Director Ross Higashi, Hawai'i Department of Transportation Airports Division.
60. https://hidot.hawaii.gov/airports/files/2013/01/20-CommercialServices.pdf.
61. Public hearings were held in Honolulu, Kahului, Kona, and Lihue. www.hawaiifreepress.com/ArticlesMain/tabid/56/ID/22158/HDoT-New-Rules-Make-UberLyft-Permanent-at-Airport.aspx.
62. https://mauinow.com/2019/01/25/rideshare-companies-ready-for-service-at-maui-airports/.
63. Senate Bill 1161 was referred out for reading to the Senate committees on Commerce, Consumer Protection, and Health (CPH) and Transportation (TRS). The bill was amended twice (SD1, SD2) and crossed over to the House committee in its SD2 amended form. On March 7, 2019, the bill stalled as it was referred to House Committees of Transportation (TRN), Consumer Protection and Commerce (CPC) and Finance (FIN). The bill failed to get scheduled for a reading. www.capitol.hawaii.gov/measure_indiv.aspx?billtype=SB&billnumber=1161&year=2019.
64. The bill was referred to the House Committees of Transportation (TRN), Consumer Protection and Commerce (CPC), and Finance (FIN). House Bill HB1093 passed several readings and was transmitted to the Senate. The bills history shows that it passed Senate Committees TRS and CPH, and Ways and Means (WAM). However, the House disagreed with the Senate's version, Senate and House conferees were selected, and the bill was scheduled for a Conference Committee Meeting in the last days of the Legislature. www.capitol.hawaii.gov/measure_indiv.aspx?billtype=HB&billnumber=1093&year=2019.
65. www.capitol.hawaii.gov/session2019/bills/HB1093_HD1_.HTM.
66. www.capitol.hawaii.gov/Session2019/Testimony/SB1161_TESTIMONY_TRS_02-11-19_.PDF.
67. Ibid.
68. Lyft's Express Drive program offers eligible drivers without a qualified vehicle an opportunity to start earning money. Lyft's Express Drive is an innovative short-term vehicle access program that offers fuel-efficient vehicles for rent to TNC drivers. Drivers can also use the vehicle for personal household needs. Express Drive rentals include insurance, routine maintenance, and a total cost of ownership that is similar to leasing a new car from a dealership. Also see: www.capitol.hawaii.gov/Session2019/Testimony/SB1161_SD1_TESTIMONY_CPH_02-26-19_.PDF.
69. www.capitol.hawaii.gov/hrscurrent/Vol09_Ch0431-0435H/HRS0431/HRS_0431-.htm.

70. Testimony dated February 26, 2019. www.capitol.hawaii.gov/Session2019/Testimony/SB1161_SD1_TESTIMONY_CPH_02-26-19_.PDF.
71. www.capitol.hawaii.gov/Session2019/Testimony/HB1093_HD2_TESTIMONY_TRS-CPH_03-20-19_.PDF.
72. Late testimony dated February 26, 2019. www.capitol.hawaii.gov/Session2019/Testimony/SB1161_SD1_TESTIMONY_CPH_02-26-19_.PDF.
73. https://cca.hawaii.gov/dca/hrs/hrs271/ & www.capitol.hawaii.gov/hrscurrent/Vol05_Ch0261-0319/HRS0271/ & www.capitol.hawaii.gov/hrscurrent/Vol05_Ch0261-0319/HRS0271/HRS_0271-.htm.
74. www.allwayscharleys.com/.
75. www.capitol.hawaii.gov/Session2019/Testimony/HB1093_SD1_TESTIMONY_WAM_04-03-19_.PDF.
76. Miculka, Cameron. "Taxicab drivers say Uber, Lyft putting them at unfair disadvantage." *West Hawaii Today*, November 24, 2018. *Accessed at*: www.hawaiitribune-herald.com/2018/11/25/hawaii-news/taxicab-drivers-say-uber-lyft-putting-them-at-unfair-disadvantage/.
77. Hawaii County Codes, Chapter 18, PUBLIC TRANSPORTATION, Common Carriers, Article 2, Taxicabs, Section 18-31 to 18.37.17 and Section 18-38 to 18-55. www.hawaiicounty.gov/lb-countycode.
78. This certification can only be granted after a public hearing determining that "public convenience and necessity" require the operation of a taxi.
79. The Hawaii Insurers Council is a non-profit trade association of property and casualty insurance companies licensed to do business in Hawai'i. Member companies underwrite approximately 40 percent of all property and casualty insurance premiums in the state.
80. https://wearemaui.org/technical-resource-papers-land-use.
81. https://climate.hawaii.gov.
82. https://dlnr.hawaii.gov/wp-content/uploads/2018/12/OCCL19-Hawaii-Climate-Change-Rpt-FY18.pdf & https://climateadaptation.hawaii.gov/wp-content/uploads/2017/12/SLR-Report_Dec2017.pdf.
83. www.mauicounty.gov/DocumentCenter/View/111851/032718_Item-E_-DLNR-OCCL-Sea-Level-Rise-Rpt_SLR-Proclamation.
84. https://governor.hawaii.gov/newsroom/press-release-governor-ige-signs-bill-setting-100-percent-renewable-energy-goal-in-power-sector/.
85. https://bylaws.vancouver.ca/11674c.PDF & https://en.wikipedia.org/wiki/Bill_28_(British_Columbia).
86. www.capitol.hawaii.gov/Session2019/Testimony/HB1093_SD1_TESTIMONY_WAM_04-03-19_.PDF.
87. www.capitol.hawaii.gov/hrscurrent/Vol05_Ch0261-0319/HRS0269/HRS_0269-0001.htm.
88. Phone conversation with PUC Maui and Oahu Branch, June 27, 2019.

89. www.mauinews.com/opinion/letters-to-the-editor/2017/06/law-regulating-taxis-not-enforced/.
90. Email to Director Marc Takamori regarding Maui County oversight on TNCs, July 6, 2019; email to Michael Du Pont on July 27, 2019.
91. Phone conversation July 16, 2019 at 9 AM.
92. Phone conversation with Kauanoe Batangan, July 16, 2019.
93. www.hawaiitribune-herald.com/2018/11/25/hawaii-news/taxicab-drivers-say-uber-lyft-putting-them-at-unfair-disadvantage/ & www.hawaiicounty.gov/lb-countycode.
94. www.honolulu.gov/rep/site/csd/PTC_Transportation_network_company_pg8.pdf.
95. Conversation with Senate Clerk regarding Senate Bill 1161 S.D. 2 on June 4, 2019; conversation with House Chief Clerk's office regarding HB1093 HD2 SD1; www.ncsl.org/research/about-state-legislatures/2018-state-legislative-session-calendar.aspx-.
96. "Bills would establish statewide regulations for 'transportation network companies' including Uber and Lyft." *Hawaii Tribune-Herald*, June 25, 2019. *Accessed at*: www.hawaiitribune-herald.com/2019/02/26/hawaii-news/bills-would-establish-statewide-regulations-for-transportation-network-companies-including-uber-and-lyft/.
97. Author phone interview with Ms. Alexander, June 7, 2019.
98. https://blog.lyft.com/posts/viaduct-closure.
99. https://mynorthwest.com/1250102/viadoom-rideshare-bike-numbers/.
100. Valley Regional Transit: Lyft Transit Connections. https://valleyregionaltransit.org/about-us/lyft-transit-connections/.
101. "Valley Regional Transit partnering with Lyft to help residents." *Boise Weekly*, January 22, 2019. *Accessed at*: www.idahopress.com/news/local/valley-regional-transit-partnering-with-lyft-to-help-residents/article_161289bc-d78a-594f-838e-03b74e9db392.html.
102. www.transit.dot.gov/research-innovation/fiscal-year-2016-mobility-demand-mod-sandbox-program-projects.
103. https://blog.lyft.com/posts/2018/6/6/how-lyft-works-with-public-transit-agencies-across-the-country-to-eliminate-transportation-barriers.
104. The author was referred to the City Works link: www.lyft.com/blog/posts/city-works-la.
105. https://www.lyft.com/city.
106. Ms. Alexander referred the author to the blog post "A Year of Carbon Neutral Lyft Rides": https://blog.lyft.com/posts/2019/5/29/a-year-of-carbon-neutral-lyft-rides?rq=Carbon%20neutral.
107. https://blog.lyft.com/posts/2019/earth-day.
108. www.moneyunder30.com/true-cost-of-owning-a-car.

Chapter 4

THE AHUPUAʻA AND THE HOUSEKEEPER

Benjamin Treviño and Victoria Larson Treviño

On a rainy day in June 2018, a group of about 70 youth, residents, and advocates pushed off from the top of the Kalihi ahupuaʻa. The entire group was on bikes. Kalihi, home to a population of 95 percent Native Hawaiian, Pacific Islander, and Asian ancestry, is not a typical backdrop for a large bicycle ride, even in Hawaiʻi. The riders, most of them under the age of 25, were participating in the second annual KAR (Kalihi Ahupuaʻa Ride), organized by the Kalihi Valley Instructional Bike Exchange (KVIBE). The inaugural ride had been held in 2017, and it would be held again in June 2019.[1]

What does a youth-led bike ride on Oʻahu have to do with traffic congestion in West Maui? For one, Kalihi may be both a glimpse of West Maui's future and a reminder of parts of its past. While West Maui will probably never include as much light industrial activity as today's Kalihi, it is already starting to mirror Kalihi's intense built environment and traffic congestion. Meanwhile, Kalihi's continuing role as a landing spot for people migrating to Hawaiʻi from other cultures around the Pacific reminds us of West Maui's historic plantation village housing during its sugarcane heyday.

But the connection between West Maui and the KAR isn't either of those things. What Kalihi, Olowalu, Ukumehame, Lahaina, Kāʻanapali, and Kapalua have in common is what lies beneath them, both physically and historically. Buried underneath the day-to-day bustle of West Maui is a much-needed technology in the struggle to achieve the community's goals—the elimination of traffic congestion among them. The connection between the Kalihi Ahupuaʻa Ride and traffic in West Maui is subtle—a hint of a suggestion—but powerful. The suggestion is powerful because the technology, dormant for decades waiting to be reclaimed, is powerful. The hint is subtle because it is about an unexpected role that one often forgotten road occupant—the humble bicycle—can play as a tool of that reclamation.

Stewards of the Land

> *I'm a rooms runner. I get the call that there is a clogged toilet in 3202. I get my plunger. I go to the room. I knock on the door. The guest opens the door. They're happy to see me. I go into the room, into the bathroom. Joo joo joo [imitates plunging a toilet]—thirty seconds later, the toilet is unclogged. The guests are happy I came in and are happy to see me leave. I walk down the hall with a sense of fulfillment that is my job. And you know what? As funny as that sounds, it's the truth.*[2]
>
> —Josh

West Maui is composed of two districts—Lahaina, from Ukumehame to Hanakaʻōʻō, and Kāʻanapali, from Honokōwai to Kahakuloa—which also comprises the second-largest job center on the Island of Maui.[3] The story of West Maui is largely a story of the people who work in these jobs, many of whom are also residents of the region. We spoke to several Kāʻanapali-area workers to learn more about their experiences, and their voices are interspersed throughout this chapter.

The intensity of visitor activity in the region means that the majority of these jobs are in the service industry. We have a tendency in our conversations on economic development to bemoan our statewide dependence on the visitor and services industries and how vulnerable it makes us. Chapter coauthor Benjamin Treviño has spent half his career as a professional software developer and has followed these conversations in Hawaiʻi for over a decade. The argument goes: *We are too dependent on the low-wage tourism industry. What we need is diversification into more innovative and economically productive sectors such as high tech. We need innovation!* The notion that a tech sector will invent new industries, opening the door to diversification, growth, and high salaries for Hawaiʻi's residents seems to be contradicted by Silicon Valley—the epicenter of this mentality—who have innovated themselves into some of the best documented social and labor problems surfacing today.[4]

Instead, we wonder if a closer look at the oft-dismissed service industry jobs might reveal a latent resource that is much more valuable when it comes to innovation. Perhaps our service industry has been supporting the development of human resources that can advance an indigenous concept of innovation—one that relies on the practice of stewardship and the observation of and response to environmental factors.

In pre-contact Hawaiian society, it was the role of the makaʻāinana to be the "eyes of the land," to tend and care for that which feeds us. Modern housekeepers, groundskeepers, and other resort employees literally do this today. Their care for the rooms, grounds, and recreational experiences enjoyed by West Maui's visitors are what keep these lands productive in today's economic systems.[5]

These workers are grounded in the land and the experience of the natural environment. Any housekeeper will know both the impact of an anticipated storm (based on who stays in their room) and its results on towels, sheets, and bathroom supplies. Groundskeepers have a similar skill, except they are connected to their ecological and stewardship predecessors in a much more literal way. They will know which windows or doors they need to close in the event of a thunderstorm, or which plants do the best in specific parts of the hotel grounds. Chapter coauthor Victoria Larson Treviño recalls cleaning up trash around Puʻu Kekaʻa (Black Rock) with a hotel engineer because it was the time of year when birds were nesting in the rocks and the engineer was afraid they would stop coming back if there was trash.

These skills and sensitivities developed over time are the basis for an indigenous style of innovation. These kinds of innovations don't make today's headlines. They don't meet venture capitalists' investment criteria. But they add up to sustainable systems that work. They also lead to the breathtaking complexity and sophistication of the Native Hawaiian society's technological achievements. Both of these features—sustainability and sophistication—are exemplified by the technology we are focused on here: the ahupuaʻa.

Island Urbanism

In the spring of 2017, the Maui County Planning division kicked off a multiyear effort to update a long-range plan for West Maui. The West Maui Community Plan is intended to guide future development of West Maui and inform decisions about land use, parks, and infrastructure for a 20-year time horizon. The development of the plan included an extensive and thoughtful community engagement process. That process integrated the voices of the engaged stakeholders and residents into the following vision:

> West Maui has everything its residents need to thrive, including a range of affordable housing options, community services, a diversified economy with family-wage jobs, and ample access to open spaces and parks, mauka to makai. Conscious of the region's rich cultural heritage, care is taken to protect and restore historic sites and to incorporate traditional Hawaiian practices that made the Island sustainable for generations. Visitors are welcomed with Aloha, and everyone enjoys an active lifestyle with safe walking, biking and public transit routes within and between West Maui's communities, and a healthy environment with resilient shorelines.
>
> - Ready and resilient systems.
> - A complete, balanced and connected transportation network.
> - Responsible stewardship of resources, culture and character.
> - Economic opportunity through innovation and collaboration.
> - Safe, healthy, livable communities for all.
>
> With this plan, the community places a greater emphasis on the interconnectedness of the natural and human-made systems, structures, and services that make West Maui a community and are vital for planning for the future.[6]

A few years prior, in March of 2014, the University of Hawai'i Press published a collection entitled *The Value of Hawai'i 2: Ancestral Roots and Oceanic Visions*.[7] One of the contributors was artist/architect Sean Connelly, whose chapter was titled "Urbanism as Island Living." In it, Connelly asserts that pre-contact Hawaiian living quarters—described as "scattered about without any order" by Captain Cook upon his arrival to Hawai'i, and incorrectly categorized as rural—were actually an expression of urbanism. His essay goes on to lay out the elements of an urban possibility in Hawai'i that does not include the images of what we consider urban today: "buildings, streets, power lines, congestion."

> To summarize a future vision for an urban island living: Hawai'i is a place where healthy neighborhoods raise resilient communities on clean, renewable energies and locally grown organic foods and materials, with less congestion and lots of open space. A place where our robust economy supports innovative local businesses and artists, and provides fulfilling jobs for everyone, with opportunities to invent new kinds of jobs for those who choose to pursue them.[8]

If it strikes you as an echo of the West Maui Planning vision, we agree. As Connelly points out, to some extent, today we define urbanism as congestion. Urbanism, from this view, does not provide a solution to congestion; they are inseparable. But this isn't really acceptable: ninety percent of the population of Hawaiʻi is now urban, West Maui being no exception. Successful, livable urbanism is thus paramount for a successful, livable West Maui.[9]

If Connelly's vision is achievable, it provides an urban—and thus practical—way forward that is consistent with West Maui's vision. So, what exactly is Island Urbanism, and how do we achieve it? Simply put: Island Urbanism is an urban form based on the technology of the ahupuaʻa, and it is achieved through their repair and recovery.

> *Ahupuaʻa are among the largest moving structures on Earth. Their surfaces emerge from the genealogy of the planet itself, making them infinite and universal. When utilized as a technology, the massive, watery, and viscous architecture of ahupuaʻa directs an island economy to operate at a planetary magnitude.*[10]
>
> —Sean Connelly

> *You can think of stream restoration as a tactic; it's not necessarily the end goal. It's one component of a larger effort to actually reclaim the entire watershed as something of a technology that we use to produce the resources we need to live on an island.*[11]
>
> —Sean Connelly

The March 2004 issue of *Maui* magazine published an article by Michael Stein titled: "Ahupuaʻa, Land for the Good of All." Stein's discussion of ahupuaʻa was framed by West Maui. It included West Maui history: aliʻi fleeing Kamehameha I through Olowalu Pass. It described sacred places in West Maui: Keōpūolani's burial site at Mokuʻula. It featured West Maui cultural practitioners: Keʻeaumoku Kapu sharing the story of Kauaʻula Valley's historic abundance.[12]

Stein goes on to describe ahupuaʻa as: "Hawaiian land divisions, usually more or less pie-shaped sections of land that extend from mountain summits through the valleys down to the outer edge of the ocean reef. Historically (and ideally), within an ahupuaʻa, the people could grow or gather and exchange everything they needed for survival." He extols their "ecological good sense." A perspective he shares from Hokulani Holt-Padilla explains that ahupuaʻa emerged as a social and management tool to carry out a cultural ethic of caring for the land.

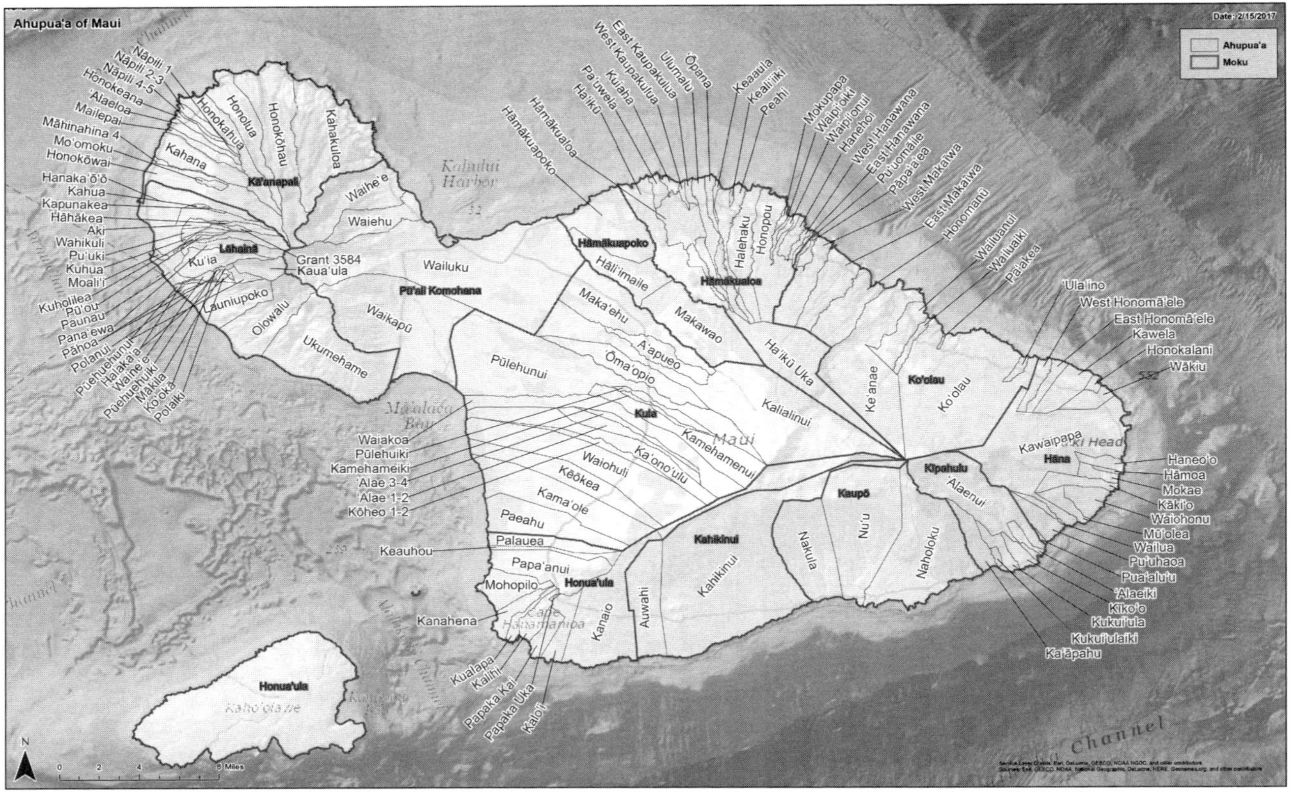

Figure 4.1. "Ahupuaʻa of West Maui." Hawaiʻi Department of Land and Natural Resources, February 10, 2017

Stein's coverage is a good review of various ways the ahupuaʻa has been discussed, studied, and celebrated. Many discussions focus on the intricacy of biological resource zones and how their arrangement and development resulted in an increase in human carrying capacity.[13] Others dig into fascinating details of governance and biocultural resource management.[14] Still others are more interested in history, such as how the introduction of the ahupuaʻa system to Hawaiian society was tied to a successful distribution of power resulting in widespread abundance.[15] Contemporary discussions of sustainability, conservation, spirituality, and civic values in Hawaiʻi all find precedent or inspiration in what is referred to as the "ahupuaʻa system."

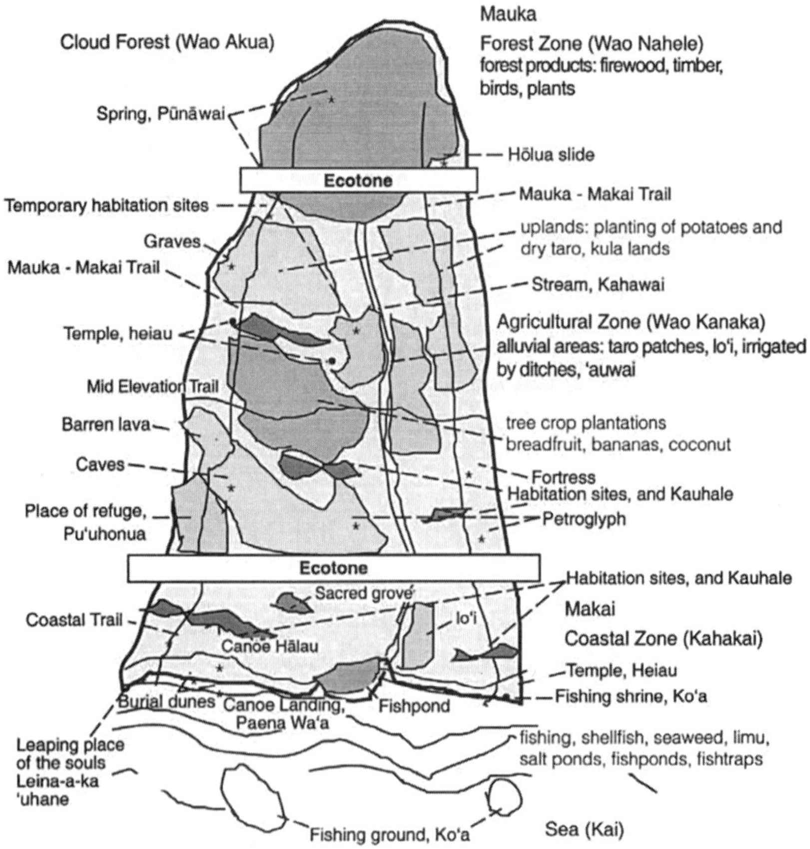

Figure 4.2. Biological resource zones in an ahupuaʻa. H. Van Tilburg et al., "A Guidance Document for Characterizing Native Hawaiian Cultural Landscapes," p. 103. Honolulu: Honua Consulting, August 18, 2017

Connelly's conceptualization of the ahupuaʻa as technology, and the ahupuaʻa system as urbanism, open the door to considering ahupuaʻa in this discussion of congestion and bicycles. These framings are relatively unique—there is certainly an understanding of ahupuaʻa in the context of Native Hawaiian technology, but Connelly's connection to urbanism is a distinct contribution that bridges the professional and academic disciplines of urban planning and community building to ecological conservation, sustainability, and spiritual practice.[16]

More importantly, the way he considers technology and urbanism together is instructive in how we might approach problems we consider both urban and technological. Let's say we were considering the development of a renewable energy project near a community. Concern about large-scale renewable solar and wind projects are often characterized by their "tradeoffs" with respect to environmental, biodiversity, and conservation land-use impacts.[17] Solar and wind projects that drastically alter their sites may disrupt the area ecosystems and compromise conservation efforts. Contrast that with a statement from Connelly in a 2016 interview: "Watersheds are much more than the drainage basins for streams; *they are the most complex and important form of solar energy that we have available today*."[18] From this perspective, watershed conservation and renewable energy development are equivalent.

In his more recent work, Connelly has honed his conceptual framework into a detailed program aimed at achieving the vision of Island Urbanism: a program he calls "ahupuaʻa recovery."

> Ahupuaʻa recovery—the process of regaining possession of land, water, and other resources that have been lost, stolen, erased, corrupted, or even destroyed—provides a framework for an ecological approach toward achieving a culture of climate resilience. It is not a nostalgic pursuit or utopian effort. It is not about ecosystem restoration, but rather an ecological revolution. Ahupuaʻa recovery names a spatial, intellectual, and responsive approach to community organizing, design, and engineering that encompasses a native resurgence to secure egalitarian, justice-advancing economies for the people of Hawaiʻi and beyond. It emerges from a consideration that every investment and expenditure—whether monetary or spiritual—is a precious resource.[19]

What do island urbanism and ahupuaʻa recovery have to offer the conversation about congestion? They offer a new vision of urban communities where the dynamics that create the traffic we experience today do not exist. Furthermore, they offer a philosophy and approach that allows us to find resources where we previously saw problems. But what about bikes?

A Housekeeper in Kāʻanapali

The very first job I had, in Kahului, I was dropped off because I was fresh from the Philippines and couldn't drive. So I was picked up and dropped off for the next four months. Then my family and friends taught me how to drive. Even the owner of the restaurant I worked at and his wife helped teach me how to drive, because they needed me to be able to get to work. I have worked in Lahaina for 19 years and I have almost always driven. There was one point when I chose to take the bus, but it was only for about six months. I liked it a lot, but then there was the inconvenience of waking up that early in the morning to be able to catch the desired bus for a shift that starts at 6 o'clock. It just felt like too much.[20]

—Liezl

To understand West Maui's potential for bicycles, island urbanism, and ahupuaʻa recovery, we must understand all these things in the context of the lives and experiences of those individuals employed in West Maui. All of these individuals (and many of their families) must either travel to or travel within the area on a daily basis.

A typical work schedule for a housekeeper living in Kahului or Kīhei and working in Kāʻanapali requires them to wake up around 6 am to get ready for the day, then leave their house around 7 am in order to drive and be ready for their shift at 8 am. Their job consists of eight hours of cleaning guest rooms and common areas, a very strenuous task, and then driving home in rush-hour traffic, which, depending on the time of the afternoon, can take an average of one and a half hours. Most of the housekeepers we spoke to described their morning commute as very pleasant. They listen to audiobooks and music, or chat with the people they are carpooling with. It's the afternoon rush-hour traffic, after a day of labor-intensive work, that is exhausting. The biggest problem, they explain, is that Honoapiʻilani Highway is the only route that residents and commuters are able to use to get in and out of West Maui. When there are incidents that affect the road such as collisions or natural disasters, the people commuting to and from West Maui are stuck.

When the fire started in Maka'ala the other day, I sat in standstill traffic on Honoapi'ilani Highway for 45 minutes. I finally decided to turn around and had to sleep on my friend's couch in Lahaina.[21]

—Kevin

But West Maui commuters explained that even on a day on which there are no natural disasters or collisions, traffic is still an issue. Some attribute it to the bottleneck where the ocean road and the new Maui Bypass converge. Others say that adding a lane on both sides of the highway would solve the issue. Many were looking for solutions to the problem that did not involve driving, and seemed excited by the idea of biking as a transportation option. Their concerns with this alternative had to do with infrastructure and distance.

If work was only a mile or two away, I would bike. But with a bike lane that is safe—a special route for bikers, away from the highway. Like in Portland, Oregon, it is so green and much cooler. If the bike lane were like that, I think more people definitely would bike to work.[22]

—Liezl

I would bike if I lived closer to work. I think I could bike 10 miles round-trip. It would be a beautiful view. But it would be too scary. I would need to have my own bike lane, not just the shoulder on the side of the road.[23]

—Marina

The sentiments above echo common concerns we have heard in our work in transportation and bicycle advocacy. We also believe they support the idea that we should explore riding bikes not as a direct alternative to driving cars, but as a tool for something altogether different. They are not likely to help us if we treat them as a smaller, lighter, cleaner, healthier, and quieter way to move around our islands the exact same way we do today. Bicycling as a mode of transportation is all of those things, but none of that changes the fact that it is our pattern of movement that makes driving so compelling.

Instead, we believe bicycles can be far more useful as a tool to radically change those patterns, ushering in (or perhaps restoring) an urban concept that is a better fit for both our urban reality and for this place.

What follows is a sampling of ideas and interventions using bicycles to support ahupua'a recovery and thus ahupua'a-based island urbanism. These are ideas we find exciting, if at times ambitious or even radical. This is not a comprehensive list of suggestions for implementing bicycle-related congestion mitigation strategies, nor is this a comprehensive list of strategies for ahupuaʻa recovery. It is an open-ended exploration of roles that bikes could play in Ahupuaʻa recovery such that not only will traffic be addressed, but that many layers of livability can be addressed at the same time.

> The notion of ahupuaʻa recovery is meant to help consolidate purposeful actions to produce an enormous cumulative economic and cultural effect in ways that are robust enough to mitigate new circumstances that result.[24]

These are our ideas for those purposeful actions that might utilize bikes, address vehicle congestion, and develop the resources needed to take on the future.

Containing West Maui's Intensity

To make this story short: I had no plans to buy a house here in Hawaiʻi because I eventually wanted to go back to the Philippines. One time we looked at buying a house in Lahaina, but the prices were so high, so we decided to rent. We rented our house in Lahaina for 21 years. I told my kids, "If you are planning on buying a house I will help you pay for it." And when they finally decided to buy the house I helped them, because that's what parents do. So now I live in Kahului with my wife and my daughter's family in the house we bought.[25]

—Nelson

I really wanted to live in Lahaina because my job is here, my parents work here—everybody works here! I asked my husband if we could sell the house in Kīhei and get a house in Lahaina. So we started looking through a realtor, but everything was just so expensive![26]

—Marina

Unlike twentieth-century engineering, the system was "engineered to plug into the hydrology of the watershed, and designed to assist the natural flow of water, reinforcing the relationships between forests that attract and capture the rains, the streams and wetlands that filter it, and the shorelines that eventually receive it," Connelly writes. "This system was so effective; it intensified the cultivation of food by 100 times the previous amount."[27]

If the commute to West Maui is so unpleasant, why not just live in the area? Wouldn't it make more sense to just move closer?

People want to live where they feel it is affordable. People want to live near their families. People want to live a particular lifestyle—having a larger house, being closer to shopping, being closer to activities. Cars allow West Maui workers to live in areas of the Island that have housing that meet these criteria. This particular liberty is a distinctly American, perhaps even continental, notion. As New Yorker writer Nathan Heller put it, "cars let Americans cross cities, states, woods, mountains, deserts, and, ultimately, the nation in reasonable time. Cities and towns thrived with the flow."

Maybe West Maui thrived with the flow as well—until it started to choke with congestion. As we know from stories around the country, congestion is not a problem experienced only in West Maui. In fact, the title of Heller's article quoted above is, "Was the automobile industry a terrible mistake?"

Cars are only one ingredient in the recipe for congestion. As we have mentioned before, West Maui is the Island's second-largest job center, and the region relies on cars to deliver that workforce. Resort development in the '60s after Hawai'i became a state and American car culture both hint at the influence of a continental approach to development. Alternatively, what would an island approach look like?

To answer that, let's take a look at one particular aspect of the ahupua'a technology: intensification. It can be useful to think about ahupua'a in terms of how they foster intensification—more homes per square foot, more taro cultivation per square foot, more fish per square foot, more language innovation per square foot, more humans per square foot—and how they handle the byproducts of that intensity.

Those byproducts, the second-order effects of one aspect of the ahupua'a system intensifying, are central to the technology and its genius. Take the relationship between upland taro cultivation and nearshore fishpond aquaculture. Increased taro cultivation led to increased nutrient content for the streamwater supporting that cultivation. This increased nutrient content was carried downstream and resulted in algal explosions at stream mouths. This algae could be used to attract and cultivate fish. The intensification of taro cultivation upstream led to the intensification of fish cultivation downstream.

Notably, in this technological philosophy, second-order effects are not "problems" to be discarded, diverted, or ignored. They were not externalized as waste products, shoved off to some other part of the system to be forgotten (because on an island, where would they go?). Quite the opposite, they were internalized as resources, contained within the ahupua'a.

Compare this to a parallel situation on the US continent. The Gulf of Mexico at the mouth of the Mississippi River is experiencing hypoxia—known colloquially as the "dead zone." Here's a description from NOAA's website that starts off sounding pretty familiar. "Excess nutrients that run off land or are piped as wastewater into rivers and coasts can stimulate an overgrowth of algae." The contrast is in what happens next: "[. . .] which then sinks and decomposes in the water. The decomposition process consumes oxygen and depletes the supply available to healthy marine life." The same biological phenomenon that spells devastation in the Gulf of Mexico was abundance to the Native Hawaiians. The difference, we believe, was the ahupua'a system.[28]

Today West Maui experiences the economic intensification created by world-class resorts and a thriving visitor industry. West Maui's coastal lands house resort operations that in turn host hundreds of thousands of guests over the course of the year. The resulting economic productivity supports the wages and livelihood for a large workforce of resort associates and staff that operate the resorts.

Much of what West Maui experiences as congestion is induced by this intense economic activity. Housekeepers, groundskeepers, service associates, cooks, bartenders, engineers, and managers that live in south or central Maui come to these lands to work on them. The modern system of transportation has intensified along with it, but it has not been contained to the ahupua'a. Auto-enabled land use patterns have allowed it to bleed far outside the boundaries of the ahupua'a that house any given Kā'anapali, Honokōwai or Kapalua resort.

Is it even possible to contain transportation intensity within the ahupua'a of the resort that is inducing it?

Returning to the idea of housing, it would certainly require more of that. In other words, containing the intensification of transportation caused by resorts would mean intensifying housing in the area as well. The value and impact of substantially more housing in West Maui is outside of the scope of this discussion. However, we can comment on the feasibility of containing all of the transportation intensity if housing were available. And when you consider that workforce housing within an ahupua'a would vastly decrease travel distances compared to any commute out of West Maui, bicycles start to become a factor.

Bicycling, by virtue of its "geometry" (small size), increases capacity.[29] Bicycles have a higher throughput than automobiles given the same amount of right-of-way (road width). Bicycling, by virtue of its weight, makes building new "roads" and paths easier. There are more and cheaper options for accommodating bikes than automobiles or traditional transit vehicles. These pieces of infrastructure also require less maintenance than those under the constant stress of heavy transit and freight vehicles.

An even higher throughput mode would be walking—although because bikes move faster, not by much.[30] Workforce housing within walking distance of the work to be done is not only the most efficient, most sustainable and healthiest provision of transportation infrastructure, but it was inherent in the ahupuaʻa system. However, where walking is not practical, bicycling can extend the travel range but still fit within the scale of an ahupuaʻa while accommodating a comfortable separation of residential and employment sites. Walking is typically considered attractive for about half a mile of travel distance, whereas bicycling can be an option for one to three miles—perhaps the width of most ahupuaʻa.

Another thing that vastly increases the range of bicycling is the relatively recent introduction of pedal-assist bicycles. These bikes include electric motors that can be used to augment the power needed to start a bike from a stopped position, accelerate to a higher speed, or travel uphill. Given that traveling makai-to-mauka in an ahupuaʻa is almost always uphill, these electric-assist bikes are extremely attractive for residential locations that are further inland and upland. One only need attempt to bike to Lahainaluna High School on an unpowered bike and then again on a pedelec (pedal electric) to physically internalize the power (and joy) of these vehicles.

This vision would require the addition of considerable workforce housing in West Maui. The addition and protection of workforce housing is something West Maui is already actively working on. [31] However, a scheme wherein each resort job is matched with housing units (and other civic infrastructure that families would need, like schools) is housing intensification on a radically different scale. As we noted previously, the question of how to implement that kind of housing program is out of scope and really the topic of its own extended discussion.

However, here we think it is important to recall that ahupuaʻa technology not only internalized intensity, it incorporated it as a resource. What community benefits could be built on more residential housing? If the resulting transportation intensity was addressed by replacing car travel with bikes, would health be a benefit? Safety and reduced traffic deaths? More time spent outdoors? There would more than likely be benefits (in addition to those) we cannot anticipate, but to which we could adapt and readily internalize.

Spreading our Spirit Around

I think I get enough exercise on my days off. I walk 30 minutes a day on the weekends and after work. I like to walk to the end of my driveway or around the block in my neighborhood. [32]

—Marina

I'm not able to bike anymore because of several surgeries that I had. But I used to love it! I also loved to run. I used to be able to run and bike 10 miles easy! If I could bike to work I would do it in a heartbeat. [33]

—Joe

Centuries before the Hawai'i Department of Highways was established, Piilani—after unifying the 12 moku of Maui—commissioned "The Kings Highway," a footpath to connect the entire Island of Maui with a coastal road wide enough to accommodate "six men side by side." The Alaloa Kihapi'ilani was regional transportation infrastructure for a different mode of transportation than we prioritize today—a human-powered mode: walking.[34]

Another key mode of transportation during the construction of the Alaloa Kihapi'ilani, over 500 years ago, was the paddling of dugout ocean canoes that could travel between islands. These wa'a—smaller than the plank-lashed ocean-voyaging canoes that brought Polynesians to Hawai'i—were not only used to go from one island to another. They could also efficiently transport people and resources (and wars) between communities on the same island.

Whether walking along coastal paths like Alaloa Kihapi'ilani or paddling a canoe just offshore, traveling between communities meant that the nearshore ecosystems were always in view. The movement of people thus created the additional benefit of regularly monitoring these ecosystems' health. Moreover, this integration into daily life meant that conditions and change could be monitored at a speed and scale at which it is natural to intervene.

In contrast to today, pre-contact travel in Hawai'i was almost an end unto itself. People surely had their reasons to travel, but in doing so they engaged in an activity that allowed them to care for precious resources, their bodies, and their 'āina. Even today, walking and canoe paddling are both regarded as spiritual activities as much as practical ones—literal manifestations of the idea that it is the journey, not the destination that is important.

This tradition of movement underscores two aspects of bicycle riding that are familiar to anyone who regularly rides: the joy and spiritual fulfillment of riding, and the connection to nature. Both are assets in the recovery of ahupua'a.

To understand why, let's take a quick detour and look again at walking. A woman decides she will walk to work. On her commute she passes through both a park and a farmers' market. On her way through the park, she notices a bottle left on the path and moves it to a recycling bin. She notices a broken sprinkler that she calls to report to the parks department. She patronizes a local farmer and a local bread maker at the farmers' market. Her presence all along the commute not only creates more engagement and satisfaction for her, but also distributes her impact along the entire path. Had she driven in a car, separated from the natural environment and moving quickly through it, none of these interactions would have happened. This has long been held up as one of the benefits of walkable urbanism, and by extension, transit-oriented development.

Biking in the open air connects the rider to the outside world—expanding their attention and awareness to an infinite collection of creations, activities, and interactions not designed by humans. To observe and monitor, tend and cultivate nature is far easier on a bike than in a car. Yes, a person on a bike still moves faster and notices less than a person walking, but for many reasons—speed, separation, safety, and noise being a few—a person in a car is far more disadvantaged than either bicyclist or walker.

To this same end, biking can also put people into different areas. All things being equal, maybe we would travel out of our way to enjoy a scenic park route farther away from our house than if we were walking because we could cover the distance faster. If we could put more bike paths through parks (or build more parks around bike paths) regular visits to these areas could lead to thriving green spaces in our urban areas.

This is especially relevant in light of our previous discussion about the significance of West Maui's resort and hospitality workforce. These workers, stewards of the land, could be uniquely effective in this role.

The central feature of many ahupua'a was the natural stream and network of waterways ('auwai) used to distribute water to the productive activities of the integrated system. Just like 'auwai systems can be thought of as facilitating the flow of the critical water resource, transportation can be thought of as facilitating the flow of the critical human resource. Just like a concrete channelized stream interrupts the natural processes that allow that water to enrich all of the areas and activities it passes through, automobile glass and steel separates our stewards from the areas they could be enriching every time they pass through them.

E Kaʻapuni A Hoʻa Kukui Na Moku ʻĀina

At 1:30 am on February 21, 2009, over a hundred people gathered on Front Street in Lahaina at Mokuʻula. According to *Maui Now*'s Wendy Osher, who was reporting on the scene, "Participants took turns rubbing sticks together before a flame was ignited." The flame was used to light a torch that would be carried 193 miles on a spiritual journey to encircle the entire Island of Maui on foot.[35]

Organizers of the event, named E Kaʻapuni A Hoʻa Kukui Na Moku ʻĀina, had this to say about it. "We mālama each other, our land, our ocean and it is our hope that this kaʻapuni will awaken the essence of how we can mālama ourselves to prepare for what lies ahead."

Each day, thousands of Maui visitors and residents traverse some portion of the Kaʻapuni's path. Each of those trips holds the potential for enlightenment, connectedness, and spiritual engagement that the participants of E Kaʻapuni A Hoʻa Kukui Na Moku ʻĀina demonstrated over seven days in 2009 and again in 2015. What can we be doing to access that potential more regularly? And what could happen if we did?

Ahupuaʻa are a technology to enrich human lives on these islands, but also a reciprocal expression of a commitment to care for the land.[36] Moving through these spaces on a bike connects us to them and gives us time to contemplate that commitment. It gives us the space to consider where we dedicate our energy, our breath, our hana.

Imagine if instead of enduring hour-long bus rides or commutes across Central Maui, our most skilled natural observers were regularly also watching over linear parks, street trees, and public resources actively being restored and cared for in the West Maui community. How much richer would we be for their impact?

If we were challenging our bodies en route to visit the most important people in our lives, would we bring with us more appreciation and kindness? If we were feeding our spirits as we moved toward the work we cherish, would we find more strength and courage to really meet those tasks? Most importantly, can we really achieve our community goals if we don't?

Restoring Forgotten Stories and Places with Bikeshare

My grandparents on my mother's side were immigrants from Japan. They were born in Japan and made their way to Hawai'i separately. My great-grandparents sort of arranged their marriage. They set up on O'ahu and then my grandparents moved to Wailuku around 1930 when Baldwin Packers opened up the Maui Pine Cannery.[37]

—Josh

I was born in Wai'anae on O'ahu. I went to high school up here in Lahainaluna as a boarder. My parents said, "It's time to get out of Wai'anae before you get put in jail!" Because you know the neighborhood in Wai'anae is a pretty tough area. But it was hot in Wai'anae, so I was used to the heat. Coming to Lahaina was easy. I had no problem with the heat![38]

—Joe

Lahaina town is so different now. We used to walk down from Lahainaluna and go down on Front Street and it was so nice. There were so many great stores. So many local people—and they were all friendly, you know? We were boarders and they knew that. Now it's not that way anymore. Everything is all jammed up and it's not like it used to be. The beaches were a lot cleaner too, and there were a lot of them. Now, everything is gone. It is so different.[39]

—Joe

It is impossible to overstate the importance of the Lahaina community as a historic resource. Lahaina, the capital of the Kingdom of Hawai'i, a critical industrial center for both whaling and plantation agriculture, is central to Hawai'i's history over the last 200 years. Moku'ula, long buried under the Malu 'Ulu O Lele baseball field in Lahaina's south end, is in a rarified class of sacred spiritual sites and its restoration one of the biggest opportunities to reconnect with pre-contact wisdom, spirituality, and cultural practice.

Similarly, the historic preservation resources in Lahaina are some of the State's most valuable and well organized. For example, the Lahaina Restoration Foundation's walking tours and interpretive sign program make Lahaina's rich history available to any visitor walking by and willing to take a look. The three historic walking trails—the Kūkulu (Founder) Trail, Holokai (Voyager) Trail and the Ho'okele (Navigator) Trail—take between 30 minutes and one hour to complete and showcase 65 distinct sites and historical gems.[40]

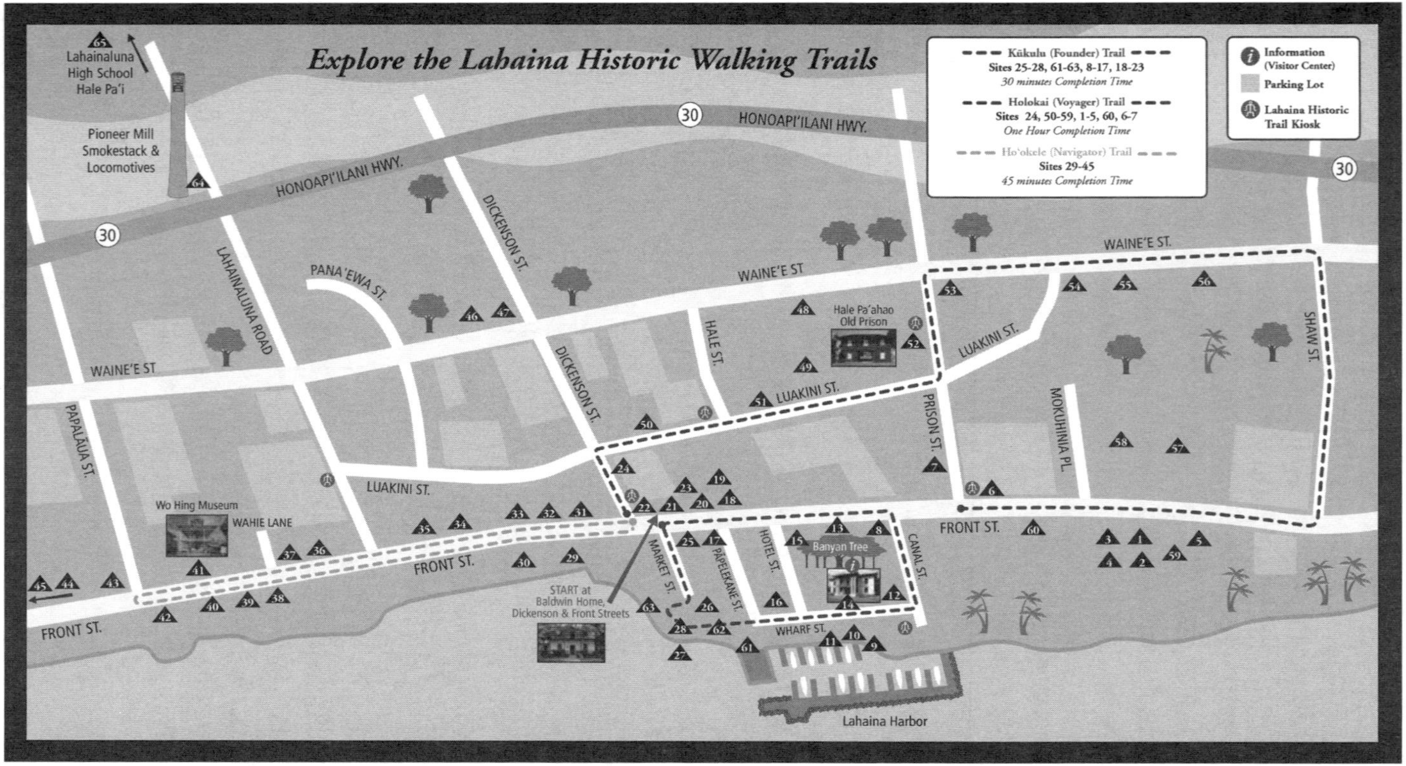

Figure 4.3. Map of Lahaina Historic Walking Trails. *Explore the Lahaina Historic Walking Trails*, Lahaina, HI: Lahaina Restoration Foundation. *Accessed:* October 20, 2019. http://lahainarestoration.org/pdf/lahaina-historical-trail-brochure.pdf

Perhaps the most powerful aspect of the ahupuaʻa system is the integration of cultural and spiritual practices in relationship with and maintenance of ecological and societal aspects of the surrounding environment. This information is so richly captured in the historic preservation of Lahaina town (elements representing both pre- and post-contact urban civilization), and the historic documentation along with the interpretive signs. Looking at it from the context of ahupuaʻa recovery, Lahaina's historic preservation provides an instruction manual and invites visitors to learn as well as make contributions to the system and community health.

Bikes, and particularly bikeshare systems, provide an intriguing opportunity here. For two and a half years leading up to the launch of the Biki bikeshare system in Honolulu, I (Ben) served as the president and chief operating officer of Bikeshare Hawaii, the nonprofit organization tasked with implementing a bikeshare system for the urban core in partnership with a coalition of stakeholders. Much of that work was investigating and digging into different business models and scenarios to find one that would work for the local conditions.

One thing we learned was that in large media markets such as New York City and San Francisco, the value and visibility of a municipal bikeshare is worth tens of millions of dollars. Bikeshare systems like NYC's CitiBike, San Francisco's Ford GoBike, and Portland's BikeTown are seen by millions of residents and visitors and as a consequence can deliver one hell of a brand impression. Fortunately, or unfortunately, Hawaiʻi's media presence does not suggest the same branding/title sponsor strategy for bikes in any of our markets, including Lahaina—there just aren't enough eyeballs to make it pencil out financially. While this was disappointing from a financial sustainability standpoint, it does make a very visible communication platform available for other uses. In the big picture, using that opportunity to leverage bikeshare to deliver a message about Lahaina's historical resources and ahupuaʻa recovery might be the most powerful branding tool of all.

Bikeshare offers many communication points and chances to deliver a nuanced and sophisticated message. The bikes themselves leave a branding impression, and can communicate a high-level message. The kiosks and station sign panels can be treated as interpretive signs, interpretive maps, or both. These can be used to reinforce the existing program of signs placed by the Lahaina Restoration Foundation. Or better yet, they can add new information—either additional sites or additional detail.

The mobile app—typically required by bikeshare systems to access bikes and let users know where to find dropoff locations—presents even more opportunities. Proximity-triggered "just-in-time" messages about nearby sites could be sent as push notifications or text messages. Walking tour elements could add multimedia content such as audio tour guidance or videos. The app could enable mobile payments, testimonials, and comments—all serving to facilitate a relationship of support between bikeshare system users and restoration efforts.

A bikeshare system designed specifically to provide a rich historic preservation experience would be like a two-wheeled version of Boston's Freedom Trail—a chance to connect with the spiritual values of Hawai'i while simultaneously accomplishing what all cities that have implemented bikeshare have found: a better way to move around.

The bikeshare, which would be a clear boon to visitors' ability to explore the area without adding motor vehicle congestion, as it has in Waikīkī, might also be an effective way to involve the visitor industry in the effort. The very premise of this chapter is that these institutions employ the individuals best positioned to spearhead the ahupua'a recovery effort. The story of the "discovery" of the forgotten moku'ula site—the late Kā'anapali Beach Hotel employee Anthony "Akoni" Akana located the site through research encouraged by the hotel's, Po'okela program—reinforces this idea.[41] The content of the restoration and recovery messages delivered by the bikeshare system could similarly be researched, shared, and produced by the visitor industry workforce. For all the reasons the famed Po'okela program's historical and cultural immersion supports Kā'anapali Beach Hotel's employees' relationships and hospitality to guests, this kind of engagement would also support the overall West Maui visitor experience by facilitating a deeper relationship with West Maui itself.

Activating Learning Assets for a Living Technology

ACADEMY describes the function of Kīpuka to engage ahupua'a as a living laboratory for learners, teachers, and practitioners. Activities may include an indigenous approach to the sciences of the environment. Educational components in addition to adjacent schools and museums include aquariums, arboretums, native plant nurseries, botanical gardens, and open pavilions.

—Sean Connelly, *Hawai'i Futures* (2008)

The current wave of '80s nostalgia (typified by the series "Stranger Things") has reminded us that the bicycle was once one of the most important symbols of youth empowerment. Steven Spielberg has perhaps most famously employed this iconography.[42] How did "kids riding bicycles" come to feel like nostalgia, and in turn lose its iconic meaning? Because of our society's increased urbanism, or perhaps because we've surrendered our urban spaces to motor vehicles, it's just not something we see as much as you might in the world of *E.T. the Extra-Terrestrial*, *IT*, or *The Goonies*.

Or is it? The Kalihi Valley Instructional Bike Exchange (KVIBE), where we started this chapter, is making "kids riding bicycles" a staple of life in the area around their shop at Kamehameha IV Road. In fact, they're making it a staple of the entire Kalihi Ahupuaʻa during their annual Kalihi Ahupuaʻa Ride. When it comes to youth empowerment, KVIBE's popular education-based program is revelatory (and deserves to be the topic of yet another extended review)—and they do as much to make the symbol of the bike deeply empowering to youth as Spielberg did to make it broad.

In the information about the 2019 ahupuaʻa ride, KVIBE states, "Participants will learn about the cultural and historical significance of the storied places of Kalihi and their roles in the changing face of Kalihi." Earlier, we proposed a bikeshare system that communicates Lahaina's rich history to provide the cultural context and historical knowledge required to recover ahupuaʻa. KVIBE's statement about the ahupuaʻa ride is made in the same spirit, acknowledging the connection between history and engaging the ahupuaʻa. But it also points out something else. It states that "participants will learn," calling out that it is not sufficient to communicate information; someone has to come to that information with the intention to learn.

Learning is inherent in the ahupuaʻa system. As a living technology that is capable of adapting to both the changing environment and incremental innovations, the survival of the ahupuaʻa depends on learning. Much like the iterative approach to today's cutting-edge software development, functioning ahupuaʻa require a technological philosophy that is fundamentally experimental. One imagines that historically, when one part of the ahupuaʻa system changed and another part of the system was affected (the "second-order" effects discussed previously), integrating those effects must have been achieved through trial and error. In more relevant terms, the continuous adaptation of the ahupuaʻa system required constant kilo (observation) and hana (craft)—learning feedback loops across the entire system.[43]

Much of what was learned about ahupuaʻa operation was encoded into the cultural practices of Native Hawaiian society. Over the years, as we have lost these practices, we have also lost this knowledge. What remains is carried by practitioners, conservationists, laborers, planners, and most importantly, educators like Keʻeaumoku Kapu of Nā Aikāne o Maui. In fact, any of the stewards of this knowledge can be educators, and many, if not all of them, double as such. What is important to the recovery of ahupuaʻa is the commitment to passing the knowledge on and as we pointed out earlier—a reciprocal commitment to learning it.

Thankfully, efforts to engage in just this kind of learning are already taking place in West Maui. In the summer of 2019, Ka Malu o Kahalawai hosted 150 canoe paddlers from the Lahaina, Kahana, and Napili Canoe Clubs on Kahoma Stream to talk about the once-thriving loʻi kalo in the area. Their stated mission: "to perpetuate the culture through the paddling clubs and bring awareness of the importance of Kahoma Valley."[44] For our purposes—relating bicycles and mobility to ahupuaʻa recovery—this effort not only supports the perpetuation of operational knowledge, it has the added benefit of connecting those with an appreciation for the spiritual potential of transportation (see section above) with another aspect of the system.

We can also be grateful for the many existing educational institutions well situated to monitor and learn about West Maui's ahupuaʻa. At the foot of what was once Mokuhinia—the sacred pond in which Mokuʻula was situated—are not one, but two schools: Kamehameha III Elementary School and Holy Innocents Episcopal School. Across the street just mauka is the Nā Aikāne ʻO Maui Cultural Center—already actively working to restore the stream (currently mostly underground) that once fed this historic and remarkable site. Meanwhile, in the upland areas, the Lahainaluna High School and the Princess Nahienaena Elementary/Lahaina Middle School campuses both abut Kahoma Stream.

Networking these educational institutions as centers of learning would allow students experimenting in one area of the system to understand the impacts observed by students in another. This connectedness is also central to the technological philosophy of the ahupuaʻa. It is why the system was so well integrated and sustainable—and will need to be present if the technology is to be repaired.

It's exciting to think of leveraging our educational resources this way. It provides valuable project-based learning experiences for students and improvements to the community as a result of those projects. It creates another exciting connection as well: to the roles of stewardship of the land. The students at these schools are the children of the workers in the area—the workers who are the focus of this chapter. This is especially true if more and more workers are able to find housing in West Maui. When students learn about the different aspects of their ahupuaʻa through their work at school, they will be able to connect what they learn to the knowledge their parents have in order to do their professional work. By entering into conversation with their parents and families, West Maui's students, who are for all intents and purposes professional learners, will be able to exchange professional knowledge. Their joint profession: to be stewards of the land as a family—as an ʻohana.

Students, then, are in the ideal position and frame of mind to observe and understand these impacts and connections, and are essential technicians for the recovery of ahupuaʻa. However students, young students in particular, are limited by automobiles in their ability to visit other locations.

Here, perhaps, the answer is entirely obvious both symbolically and pragmatically. If the recovery of ahupuaʻa requires the technical empowerment of youth, what better way to move them around than youth empowerment's two-wheeled mascot?

What if these academy networks within ahupuaʻa included a transportation network of safe walking and biking paths and shared electric bikes to travel up and down the watershed? How much more inquiry, exploration, and independent learning would be facilitated? As we've discussed previously, this movement would also produce all of the benefits of observation and intervention made possible by mauka-to-makai movements on bikes made by other stewards of the land. It's strange, and perhaps a little uncomfortable, to think of our youth zipping up and down the mountain on bikes unsupervised. But while we're in the mindset of learning from our past, why not remember that little tidbit from the '80s?

The West Maui Greenway: A Kīpuka for the Recovery of West Maui Ahupuaʻa

> *I take pride in working here and the landscaping part of the hotel. I love the colors, and I think all of the flowers and all of the plants should just be bright as can be. I don't want just green; I want colors. Why do you have to go all the way to Hāna to see these beautiful plants when you can bring them right here?*[45]
>
> —Joe

130 years ago, the Pioneer Mill Company began purchasing easements and rights of way to operate a sugar cane train that would be used to transport the products of Maui's plantation-based agriculture.[46] The path of what we now

know as Cane Haul Road foreshadowed the Honoapiʻilani Highway that now runs alongside it. The volume of products being transported across ahupuaʻa boundaries signaled a departure from the traditional terrestrial movement patterns in the mauka-makai direction. The plantation system overall signaled a much larger departure from ahupuaʻa-based urbanism.

If the sugarcane train helped lead the way out of the ahupuaʻa system, it only seems fitting that the way back might pass over Cane Haul Road as well.[47]

"The 25-mile West Maui Greenway will be a multi-use trail that uses and transforms the abandoned cane haul into a recreational ribbon connecting residents and visitors alike to the outdoors and community destinations."

From the West Maui Greenway Conceptual Plan:

"A family-friendly multi-use trail that travels along the west coast of Maui, providing cultural and recreational experiences within this hidden gem."[48]

Plans for the West Maui Greenway (WMG) began in 2014 and quickly gained support in the community. Multiple community outreach events have been held by the group since its creation, including exploration rides with Maui County councilmembers, former mayor Alan Arakawa, and the director and deputy director of the Maui Department of Public Works. In 2016 and 2017 the

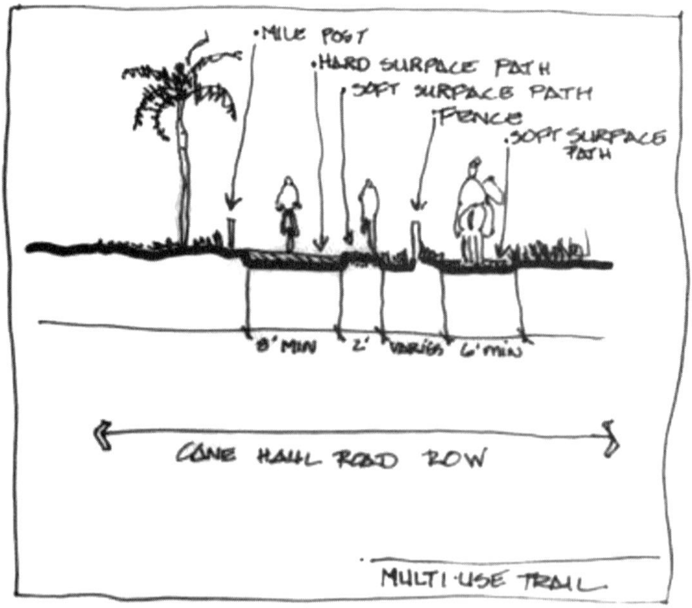

Figure 4.4. Proposed elements of a multiuse path from the West Maui Greenway Conceptual Plan

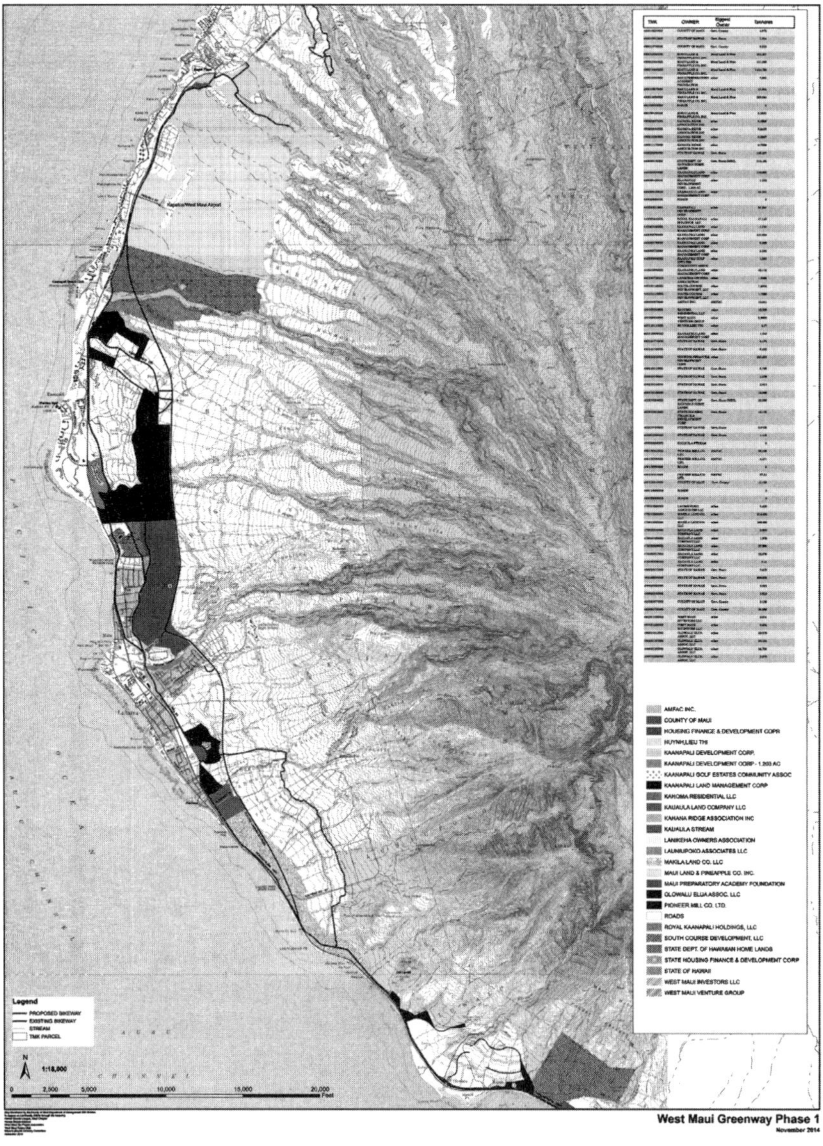

Figure 4.5. Proposed Bikeway from West Maui Greenway Alliance. “Maps.” West Maui Greenway Alliance, 2017. *Accessed at*: www.westmauigreenway.org/maps.html)

West Maui Greenway received a grant from the National Park Service's Rivers, Trails and Conservation Assistance (RTCA) program, which provides technical assistance to community groups.[49,50] In 2017 West Maui Greenway received a grant from the Hawai'i Tourism Authority to hold a "Love the West Maui Greenway" community outreach event, which offered information about the vision and mission of the project to address the importance of safe, walkable, and bikeable communities.[51]

The Hawai'i Department of Transportation lists the West Maui Greenway as a Priority I proposed project in the Hawai'i Bike Plan for the near-term future.[52]

Which is all to say that of all of the bicycle-driven ahupua'a recovery interventions discussed herein, the West Maui Greenway is easily the most achievable. As a project, it may also be a keystone, the single building block useful for realizing all of the other ideas—a foothold to begin each respective climb.

In the scenario where economic and housing intensity were both contained within ahupua'a, the West Maui Greenway would serve as a safe and reliable trail to connect residents with their workplaces as well as grocery stores, laundromats, and other necessities of life. As a separated and protected bikeway, both bikers and walkers would have a completely different and remarkably safer experience compared to the alternative of traveling along the Honoapi'ilani Highway.

The Greenway's path travels through a variety of ecosystems and environments, all relatively close to West Maui's urban features, creating the opportunity to engage residents' previously discussed aptitude for stewardship of the ahupua'a, invoking their role as caretakers of the land. A connection to nature could be experienced on the way to the post office. The enhanced sense of place that comes from biking would be available to riders of all ages, including students who could begin to travel between ahupua'a-networked schools.

The West Maui Greenway conceptual plan includes educational kiosks along the path, not unlike the bikeshare system map panels and the signage we proposed to display information about Lahaina's historic resources.

Interpretive expressions would be located at key locations and offer a variety of messaging techniques, whether subtle or instructional. Native iconic trees and plants, traditional markers to delineate the ahupua'a, or structures such as bridge railings can be used to symbolize important practices and uses of the land. Public art and care of the 'āina could be integrated into these sites, potentially inspiring a desire and responsibility to care for the greenway and surrounding areas.[53]

Using these kiosks and other amenities such as comfort stations, water fountains, rest areas, and bike fixit stations to mark streams and ahupua'a boundaries could provide almost limitless opportunities to communicate aspects of the ahupua'a system and enlist people in the recovery effort by providing them both information and access to sites.

The Greenway will cross every stream in West Maui as on its way to the ocean. By drawing attention to the streams rather than hiding them, the greenway supports connected educational efforts. Downstream of the lo'i kalo cultivation happening on Kahoma, information can be provided about the last harvest and how to support the continued healthy recovery of that practice. Upstream of Moku'ula, a water fountain can describe the underground springs that historically fed Loko Mokuhinia, and how to fund their increasing restoration.

Finally, to refer back to an earlier point made about residents choosing housing for lifestyle, building the West Maui Greenway could not only benefit current residents, but also make living in West Maui more appealing to potential residents who desire more outdoor experiences. These can be enhanced even more over time. Where stream access is possible, recreational mountain biking or off-road trails can gradually be built in partnership with trail-making organizations. As designed, the West Maui Greenway already connects to the Launiopoko and Hokioko trailheads. The conceptual illustration (see Figure 4.6) showing these trailhead connections poetically captures the idea of kīpuka

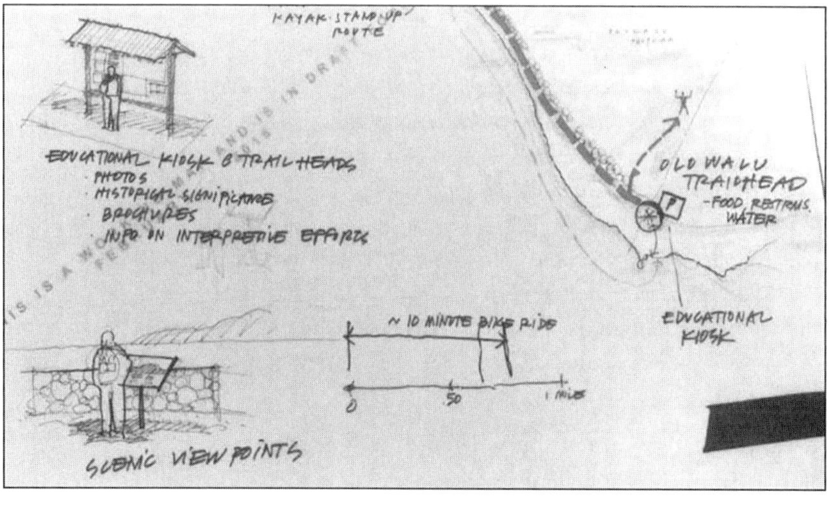

Figure 4.6. Proposed educational kiosks and other trail elements from the West Maui Greenway Conceptual Plan

and revegetation—tendrils of tree-lined recreational paths emanating from the greenway.

The original Phase 1 of the West Maui Greenway was intended to be a 7.5-mile (39,600 feet) multi-use road from Olowalu Village to Lahainaluna Road.[54] However, a revised Phase 1 was created that spans approximately 3,800 feet (36,100 feet less than the original proposed Phase 1), from the vicinity of Fleming Road south to the vicinity of Keawe Street. Completion for the shorter Phase 1 is still to be determined, according to Lee Chamberlain, longtime advocate for the West Maui Greenway.

The relative ease of implementation and tremendous benefits make the West Maui Greenway a no-brainer. The longer it takes to implement the West Maui Greenway, the longer the West Maui community is without a safe way for residents and visitors of all ages to explore experiences built around clean and sustainable transportation. This makes it urgent.

The longest-term benefit of the WMG, however, may be reestablishing mauka-to-makai movement that supports the practice and health of the ahupua'a. Perhaps 200 years from today, as sea level rise has driven the shores of Maui well beyond where Cane Haul Road used to be, we'll consider the logic of shoreline-adjacent travel paths with the same perplexity that we view the ahupua'a mauka-to-makai routes today.

Wayfinding: Getting (un)Lost in Time and Space

We found that there was one old man left who was familiar with the route and who assured us that he was able to guide us through, so we engaged him with all confidence. Starting early, with as light a pack as possible, we made our way up the valley without mishap and undertook the climb to the top of the pass—a narrow saddle separating Oluwalu from Iao Valley. The way became more and more precipitous and our old man became more and more managua—doubtful—until we finally faced an inaccessible pali. Then the old man gave up and declared that we were lost and had better return home.[55]

—Elspeth P. Sterling, *Sites of Maui*

We know that we cannot stay where we are. The need for this book is evidence of that. Traffic in West Maui, as we experience it and as it affects our lives, must be solved. In other words, the status quo is not acceptable. It is projected that 20 years from now, in 2040, Maui's population will have grown by over 20 percent.

The Kahului airport recently debuted a consolidated rental car center with a capacity for 3,800 rental vehicles.[56] Amazon is making more and more products available at the push of a button—and the dispatch of a delivery truck. If everything stays the same, these things will only make congestion worse.

Where was it that we were hoping cars would take us? Did we arrive at the place we were looking for? When we read the West Maui Community Plan, it did not seem so. It seems that we are lost. Perhaps it's time to turn back.

Legendary State Senator Kenneth Brown guided Hawai'i through the transition to our current visitor-driven economy. His Mālama speech articulated Hawai'i's values in the context of that transition. Notably, he opened with a historical perspective.

> *A couple of thousand years ago, these islands lay in the sea and the sun, unknown to man, and not knowing man. Three million years before, they had emerged from the sea as flaming, hostile volcanoes, connected with the rest of the world only by the mindless and infinitely slow vagaries of the winds of the air and the currents of the sea. Yet, in the three million years that had passed, nature had brought forth on these islands a rich assortment of creatures and plants spread over the land, from the mountain peaks down to the sea, and out to where the coral gave way to the cold black ocean depths. Carrying on their timeless, intricate, interwoven cycles of life, death, and birth, they had completely transformed the landscape, replacing the lava with verdure, populating the bays with sea creatures, and the air and land with birds, animals and insects. All this in a totally self-contained environment, and without that ultimate creature, man.*[57]
>
> —Kenneth Brown

If we do discover that we are lost, looking at the path behind us, how far back do we go to see a place where we can start on a more successful path? When was the last time that humans, transcendent as Senator Brown suggests they may be, transformed the Hawaiian Islands beautifully, poetically, the way they transformed over the centuries before the arrival of humans? We have every reason to believe that it was prior to Western contact when Kānaka Maoli lived in abundance for centuries.

Another question: who will guide us on this new path? Up to this point we have entrusted our land use, economy, and governance to continental, transactional, and Western models. A thousand years ago, when the ancestors of Native Hawaiians were just getting set up, they too were faced with intense population pressure and subsequent ecosystem collapse. They were able to connect with a guide that showed them where to go. They listened to ʻāina. They let ʻāina lead. We know that, because that reverence is central to what it means to be Hawaiian.

> *This respect is also reflected in traditional sayings that confer prominence and superiority to the natural world in people's relationship with nature. The classic example is "He aliʻi ka ʻāina, he kauā wale ke kanaka." (The land is the ruler, the people merely servants.)*[58]
>
> —Sam ʻOhu Gon and Kawika Winter

The moku system, the ahupuaʻa technology and urban form—these successes shaped the Hawaiʻi we still know today. They emerged from receiving ʻāina's leadership. Hawaiʻi has changed many times and in many ways since ʻāina was our primary guide. We are again facing population pressure and ecosystem collapse—and we exacerbate those issues every time we turn the ignition on our cars. To this point, Senator Brown left us a deeply insightful point about our economic path along with a prescient sentiment about the topic of this collection.

> *It is important for us, then, not to be bemused by the fact that we have money to buy almost anything we want from overseas. We must remember to determine where the money comes from, and remember that if it doesn't come from a product of the land, it may be one-shot money, and the car we buy might be costing us an irreplaceable piece of Hawaiʻi.*[59]
>
> —Kenneth Brown

The video of KVIBE's Ahupuaʻa ride shows the group of bicyclists winding their way down tree-lined streets, a visual callback to the flowing streams that are the lifeblood of Island Urbanism. Connelly, whose work around ahupuaʻa recovery is the primary inspiration for these ideas, is not the only person thinking about the function of ahupuaʻa in our urban communities. Two students were recently recognized with an international award for their concept for the same Kalihi community that KVIBE rides through: an ahupuaʻa.[60]

West Maui's congestion is painful—especially to its workforce. There is a silver lining, though, particularly if you can look at it the same way ahupuaʻa technology might. Congestion presents an opportunity to lead, to build a different kind of community—because it is necessary, but also because it is better. It can be a community that achieves all of the aspirations today's West Maui residents have expressed.

Bikes can play a role in that. To do so, West Maui will need them to be time machines. We will need bikes to carry us to the places we know but haven't visited in a while. We will need bikes for expeditions into the future—to navigate uncertain and changing terrain. We will need them to warp time . . . to make the past and the future simultaneous. If they could, we could finally see our place in history—how to use what our parents left us, how our actions today will impact us and our children tomorrow. That may seem like a lot to ask of two wheels and a metal frame. But like us humans, they are not alone, or at least don't have to be. We both have ʻāina to guide us.

Notes

1. KVIBE, Kalihi Ahupuaʻa Ride 2018. *Accessed at*: www.youtube.com/watch?v=Coe-_om_d4k.
2. Author interview with a West Maui Hotel Engineer, August 16, 2019.
3. "West Maui Community Profile Draft, p. 5: Wailuku (County of Maui Department of Planning, 2018).
4. Nitasha Tiku, "The Year Tech Workers Realized They Were Workers," *Wired*, May 10, 2019. *Accessed at*: www.wired.com/story/why-hotel-workers-strike-reverberated-through-tech/.
5. Hawaiʻi Green Growth, "Senator Kenneth Brown's 1973 Speech," April 18, 2019. *Accessed at*: www.hawaiigreengrowth.org/senator-kenneth-browns-1973-speech/.
6. Draft West Maui Community Plan, "We Are West Maui." County of Maui Department of Planning, July 19, 2019. *Accessed at*: https://wearemaui.konveio.com/draft-west-maui-community-plan.
7. Sean Connelly, "Urbanism as Island Living: Architecture and Urban Design" In *The Value of Hawaiʻi 2: Ancestral Roots, Oceanic Visions*, pp. 88–99. University of Hawai'i Press, 2014.
8. Connelly, "Urbanism as Island Living," p. 90.
9. Sean Connelly interview by Tina Grandinetti: "Re-scape the City." *Summit*, December 15, 2016. *Accessed at*: https://web.archive.org/web/20170509071216/http://www.summitzine.com/posts/re-scape-the-city.
10. Sean Connelly, *Hawai'i Futures: An Intervention for Island Urbanism*, 2008. *Accessed at*: www.hawaii-futures.com.
11. Timothy A. Schuler, "Uncovering the Potential of Honolulu's Hidden Streams," *Next City*, August 22, 2016. *Accessed at*: https://nextcity.org/features/view/honolulu-sustainable-development-auwai-howard-hughes.
12. Michael Stein, "Ahupuaʻa: Land for the Good of All," *Maui* magazine, 2004. *Accessed at*: https://web.archive.org/web/20111008140941/http://www.mauimagazine.net/Maui-Magazine/Winter-2004/Ahupuaa/.
13. Dieter Mueller-Dombois, "The Hawaiian Ahupuaʻa Land Use System: Its

Biological Resource Zones and the Challenge for Silvicultural Restoration," in *Biology of Hawaiian Streams and Estuaries* (Bishop Museum Bulletin in Cultural and Environmental Studies 3, 2007), pp. 23–33.

14. Kawika Winter et al., "The Moku System: Managing Biocultural Resources for Abundance within Social-Ecological Regions in Hawaiʻi," *Sustainability* 10, no. 10, 2018, p. 3554. https://doi.org/10.3390/su10103554.
15. H. Van Tilburg et al., "A Guidance Document for Characterizing Native Hawaiian Cultural Landscapes," p. 103. Honolulu: Honua Consulting, August 18, 2017.
16. Nālani Minton, *Ahupuaʻa, Fishponds and Loʻi*, DVD. Nā Maka o ka ʻĀina, 2010.
17. Eliza Larson, "Are Wind Farms in Hawaiʻi Hurting or Helping the Native Bat Population?" KITV, September 18, 2019. *Accessed at*: www.kitv.com/story/41063526/are-wind-farms-in-hawaii-hurting-or-helping-the-native-bat-population.
18. Connelly and Grandinetti, *Re-scape the City*, 2016.
19. Sean Connelly, "AWC," *Hawaiʻi Futures,* 2008. *Accessed at*: www.alawaicentennial.org/ESSAY.
20. Author interview with a West Maui hotel housekeeping manager, August 16, 2019.
21. Author interview with Kevin Hancock, director at a West Maui resort, August 15, 2019.
22. Author interview with a West Maui hotel housekeeping manager, August 16, 2019.
23. Interview with a West Maui hotel housekeeper, August 16, 2019.
24. Connelly, "AWC," *Hawaiʻi Futures*, 2008.
25. Interview with a West Maui hotel housekeeper, August 16, 2019.
26. Author interview with a West Maui hotel housekeeping manager, August 16, 2019.
27. Schuler, "Uncovering the Potential of Honolulu's Hidden Streams," August 22, 2016.
28. U.S. Department of Commerce, and National Oceanic and Atmospheric Administration,"Responding to Hurricanes." NOAA's National Ocean Service, October 6, 2014 *Accessed at*: https://oceanservice.noaa.gov/hazards/hypoxia/.
29. Social Ink, "Designing to Move People," National Association of City Transportation Officials, May 17, 2016. *Accessed at*: https://nacto.org/publication/transit-street-design-guide/introduction/why/designing-move-people/.
30. Social Ink, "Designing to Move People," May 17, 2016.
31. Lance D. Collins, "Fast Tracking the Luxury Housing Crisis in West Maui" in Bianca Isaki and Lance D. Collins, *Social Change in West Maui*. Lahaina: North Beach West Maui Benefit Fund, 2019.
32. Interview with a West Maui hotel housekeeper, August 16, 2019.
33. Author interview with a West Maui hotel lead engineer, August 16, 2019.
34. "Kaʻapuni Maui Week-Long Torch-Lit Journey to Begin," *Maui Now,* February 7, 2015. *Accessed at*: https://mauinow.com/2015/02/27/kaʻapuni-maui-week-long-torch-lit-journey-to-begin/.
35. Wendy Osher, "Kaʻapuni Updates: Opening Ceremonies 2/21/09 12am Midnight

Report," *Maui Now*, February 23, 2009. *Accessed at*: https://mauinow.com/2009/02/23/ka'apuni-updates-22109-12-am-midnight-report/.

36. Stein, *Ahupua'a: Land for the Good of All*, 2004.
37. Interview with a West Maui hotel engineer.
38. Interview with a West Maui hotel engineering lead.
39. *Ibid.*
40. *Explore the Lahaina Historic Walking Trails*, Lahaina, HI: Lahaina Restoration Foundation. *Accessed*: October 20, 2019. http://lahainarestoration.org/pdf/lahaina-historical-trail-brochure.pdf.
41. Ronald Williams, "Raising Moku'ula," *Hana Hou!*, 2014. *Accessed at*: https://hanahou.com/17.5/raising-mokuula.
42. Paul Bullock, "Kids Riding Bicycles: Steven Spielberg and the Empowerment of Children," Medium, July 1, 2017. *Accessed at*: https://medium.com/from-director-steven-spielberg/kids-riding-bicycles-steven-spielberg-and-the-empowerment-of-children-f9e4f35cf062.
43. Jan Wizinowich, "Kawaihae I: Bringing an Ahupua'a Back to Life," *Ke Ola*, 2019. *Accessed at*: https://keolamagazine.com/sustainability/kawaihae-i/.
44. Walter Chihara, "Canoe Clubs Visit Kahoma Valley to Learn about Taro Farming and Water Rights," *Lahaina News*, June 6, 2019. *Accessed at*: www.lahainanews.com/page/content.detail/id/565804/Canoe-clubs-visit-Kahoma-Valley-to-learn-about-taro-farming-and-water-rights.html?nav=19.
45. Interview with a West Maui hotel engineering lead.
46. "About Us," West Maui Greenway Alliance, 2017. *Accessed at*: www.westmauigreenway.org/about-us.html.
47. West Maui Greenway Alliance, "West Maui Greenway Conceptual Plan," p. 6. Lahaina: West Maui, Greenway Alliance, March 2016.
48. "West Maui Greenway Conceptual Plan."
49. "Milestones." West Maui Greenway Alliance, 2017. *Accessed at*: www.westmauigreenway.org/milestones.html.
50. "RTCA in Hawaii." Pacific West Region - Hawaii: National Park Service, 2016.
51. "Love the West Maui Greenway Day." *Maui Now*, April 13, 2017. *Accessed at*: https://mauinow.com/2017/04/13/love-the-west-maui-greenway-day/.
52. "Appendix G: Proposed Bicycle Facilities by Priority Level," n.d., Hawai'i Department of Transportation.
53. "West Maui Greenway Conceptual Plan,", p. 11.
54. "Plans," West Maui Greenway Alliance, 2017. *Accessed at*: www.westmauigreenway.org/plans.html.
55. Elspeth P. Sterling, *Sites of Maui*, p. 26. Bishop Museum Press 1998.
56. "OGG Airport, Kahului Airport, Island of Maui." *Accessed*: October 20, 2019. www.oggairport.com/.
57. Hawaii Green Growth, "Senator Kenneth Brown's 1973 Speech."

58. Sam ʻOhu Gon and Kawika Winter, "A Hawaiian Renaissance That Could Save the World," *American Scientist*, 2019, p. 232. *Accessed at*: www.americanscientist.org/article/a-hawaiian-renaissance-that-could-save-the-world.
59. Hawaiʻi Green Growth, "Senator Kenneth Brown's 1973 Speech."
60. "Architecture Students Win National Award for Reimagining Kalihi," *University of Hawaiʻi System News*, September 24, 2018. *Accessed at*: www.hawaii.edu/news/2018/09/24/architecture-students-award-reimagining-kalihi/.

Chapter 5

USING LIGHT RAIL TO SHAPE A MORE SUSTAINABLE FUTURE FOR WEST MAUI

Ryan Tam

Maui's development patterns have long been shaped by transportation. Historically, one of these major economic transformations occurred with the advent of the railroads in the late nineteenth century. In 1882, the Pioneer Mill began operating a steam railway to transport sugar cane between Kāʻanapali and Lahaina. This would facilitate the growth of agriculture and eventual development of the region.[1] By 1929, there were over 140 miles of railway tracks throughout the island,[2] with tracks in West Maui stretching up to Nāpili and down to Olowalu. To this day, a six-mile portion of this line is the only remnant of Maui's railroad history. The Sugar Cane Train carried over five million people between Lahaina and Puʻukoliʻi from 1970 to 2014, and continued to operate occasional holiday services through 2019.[3]

Elsewhere on Maui, the Kahului Railroad was actually the first commercial railway in Hawaiʻi when it was established in 1879 to haul sugarcane and other freight along a three-mile route between Wailuku, Puʻunēnē, and Pāʻia.[4] By 1908, the railroad was also transporting 55,000 passengers annually.[5] Passenger services in 1911 included six trains per weekday to Wailuku and five trains per day to Pāʻia.[6] With the advent of pineapple cultivation, the Kahului Railroad was even extended to Haʻikū and Kuiaha. The Kahului Railroad ended regular passenger rail service in 1936, however, due to the Great Depression and the opening of new highways. The company continued to provide passenger transportation until 1952 using a fleet of 60 transit buses. Freight trains continued to run until May 1966, when pineapple shippers switched to trucks and the entire railway was abandoned.[7]

Automobiles and trucks replaced the railways, and the Honoapi'ilani Highway is now the primary transportation corridor into and out of West Maui. On a typical day in 2018, over 43,000 vehicles traveled this highway.[8] The 24-mile trip from Kahului to Lahaina can take 35 to 55 minutes, depending on peak-period traffic congestion or other factors.[9] This highway is also subject to closures due to vehicle collisions, brush fires, rockfalls, and even coastal flooding. These closures can cause hours of delay and significant disruption to everyday activities. In the future, travel along the highway may also be affected by expected climate change and sea level rise. Analysts predict that with the 3.2 feet of sea level rise expected by the year 2100, about six and a half miles of the Honoapi'ilani Highway will be vulnerable to coastal erosion, passive flooding, and annual high wave flooding.[10]

There are currently very few practicable alternatives to the personal automobile in West Maui. Buses and shuttles can get stuck in the same traffic that affects cars. Perhaps more importantly, today's bus trip can take up to twice as long as the automobile. By car, the travel time between the Nāpili Market and Kahului Airport is typically 50 to 90 minutes.[11] By bus, it's over a two-hour ride. From Kapalua, it's a one-hour bus ride to Lahaina, followed by a connection to another one-hour bus ride to the Queen Ka'ahumanu Center shopping mall in Kahului. Getting to the airport requires a second connection and another 10-minute bus ride. In addition, the buses only run hourly between 6:30 am and 7:30 pm—making it necessary to plan ahead while being unusable for people who need to travel outside of those hours.

Faced with issues with congestion, community leaders continue to dream about alternatives such as monorails and other forms of transit systems.[12] A light rail system running on its own dedicated tracks could whisk riders between the Kahului Airport and Lahaina in about 30 minutes, with another 15–20 minutes to get up to Kapalua. Rail stations could be surrounded by new and redeveloped buildings and streets that make it easier and more convenient to walk and bike to get services, shops, and restaurants. Organizing commerce and other activities around walking, biking, and transit would be more economically and environmentally sustainable than today's automobile-oriented communities. This will require new land use policies and urban design changes, however, in addition to major changes to transportation infrastructure. This chapter looks at the potential of light rail and more compact communities to create more reliable mobility and shape a more sustainable future for West Maui.

Part I: Mobility and Community Today

Today, autos and highways are essential parts of our communities—enabling people to travel between jobs, homes, services, and recreation. The automobile shapes how and where we earn a living, how we get our goods and supplies, and even how we interact with our families and friends. We've essentially built our lives and our communities around this transportation system. But this is all by design, and the automobile is a costly system to operate.

Like almost every other community in the United States, the automobile is a fundamental component of Maui's transportation system. In 2018, there were about 176,300 passenger vehicles and trucks registered in Maui County.[13] That's about 2.3 vehicles for each of Maui County's 76,000 occupied dwelling units and visitor rooms. Over 62 percent of occupied dwellings in Maui County had two to four vehicles in 2017. Another 31 percent of dwellings had one vehicle available.[14] About 86 percent of all workers on Maui use an automobile to get to work—either driving themselves or sharing a ride with someone else.[15] Less than three percent of commuters ride the bus to get to work, although work trips account for over half of all regular Maui bus riders.[16] Less than five percent of all workers walk, bike, or take some other form of transportation to get to work, while another six percent work from home. The pervasiveness of the automobile even extends to the visitor industry. The Kahului Airport rents more cars than any other airport in the state, with an average of 2,200 cars rented daily—more than twice the amount of cars rented in Honolulu.[17]

For most of the 24,000 residents of West Maui, owning a car and driving along the winding Honoapiʻilani roadway is a necessity to get to work or see family and friends in Kahului, Kīhei, or elsewhere on Maui. With more than two jobs for every occupied housing unit, businesses in West Maui are forced to draw in workers to commute from other areas on the island.[18] About 7,400 people use the Honoapiʻilani Highway to get to jobs in West Maui from other areas of the island, as shown in Table 5.1.[19] And an estimated 36,000 visitors in the 12,000 hotel rooms in West Maui also use this highway to get to the Kahului Airport and other tourist destinations around the island (Table 5.2).

As a transportation system, the automobile has surprisingly large operating costs—most of which is borne by individual users. In 2017, each of the 180,000 registered vehicles in Maui County traveled an average of 8,900 miles—or a total of about 1.6 billion vehicle-miles travelled.[20] Roadway maintenance is only a small fraction of the total operating cost of the automobile transportation system. In 2017, for example, the State of Hawaiʻi spent $7.8 million on the

Table 5.1. Estimated Commuter Flows Within and To/From West Maui, 2017

CATEGORY	EMPLOYEES[a]
Live and work within West Maui	9,200
Live in West Maui, work elsewhere	7,300
Live elsewhere, work in West Maui	7,400
Total	23,900

Source: Longitudinal Employer-Household Dynamics Origin-Destination Employment Statistics, 2017.

[a] Includes all reported employees, including those with reported off-island jobs or homes.

Table 5.2. Estimated Residents, Workers and Visitors in West Maui and Islandwide, 2018

AREA	RESIDENTS	JOBS	VISITOR UNITS	VISITOR UNIT SHARE (%)	ESTIMATED VISITORS (BY SHARE)
West Maui	23,600	24,100	12,100	56%	36,400
Other Parts of Maui	130,400	41,400	9,300	44%	28,100
Total	154,000	65,500	21,400	100%	64,500

Sources: U.S. Census American Community Survey, 2017 5-Year Estimate; Hawai'i Tourism Authority 2018 Visitor Plant Inventory

operation and maintenance of Maui's highways,[21] while the County of Maui budgeted another $26.5 million for the upkeep of local streets and roads.[22] In contrast, individuals and private companies on Maui collectively spent over $850 million to operate their vehicles in 2017, or about $4,700 per vehicle. This is based on an average operating cost of $0.53 per mile, and includes individual vehicle ownership costs such as insurance, registration, depreciation, and financing, as well as operating fuel and maintenance costs.[23]

Reconsidering Auto-Oriented Communities

Over the years, Lahaina has maintained its character as a dense, lively, historic town, while the rest of West Maui has evolved as a typical automobile-oriented community. Sugarcane and pineapple fields previously confined urban development to a narrow corridor between the Honoapi'ilani Highway and the coastline. The decline of agriculture, however, has now allowed new housing subdivisions to stretch mauka up the hillsides. Scores of detached homes, townhouse apartment complexes, shopping centers, hotels, and resorts are now the norm—all surrounded by vast, inefficient parking lots. Although planners have tried to mitigate this visual blight with landscape requirements of one tree for every five parking spaces[24] or by encouraging underground parking,[25] the environment is still dominated by the automobile. Sidewalks and bicycle paths are inconsistent, narrow, or simply missing—making it a generally unfriendly environment to pedestrians and cyclists.

This urban form is not unique to Maui, but did occur by design. Over the last hundred years in the United States, we've developed a complex transportation system centered on the personal automobile. Cities and towns were rebuilt around this transportation system. Most cities in the United States dismantled their streetcar systems in the early- to mid-twentieth century in favor of buses and cars.[26] Streets were widened to accommodate ever-increasing automobile traffic, and neighborhoods were demolished to accommodate new freeways and shopping malls surrounded by large parking lots. As congestion grew, engineers added lanes or straightened highways in order to allow cars to move faster and solve the traffic problems. But inevitably, these facilities would fill up and need to be expanded again. This same story played out in communities throughout the United States and elsewhere, over and over again.

Around the 1940s and 1950s, communities began incorporating off-street parking requirements into their zoning codes in order to mitigate congestion and issues with parking.[27] Although these requirements were intended to accommodate the growing needs of automobile-based mobility, they shaped the economics of real estate and commerce. Parking regulations actually impose direct costs on businesses and indirectly affect the economics of land development. Chapter 19.36B of Maui's zoning code, for example, requires businesses to have a certain number of parking spaces based on the use and size of the building. A restaurant with a dining area requires at least four parking stalls, with one stall per 100 square feet of amusement, serving and dining area. An office requires at least three parking stalls, with one stall for each 500 square feet of space.[28] Thus, a restaurant or office needs to generate enough revenue to recoup the construction and operational cost of its off-street parking, which is estimated at an annualized cost of $1,500 to $5,000 per year per stall.[29] This parking lot also needs to be a certain size in order to ensure that there are enough parking spaces to attract the desired number of customers from its catchment area. This, in turn, tends to favor large national retail chains in large shopping malls rather than small local businesses. A large development such as a new shopping center might also be required to contribute to regional traffic improvements like a new intersection or a lane widening.

The reliance on the automobile, along with the popularity of the suburban lifestyle, has also affected the supply and demand of housing. Off-street parking requirements and other zoning regulations all govern the dimensions of allowable buildings and thus the economics of housing developments. About 1,700 acres in West Maui, or about 82 percent of residential land, is zoned for single-family homes.[30] Single-family homes require minimum lot sizes of 3,000 to 10,000 square feet, with lots 60 to 70 feet wide, front yard setbacks of 15 feet, and side or rear yard setbacks of six feet. These requirements constrain the number of homes that can be built on a given amount of land—affecting the economics of construction and the overall affordability of these homes. Parking requirements and mobility needs impose similar costs. Maui's zoning code requires that a 3,000-square-foot house have at least three parking stalls. Since the average size of an off-street parking stall and circulation space is 320 square feet,[31] this requirement can increase the required land area by a third. To put this in another context, the average rental studio in the United States is 472 square feet in size, while the average one-bedroom apartment is 714 square feet.[32] We devote almost half as much or more in land area to parking as we do for the living unit itself.

Reliance on the automobile thus directly translates into higher housing costs or fewer housing units provided. After an off-street parking requirement was implemented in Oakland, California, a 1964 study showed that construction costs per apartment unit increased by 18 percent. The study also found that the number of apartments constructed fell by 30 percent and that land values also fell by 33 percent, due to the increase in development costs and reduced development potential.[33] This also reduced property tax revenues. A 1995 study found similar results.[34] In practice, this means that for someone to be able to afford a house or apartment and a parking stall, they may also need to make tradeoffs in terms of smaller living spaces and fewer bedrooms than they might otherwise afford if they didn't own a car. Alternatively, they could choose to live in a cheaper location that is further away from their workplace, school, shopping, and recreational amenities. This further locks in a reliance on the automobile as the primary transportation system.

Back to the Future

The dominance of the automobile and the rise of low-density suburban environments have had physical, environmental, and social consequences on our communities. The manifestation of automobile-oriented zoning codes has distorted the structure and dynamics of our cities. Planner Donald Shoup, for example, noted that half of the land in downtown Buffalo is actually devoted to parking. And in downtown Albuquerque, more land is devoted to parking lots than the actual offices and business themselves.[35] In 1973, journalist Grady Clay described the evolution of the auto-focused, convenience-oriented urban-suburban commercial "strip" that had become the centerpiece of American cities and towns.[36] The strip in the 1950s and 1960s was typified by fast-food restaurants, shopping malls, motels, and almost every other type of commerce. He argues that these "strips" evolved on the basis of inexhaustible energy and simplistic views of locational decisions. Such locational decisions may not have included the full environmental and societal costs of automobile-based transportation.

Indeed, researchers have identified quantifiable evidence of the environmental ramifications of auto-oriented communities. In a study of U.S. metropolitan areas, urban economists Edward Glaeser and Matthew Kahn found a relationship between residential density and energy consumption. The average household in a low-density suburb uses an average of 1,164 gallons of gas per year, while one in a dense city uses only 687 gallons of gas per year. Sun Belt cities in the South, which tended to be spread out and had dispersed employment areas, used 75 percent more gasoline than a traditional city like New York. And households in dense urban areas emitted 60 percent less carbon than those in suburban areas.[37]

Automobile traffic has also been found to have a negative impact on urban communities. In the 1970s, urban planner Donald Appleyard examined the impacts of traffic on traditional urban neighborhoods.[38] He found that the amount of traffic through a neighborhood had an effect on the street life, sense of community (neighboring), and home life, as well as creating safety hazards and other environmental degradation. He also noted that streets could be deliberately designed to control traveler behavior (reducing cut-through traffic) and provide amenities to mitigate the impacts of auto traffic on communities. These so-called "traffic calming" measures include roundabouts, curb extensions, diverters, and other physical features that can be retrofitted into streets to change the psychology of drivers and community behavior. More recently, these measures have gained new life through the efforts to adopt "complete streets" policies that integrate pedestrians, cyclists, and other roadway users into the design and operation of streets—rather than just engineering for vehicular efficiency.[39] Examples of complete streets projects include the removal of extra roadway space to widen sidewalks and the installation of tree-lined paths and bike lanes. Over 1,450 state and local agencies throughout the United States have adopted complete streets policies. Maui adopted a complete streets policy in 2012.[40] Implementation of complete streets is a step towards creating more sustainable community mobility.

Along with efforts to redesign the streets, many architects and planners have also been promoting the benefits of denser communities and the return to the more traditional urban fabric of cities. Author Jane Jacobs celebrates urban density, lively street life, and economic diversity as all contributing factors to a flourishing city life.[41] Glaeser noted that cities and proximity (closeness) are important for economic innovation and resiliency. He found that people in more urbanized countries tend to be happier than those in more rural ones.[42] Architect David Sim argues that denser and more diverse communities make better use of infrastructure and resources by increasing the likelihood of being close to needed goods, services, and even relationships.[43] This proximity is essential to creating good neighbors and communities and creating more human-centered urban environments.

The form and design of city blocks and individual buildings affects accessibility, neighborhood walkability, and social proximity. Sim advocates for traditional styles of urban buildings that are four to five stories high, and which accommodate layers of different uses, such as ground-floor shops, second-floor offices, and upper-floor residential units. When integrated into traditional urban blocks that maximize direct street frontage, these types of walkable buildings can promote accessibility by allowing quick entrances and exits. Such traditional building forms can enable building occupants to walk between the street and an apartment, office, or hotel room in less than a minute.[44] This increases social connectedness and proximity, and creates vibrant environments. In contrast, contemporary tall buildings with elevators might take 4–5 minutes to access the outside world, or even longer when parking a car is involved.

The rise of low-density, automobile-oriented communities has also affected the economics of public mass transportation systems like buses and trains. Planners Boris Pushkarev and Jeffrey Zupan noted that the speed of the automobile allowed homes and businesses to spread out across the landscape and gave rise to suburban communities that were one-tenth as dense as traditional cities.[45] Car-oriented suburbs in the New York region evolved with densities of less than 3,000 people per square mile, or about 4.6 people per acre. This is compared to the historical densities of pre-automobile European cities that were designed around walking and transit—many of which had densities of around 20,000 to 80,000 people per square mile in the late 1930s, or 30 to 120 people per acre.[46]

In such low-density communities, it is difficult to operate cost-effective public transit services because of the high operating costs per boarding passenger. This can also make it too costly to provide good levels of service (frequency), which then makes transit services less useful or competitive to the automobile. Pushkarev and Zupan noted that denser communities with larger business districts and more residents were associated with reduced auto usage and greater public transit.[47] They also observed that transit usage was higher in communities with densities greater than seven dwelling units per acre. And in communities with densities greater than 60 dwelling units per acre, more than half of all trips were made by transit.

This observed relationship between greater density and transit usage is often cited by transit advocates as a way to ensure that transit services are useful and successful. Transportation planners Eric Guerra and Robert Cervero found that light rail is generally cost-effective in areas with about 28 residents and jobs per acre.[48] Transit planner Christof Spieler suggests that an infrequent bus service can be supported in a community with a density of about 4.6 people per acre, or about 3,000 people per square mile.[49] Spieler also argues that frequent transit service can be justified in a community with about 15.6 people per acre, or about 10,000 people per square mile.

West Maui may already have enough density to support a frequent-service transit corridor, especially when the large concentration of residents, visitors, and jobs are taken into account. About 29 percent of West Maui's 11,800 housing units are single-unit detached homes,[50] while about 38 percent of housing units are in structures with 10 or more units. This is actually much higher than the average for Maui County, and is reflected in West Maui's relatively high population density.

In 2019, there was an average of 66,000 daily visitors on Maui.[51] Almost 60 percent of Maui's 21,000 hotel units are in West Maui—meaning that there are approximately 37,000 visitors each day who are staying in West Maui. As shown in Table 5.3, this means that Kāʻanapali has a combined density of 26 people, jobs, and visitors per acre, while Lahaina has a combined density of 17.4 per acre. Nāpili and Honokōwai already have a combined density of about 21.4 people, jobs, and visitors per acre. When combined with a link to a strong traffic generator such as Kahului and the airport, a regional light rail system could be very successful. The higher density of activity in West Maui relative to other communities also suggests that it would be the best corridor for a light rail system on Maui (Table 5.4).

Table 5.3. Combined Urban Density of West Maui Communities, 2018

COMMUNITY	URBANIZED LAND AREA (ACRES)[a]	POPULATION	JOBS	VISITORS	COMBINED URBANIZED DENSITY
Kapalua	793.0	1,250	1,469	4,690	9.3
Nāpili-Honokōwai	551.9	6,243	941	4,606	21.4
Kāʻanapali	1,179.6	2,208	6,264	22,218	26.0
Lahaina	1,450.5	13,223	7,724	4,310	17.4
Launiupoko	216.5	644	8	18	3.1
Total	4,191.5	23,568	16,406	35,842	18.1

Sources: U.S. Census American Community Survey, 2017 5-Year Estimate; Hawaiʻi Tourism Authority 2018 Visitor Plant Inventory

[a] Includes U.S. Census urbanized land areas

Table 5.4. Combined Urban Density of Other Maui Communities, 2018

COMMUNITY	URBANIZED LAND AREA (ACRES)[a]	POPULATION	JOBS	VISITORS	COMBINED URBANIZED DENSITY
Māʻalaea	63.8	253	250	652	18.4
Kīhei-Wailea	5,567.6	27,935	11,920	25,546	11.7
Wailuku-Kahului	10,151.3	60,926	24,366	1,616	8.6
Pāʻia-Haʻikū	5,914.5	11,886	1,765	257	2.4
Upcountry Maui	8,274.1	26,277	3,132	61	3.6

Sources: U.S. Census American Community Survey, 2017 5-Year Estimate; Hawaiʻi Tourism Authority 2018 Visitor Plant Inventory

[a] Includes U.S. Census urbanized land areas

Part II: A Light Rail Vision

One perhaps compelling idea might be to envision West Maui as a series of close-knit urban communities primarily linked by transit and bikeways. Automobiles and parking lots could be replaced by trees and multimodal paths, while stores and restaurants could be redeveloped at a smaller, more human scale. People could walk or bike to nearby convenience stores and restaurants to meet their basic needs, or else hop on frequent shuttle buses or light rail trains to get to Lahaina or Kahului for other shopping or entertainment needs. And visitors could ride into West Maui directly from the Kahului Airport on a comfortable and spacious light rail train—a much-improved experience over driving or taking a shuttle van.

Connecting Communities

A basic light rail system from West Maui to the Kahului Airport could offer an alternative to an automobile-oriented lifestyle and provide the foundation for a more sustainable pattern of land development. A 31-mile light rail line with 14 stations could effectively connect communities within West Maui and also provide a fast regional link to Kahului. Such a line could operate as a hybrid system that combines the features of long-distance regional or commuter rail trains with the connectivity associated with more traditional urban light rail systems and streetcars. A conceptual route is shown in Figure 5.1.

The first eight miles of the system between Nāpili and Lahaina would serve to connect the communities within West Maui. Stations could be located about every mile, with more stations added as the corridor develops. This would place a majority of the hotels, resorts, and residential communities within about a 10- to 15-minute walk of the station, while still minimizing overall travel time along the route. The line would parallel the Honoapi'ilani Highway, and could

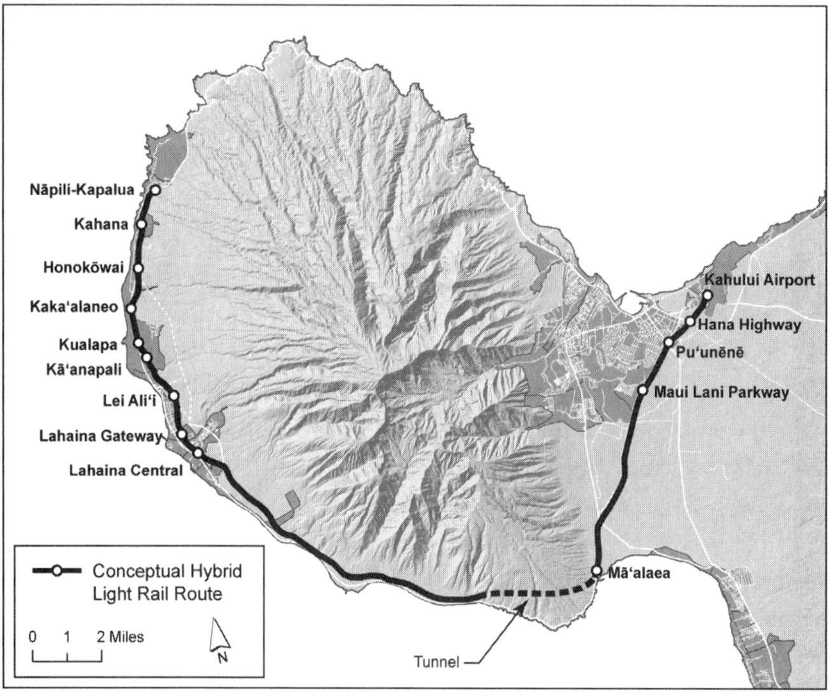

Figure 5.1. Conceptual route for a West Maui hybrid light rail system

even utilize the tracks and right-of-way for the Sugar Cane Train alongside a new multiuse path. To address climate adaptation needs, a new alternative inland route could be established that would shift activity centers away from the coastline. The planning for a new route could also be coordinated with the redevelopment of existing properties, especially as the need arises to mitigate the effects of sea level rise and coastal erosion.

From Lahaina, the light rail line would continue along a 23-mile route to the Kahului Airport within a new right-of-way alongside existing roads. Most of the rail line would be built at ground level in order to minimize construction costs. The line could be initially built as a single-track system, with passing track sections included as necessary to allow trains to operate every 15 minutes. The required right-of-way would be about 11 to 13 feet wide for a single-track section, and about 19 to 33 feet wide for a double-track passing section or station.[52] As the traffic grows, a continuous second track could be built to allow for more frequent train service.

The biggest engineering challenge would be to establish a new route across The Pali between Ukumehame and Māʻalaea. One solution might be to bore a new four-mile-long tunnel inland of the existing highway. Although costly, a tunnel would have a much smaller footprint and less environmental and visual impacts than a new highway along this route. Modern tunnel-boring machines can excavate the ground, transport the excavated spoils, and install a permanent tunnel lining at rates of 50 to 100 feet per day.[53] Such tunnels are typically lined with concrete precast segments that are manufactured off site. The City and County of Honolulu recently built a three-mile-long gravity sewer tunnel between Kāneʻohe and Kailua using this method. This tunnel was about 13 feet in diameter—slightly smaller than what would be needed for a rail line—and cost about $375 million to build.[54]

Detailed technical studies and cost-benefit analyses would help engineers establish the configuration of the tunnel and how its design would address industry standards for fire protection, tunnel evacuation, and ventilation requirements. These standards, called NFPA 130, include requirements for emergency walkways and cross-passages every 800 feet, or else an intermediate exit shaft for distances greater than 2,500 feet.[55] Many rail systems are developed with two separate tunnels—one for a train in each direction. A single large tunnel with intermediate emergency exits to the surface could potentially be a more economical solution.[56]

From Māʻalaea, the line would follow the east side of the Kūihelani Highway. Overpasses or underpasses could be built where the rail line crosses key roadways, such as at the Hana Highway, Maui Veterans (Piʻilani) Highway or Maui Lani Parkway. This would reduce delays to motorists and increase safety. The line could even be elevated for a two-mile section along the edge of Kahului in order to avoid disrupting adjacent businesses. Stations at the Maui Lani Parkway, Puʻunēnē Avenue, and Hana Highway would serve major shopping centers and provide connections to other communities on Maui. The end station would be located at the Kahului Airport, perhaps near the departures terminal.

STATIONS

Most of the stations could be simple facilities with covered waiting areas. Station platforms would likely be 200 to 250 feet long and about 12 to 20 feet wide, and would have canopies or trees for shade and rain protection. Stations would generally serve as community mobility hubs that would incorporate curb space for shuttle buses, ride-sharing services, and "kiss-and-ride" waiting areas. Other multimodal facilities could include short-term bicycle storage facilities and bikeshare rental stations. Some larger stations could include enhanced facilities such as restrooms, convenience retail stores, visitor information kiosks, and even luggage storage (as shown in Figure 5.2).

Figure 5.2. Light rail train stations, such as this example in Downtown Petaluma, could become multimodal transportation hubs (Sonoma-Marin Area Rail Transit)

Station locations are typically determined by several factors. These factors include availability of suitable land for a station, the proximity of the station to nearby activity centers and destinations, and the spacing of stations along the route. Transit systems need to have enough stops to provide good access along the corridor, but not too many stops that it slows down the overall travel time. For example, the current West Maui Islander bus service takes an hour to complete a one-way trip between Kapalua and Lahaina because it makes 22 stops along the way.[57] While this provides convenient access to individual hotels and neighborhoods along the route, this bus route is significantly longer than the 20- to 30-minute nonstop trip by car.[58]

A light rail system with nine stations in West Maui would allow most of the transit users to walk or bike to a rail station. About 60 percent of the hotel rooms in West Maui would be within a 1/2-mile walk (10–15 minutes) of a station. About 85 percent of the rooms would be a 0.6-mile walk or less from the station.[59]

Shuttle buses or shared-ride services could also provide a convenient way to access a station. Small circulators could operate shuttles between the rail stations and individual resorts, providing more direct curb-to-door service. Bikes, bikeshare, and pedestrian improvements could also help to connect the rail stations with other neighborhoods. These could include the West Maui bikeway, sidewalks and pathways. Park-and-ride lots could be developed at the terminal station in Nāpili or the other stations in Central Maui to provide connectivity to outlying areas. Park-and-ride facilities are not as important in communities with well-connected multimodal transportation networks. In Portland, OR, for example, only five percent of the 120,900 daily light riders originate at a park-and-ride facility.[60]

Shared Autonomous Vehicles (SAVs) are another emerging technology that could provide effective "first-mile, last-mile" connectivity to and from transit hubs. SAVs are small, driverless, autonomous shuttles that typically carry six to 12 people. Current applications operate in mixed traffic along existing streets as well as on dedicated guideways. Although SAV technology growth has been slow in the United States due to complex roadway hazards, dramatic media coverage of autonomous vehicle accidents, and institutional issues,[61] they could nevertheless provide effective, on-demand connectivity or serve off-peak hours when demand is lower. SAVs will probably not be able to replace the throughput of mass transit systems during peak periods or over long distances, however, because they will still be limited by the finite capacity of roadway infrastructure and parking lots.[62]

TRAIN SERVICE

Each light rail train would typically have seats for about 150–200 people, with standing room for another 400 people, as shown in Figure 5.3. Commonly used low-floor trains now provide easy, step-free boarding for all users. Passengers using wheelchairs and personal mobility devices would be able to easily and quickly board the trains without the need for slow lifts or ramps. Trains could even be equipped with toilets or even an onboard snack bar to create an enhanced experience for commuters and visitors alike.

Rail services could initially operate at frequencies of every 15 to 30 minutes. This would provide sufficient frequency for the line to serve as a regional connector. The travel time would probably be about 17 to 20 minutes from Nāpili to Lahaina, while Lahaina to Kahului Airport would be another 25–30 minutes. Total travel time from Nāpili to Kahului Airport would be about 45 to 50 minutes. With trains running every 15 minutes, the system would have a throughput capacity of 1,600 people per hour per direction. Assuming 18 hours of operation each day (5 am to 11 pm), this provides a daily capacity of 28,000 people per direction, or up to 57,600 people per day in both directions. This is a tremendous amount of transportation capacity, and would essentially be the equivalent of building a six-lane freeway.[63]

Figure 5.3. Example interior of a light rail train (Sonoma-Marin Area Rail Transit)

The system could be developed as a hybrid form of light rail using self-powered trains with diesel motors. The so-called diesel-multiple unit (DMU) trains are small, lightweight passenger trains with engines located in the passenger cars, as shown in Figure 5.4. This cuts down on the size and complexity of the system, and could also minimize the electrical infrastructure that would be needed. In contrast, traditional fully electrified rail systems require a third power rail or overhead catenary systems with support poles about every 150 to 240 feet.[64] These electrification systems also require supporting traction power substations, which are air-conditioned buildings that contain electrical transformer equipment that converts power from utility distribution lines to voltage that the system can use. Each substation is about the size of a 40-foot shipping container, located alongside the track every mile or so.

Battery-electric light rail trains are now under development, however, which could also provide an alternative, catenary-free motive power for the trains. Batteries could be charged in seven to 10 minutes, and could then run up to 30–60 miles.[65] In the future, hydrogen power could also be used.[66] A new train in the United Kingdom can travel 50 to 75 miles on hydrogen power, while a German model can travel up to 600 miles.

Figure 5.4. Example of a hybrid self-powered light rail train in Northern California (Sonoma-Marin Area Rail Transit)

CONSTRUCTION AND OPERATING COST

Recent construction costs for light rail systems have been around $100 million[67] to $200 million[68] per mile, but costs can depend on whether the chosen route alignment requires elevated guideways or subway tunnels. In contrast, urban streetcars and commuter rail systems are typically built with more limited infrastructure along existing railway lines or within existing streets, and typically cost $25 million[69] to $50 million per mile.

As shown in Table 5.5, a 31-mile hybrid light rail system on Maui could potentially cost somewhere between $1.2 and $2.3 billion dollars. This assumes overall project costs of about $30 to $60 million per mile. In comparison, a hybrid light rail project which recently opened in Texas cost about $30 million per mile to construct,[70] while another hybrid project under construction is expected to cost about $45 million per mile.[71] This assumes that most of the route would be built at ground level on current agricultural lands or in existing rights of way. This cost estimate also assumes that a four-mile Pali Tunnel would cost between $80 and $160 million per mile, or about $315 to $635 million. Other costs could vary greatly based on the selected alignment, system technology, right of way needs, and utility relocation needs.

Table 5.6 shows the operating costs of other hybrid light rail systems throughout the United States. Based on this data, the annual operating cost of a Maui hybrid light rail system could be about $30 million dollars per year, plus another $10 million dollars annually to operate the tunnel.[72] This is substantially higher than the current $13.7 million annual operating budget for the

Table 5.5. Conceptual Capital Cost Estimate for a Hybrid Light Rail Corridor Serving West Maui

		GUIDEWAY COST PER MILE[a]		
SECTION	SECTION LENGTH (MILES)	LOW ($30M)	MEDIUM ($45M)	HIGH ($60M)
Nāpili to Lahaina	8.0	$240	$360	$480
Lahaina to Ukumehame	10.0	$300	$450	$600
Pali Tunnel[a]	4.0	$315	$415	$635
Mā'alaea to Kahului Airport	9.0	$270	$405	$540
Total	31.0	$1,125	$1,630	$2,255

[a] Note: Assumes tunnel costs of $80, $105, or $160 million per mile

Table 5.6. Operating Costs for Selected U.S. Hybrid Rail Systems, 2017

SYSTEM	SYSTEM LENGTH (MILES)	TRACK LENGTH (MILES)	2017 OPERATING COST ($M)	COST PER TRACK MILE ($)
San Diego North County - Sprinter	22.3	58.0	19.8	341,170
New Jersey - River Line	33.8	89.6	32.3	360,300
Austin - Capital MetroRail	32.0	83.5	23.2	277,791
Denton County - A Train	28.7	42.9	13.7	319,190
Average Cost				324,600

Source: U.S. Federal Transit Administration National Transit Database, 2018 Operating Expenses

Maui Bus system—including regular bus services, paratransit, and commuter routes. In fiscal year 2019, the Maui Bus collected $2.1 million in revenues; this was able to cover about 26 percent of the total operating cost.[73] The concentration of hotels around the stations in West Maui and the potential integration with other commercial activities, however, could create a much larger ridership base. This tourism revenue base could potentially generate more reliable revenues that could offset operational costs and create a more sustainable operation than regular transit projects that rely on transit-oriented development to foster ridership density. A West Maui airport connection could also attract tourists by providing more comfortable and economical transportation than today's car rentals.

Examples from Other Communities

This hybrid rail concept is modeled after 10 DMU systems that currently operate in the United States and Canada. In contrast with the more traditional urban light rail systems, these DMU light rail systems provide longer-distance services in lower-density suburban and rural areas. They provide examples of the types of features that might be attractive and useful for a rail system on Maui—such as airport connectivity, on-board amenities, and downtown streetcar circulation.

FORT WORTH

The Fort Worth Transportation Authority opened the TEX Rail system in January 2019. The system links downtown Fort Worth with the Dallas–Ft. Worth Airport while also providing regional connectivity to other commuter rail, intercity rail, and intercity bus services. The 27-mile line has nine stations and six park-and-ride facilities. Travel time is approximately 52 minutes from end to end. Trains operate every 30 minutes during rush hour, and hourly during off-peak times. The system currently carries about 2,000 to 3,000 riders per day, which is less than the projected 8,300 daily trips.[74] By 2022, the route will connect to the Silver Line, which is another light rail line that will extend 26 miles from the Dallas–Ft. Worth Airport to Plano, Texas.[75] The TEX Rail system uses DMU trains on a primarily single-track alignment with double-track passing sections. Each of the eight trains has 229 seats and a total capacity of 488 people. There are four doors on each side of the train. Amenities include USB charging stations, seatback tray tables, overhead luggage storage, onboard bike racks, and a designated quiet car.[76] The system cost about $1.1 billion to construct, and will get about $499 million in federal funding.[77]

SONOMA–MARIN COUNTY

The Sonoma–Marin County Area Rail Transit (SMART) system is a 45-mile system that currently connects Larkspur Landing, San Rafael, and Santa Rosa, California. Another three-mile extension is expected to open in 2021.[78] Trains run between 12 stations every 60 to 90 minutes from 4 am to 9 pm, with more frequent services during rush hour. A fleet of 14 DMUs is operated in two- and three-car train sets, with 158 to 237 seats per train set.[79] They have on-board restrooms and snack bars offering food and beverages for purchase.[80] Seats have tray tables, overhead storage racks, and space for 24 bicycles.[81] The trains have a top speed of 79 miles per hour, and an average speed of 40 miles per hour. In January 2020, SMART carried about 2,400 passengers on an average weekday, and about 800 passengers on an average weekend.[82] Construction of the initial 49-mile system will cost $569 million in total. An additional 21-mile extension is expected to cost another $364 million.[83] What's also unique about the SMART project is that the initial voter-approved tax increase in 2008 also included a parallel bicycle and pedestrian pathway to link the rail stations.[84] Currently, 12 miles of multiuse paths are either completed or funded for construction.[85]

NEW JERSEY

Opened in 2004, the River Line was the first modern diesel light rail system in the United States.[86] The system serves as a streetcar circulator within downtown Camden and Trenton, provides regional access throughout Burlington County, and connects to regional rail systems. It was partially built on an old, underused freight railway line. This 34-mile system has 21 stations serving 13 municipalities. Service is provided every 15–30 minutes using a fleet of 19 trains making 98 trips on an average weekday. Each train accommodates up to 200 passengers, and can be linked up into a four-car train. The system carried about 8,500 riders on an average weekday in 2018. Typical weekend ridership included about 5,600 boardings on Saturdays and 4,300 boardings on Sundays.[87] Construction costs totaled about $1.9 billion in 2020 dollars.[88]

OTHER SYSTEMS

Other diesel-powered light rail lines have been built in California, Texas, and Oregon. The 22-mile Sprinter light rail line in San Diego County connects Escondido with Oceanside. The line also links with regional commuter rail systems to San Diego as well as the Amtrak system.[89] It opened in 2008 and carries about 8,300 passengers per day.[90] The eBART system in Contra Costa County is a 10-mile, three-station DMU system that opened in 2018 and serves as an extension of the regional rapid transit system.[91] The system includes over 1,200 parking spaces at two stations, with another 800 spaces under construction.

In Austin, Texas, the Capitol MetroRail system is a 32-mile line with nine stations that began running in 2010. It connects downtown Austin with communities to the north and carries about 2,900 people per day. The A-Train in Denton, Texas, carries 1,900 riders per day on a 21-mile line with six stations. The Portland, Oregon, Westside Express Service is a 14.7-mile commuter rail line that runs only on weekdays during the morning and afternoon commute hours. [92] This service connects to a branch of the regional light rail network, making it functionally similar to the eBART system. The system opened in 2009 and carries about 1,500 riders per day. [93]

Part III: What it Would Take

While the idea of a light rail system whisking people between jobs, homes, hotels, and activities may seem like a solution to traffic jams, this is more about identifying how West Maui will handle economic growth and development over the long run. Planning for economic growth involves identifying how much growth will be allowed, where it will occur, and what physical form it will take. Community leaders need to establish what type and level of economic growth is desired, and how the transportation system will be developed to support this vision. Transit projects need to be accompanied by policies to concentrate job growth and housing around transit stops in order to realize the full economic potential of infrastructure development. [94] New housing or commercial developments would need to be focused within a short walking distance of a transit station—typically about a quarter- to half-mile radius. This would enable most trips to be easily made via a combination of walking or biking and transit.

Concentrating jobs and housing within walking or biking distance of transit stations involves transforming zoning and parking requirements to facilitate transit-oriented development. This could include allowing taller, mixed-use buildings to accommodate growth while preserving valuable agricultural lands and open space. Reduced parking requirements will reduce land requirements and make buildings more compact and cheaper to build. More compact buildings will also reduce walking distances. This also has the benefit of concentrating development and preserving agricultural or other open space.

Project Development Process

Due to the large capital costs, transit projects have traditionally relied on federal and state funding sources. The Federal Transit Administration (FTA) typically provides about $2.3 billion annually in competitive grants to support the construction of transit infrastructure across the United States.[95] In 2019, these grants supported the construction of 89 major rail and bus rapid-transit projects.[96] The FTA can cover 60 to 80 percent of the construction costs, depending on the size of the project as well as the size of the funding request.[97] Obtaining FTA support involves a multi-year, multi-step process with competitive evaluations at several milestones between project conception and revenue operation. These project development phases typically include regional systems planning, corridor-level alternatives analysis, preliminary engineering, final design, and construction.[98]

REGIONAL SYSTEMS PLANNING

The first step in the project development process is the assessment of existing and projected future transportation conditions. Regional transportation planning is an ongoing process that is carried out by a federally mandated agency that develops long- and short-range transportation plans in coordination with state and local transportation agencies. These plans demonstrate that there are sufficient or reasonably available funding sources to assure that federally supported highway, transit, and multimodal systems are being adequately operated and maintained. The Maui Metropolitan Planning Organization (Maui MPO) was established in 2016 to develop these plans for the island. The long-range transportation plan identifies projects over a 20-year period, and is generally updated every five years. Long-range transportation plans generally identify regional mobility goals, analyze travel patterns, and forecast future transportation needs. The planning process includes community input and analysis of alternative projects to address these needs. The Maui MPO approved its "Hele Mai Maui 2040 Transportation Plan" in December 2019.[99] The adopted plan includes overall goals consistent with the development of a light rail corridor, such as the expansion of mobility choices, connecting communities, improving safety, and enhancing sustainability. Specific projects within the 2040 plan that could also support a future transit corridor include the development of a new transit hub in Lahaina and the completion of the Lahaina Bypass highway.

CORRIDOR PLANNING

Where the regional planning process identifies the likely need for a major capital investment to address transportation problems in a given corridor, the next step in the process is to evaluate different transportation improvements that can best meet these needs. This analysis includes all reasonable types of transportation (called modes), as well as different route alignments. The analysis starts out with a description of the basic transportation problem in the corridor.

An evaluation framework is developed to assess and compare the performance of different transit technologies and route alignments. Broad community input and feedback is typically incorporated into these analyses. Such alternatives could include studies of more cost-effective or advanced transportation technologies that could still meet the purpose and need of the proposed project. Alternatives that are commonly considered include bus rapid transit, guided busways, monorails, and even magnetic levitation trains.

- *Bus rapid transit systems* employ a range of techniques to provide faster and more efficient services than regular buses without the high capital costs of rail systems. They typically include features such as dedicated bus lanes, enhanced stations, high-capacity vehicles, high-frequency services, off-vehicle fare collection, and the use of technology to enhance reliability and convenience.[100] Special bus lanes and level, multiple-door loading platforms can dramatically reduce travel times by bus and lead to increased ridership.
- *Guided busways* are an enhanced form of bus rapid transit that utilizes special tracks to create a smooth, rail-quality ride. One system utilizes a short seven-inch high curb along the sides of the busway to physically guide special buses that are equipped with small horizontal steering wheels. Newer busways in the United Kingdom have been built using precast concrete beams that also incorporate a planting strip between

the tracks. Nagoya, Japan has a four-mile elevated busway,[101] while a busway in Adelaide, Australia, includes both surface and underground sections. One advantage of a busway is that it allows buses to circulate on existing streets through a neighborhood before joining a busway for a longer trip or to avoid congested roads. Busways could also be designed to accommodate emergency vehicles and even private shuttles or autonomous vehicles.

- *Monorails* are elevated trains supported by single, slender beams rather than conventional railroad tracks. The narrow support beams provide some aesthetic benefits in dense urban areas, and can even be integrated into buildings.[102] The lighter cars and smaller support beams can also reduce construction costs relative to subways or elevated rail systems. There are 21 monorail transit systems across the globe, and another 12 systems are under construction in Asia, the Middle East, and South America.[103] Although there are only a handful of monorail systems used for transit service in the United States, the three-mile Newark Airport monorail carries about 33,000 riders per day,[104] while the Walt Disney World monorail carries about 150,000 people per day.[105] A 3.9-mile, privately owned, driverless monorail connects seven stations in Las Vegas. The $650 million construction cost was funded entirely via tax-exempt revenue bonds supported only by farebox revenues and advertising.[106] The Las Vegas monorail operating company filed for Chapter 11 bankruptcy in 2010 due to declining ridership, and carried about 12,000 riders per weekday in 2017.[107]
- *Magnetic levitation (maglev) suspension trains* are another emerging technology that can be assessed in an alternatives analysis. Because maglev systems have no moving parts and generate less noise than conventional trains, they offer some operating advantages over traditional light rail trains using steel wheels on steel rails. There are only a few commercial maglev transit systems in operation. The driverless Linimo maglev system has been operating since 2005 along a 5.5-mile route in Nagoya, Japan. Since 2016, another five maglev systems have either opened or are under construction in South Korea and China. Passive magnetic levitation systems are also under development and could dramatically reduce the cost of this technology.[108] In general, though, maglev systems have still not achieved widespread usage due to the limited number of suppliers of a largely unknown and costly technology relative to conventional trains.

The corridor planning process includes the use of travel demand forecasting models to estimate differences in potential ridership between the various alternatives. Forecasting models are typically based on travel behavior data and transit rider surveys. Land use and population data are used to estimate the number of work, school, or other trips generated. A mode choice model estimates how someone is likely to make a trip—either by automobile, transit, or some other means of transportation. Ridership forecasts are also used to identify differences among the alternatives in terms of potential ridership, environmental impact, construction and operating costs, and other issues.

All of these factors are evaluated in order to screen out alternatives that don't address the overall purpose and need for the project. This evaluation narrows the range of available alternatives until community leaders select a locally preferred alternative (LPA) for implementation. The LPA is then reviewed by the metropolitan planning organization and incorporated into the regional short- and long-range transportation plans.

These studies are also used to help identify a minimum operable segment (MOS). An MOS is a segment of the LPA that provides the most cost-effective solution while providing the greatest benefits to the community. The MOS must be able to function as a stand-alone project and not be dependent on any future segments being constructed.[109] For a West Maui transit corridor, a MOS might be a route from Nāpili to Lahaina (eight miles in length), or perhaps from Lahaina to Kahului Airport (23 miles).

PROJECT DEVELOPMENT

Once the LPA is selected, a project can be approved by the FTA to move into preliminary engineering (PE) and final design. The FTA reviews factors such as mobility benefits, cost-effectiveness, operating efficiencies, environmental benefits, economic development, and influence on transit supportive land use. The FTA also must determine whether or not there is an acceptable degree of local financial commitment and technical capacity to undertake the project development.[110]

During the project development phase, the project scope and design is refined so that precise estimates of project scope and costs are developed to the point where the financing plan can be defined and implemented. The FTA evaluates the degree of local financial commitment and availability of stable and dependable project funding sources. The initial financial plan for Honolulu's rail transit project, for example, was based on Act 247 (2005), which enabled Hawai'i's counties to levy up to a half-percent surcharge on the general excise tax for operating or for capital costs of public transportation systems. Based on this strong financial commitment, the FTA agreed to contribute $1.55 billion to the Honolulu project.[111] In fiscal year 2019, this 0.5-percent surcharge generated $270 million for the City and County of Honolulu to fund the rail transit project and $10.5 million for the County of Kauai. The County of Hawaiʻi adopted a 0.25-percent surcharge rate, and this generated $10.2 million in collections during fiscal year 2019. Although the County of Maui has not adopted the surcharge, such a funding source could be incorporated into a financial plan for a transit corridor project or generate revenue for transit operations.

Environmental studies are also conducted to identify potential impacts to natural, biological, or community resources such as endangered species, historic buildings, and archaeological resources. Appropriate avoidance or mitigation measures are developed and codified in accordance with the National Environmental Protection Act and other local environmental regulations, such as Chapter 343, Hawaiʻi Revised Statues. In some cases, federal regulations may trigger stricter requirements than traditional state- or local-funded transportation projects. Section 4(f) of the U.S. Department of Transportation (USDOT) Act of 1966, for example, prohibits the use of land from publicly owned parks, refuges, and historic properties, unless there is no feasible and prudent alternative to that use.[112] This requires extensive planning, design, and coordination to minimize harm to any property resulting from such uses.

Section 106 of the National Historic Preservation Act also requires federal agencies to consult with community stakeholders in order to avoid, minimize, or mitigate any adverse effects on historic properties, including those considered eligible for listing on the National Register of Historic Places (NRHP).[113] Such a consultation would be required if the rail line affects the Lahaina National Historic Landmark. FTA funding also triggers "Buy America" provisions that require steel, iron, and manufactured goods used in the project to be produced in the United States. Starting in fiscal year 2020, the FTA is requiring that 70 percent of the cost for train components and associated equipment must also be produced in the United States. Waivers can be obtained under limited circumstances.[114]

Based on the project justification, financial commitment, and other evaluation criteria, the FTA assigns a rating to the project. The FTA also considers factors such as project readiness, geographic equity, and the amount of available funds versus the number and size of the projects in the pipeline. Projects with "medium" or higher ratings are then recommended to Congress for funding. The FTA then executes a Full Funding Grant Agreement (FFGA), which codifies the project cost and schedule and establishes the terms and conditions of federal financial participation, including a ceiling on the level of federal financial assistance. The FFGA covers the period of time for completion of the project and also helps to manage the project in accordance with federal law.[115]

INTEGRATING DEVELOPMENT

One potential strategy to offset the high cost of a rail system is to integrate transit stations with commercial retail and housing hubs that can then fund the operating costs of the rail system. Such a scheme has been implemented in Hong Kong. While Hong Kong's 7.5 million people[116] is a far cry from Maui's 170,000 residents[117] and 80,000 tourists, its integration of transit, housing, and commerce in a profitable venture could be a more sustainable development model.

Hong Kong's transit agency, the MTR Corporation, uses its so-called "Rail + Property" model to capture the increase in property values in the land and air rights around the rail stations.[118] The agency is able to capture a share of the profits from land sales or rental income from these lands, and then use the proceeds to cover ongoing rail operating costs and fund the construction of new transit lines.[119]

The MTR also manages over 99,000 residential units and 13 shopping malls in Hong Kong, and is developing another 20,000 residential units and three shopping malls. [120] In 2018, property rental and management services generated about US$648 million in revenue,[121] while proceeds from property development generated another US$330 million.[122] The MTR also receives revenue from 1,470 shops in 714,000 square feet of retail space and about 48,000 advertising units within the rail stations themselves. This revenue amounted to $641 million in 2018.[123] Transport operations also generate profits from passenger fares of about US$254 million.[124] Altogether, this revenue helps the MTR fund the maintenance, upgrading, and renewal of its railway assets—which amounted to US$1.2 billion in 2018.[125]

A slightly different scheme is being used to capture the increase in land values around new rail stations in order to help fund a new light rail system in Montréal, Canada. The Réseau express métropolitain (REM) is a 42-mile driverless light rail transit system with 26 stations that will begin operations in 2021. Developers building new housing, retail, office or commercial space in the vicinity of REM stations will have to pay transportation dues of about US$7.70 per square foot.[126] This fee is applied to new construction within one kilometer of the future stations (500 meters in downtown Montréal) with a value of over

US$590,000[127] and a floor area greater than 2,000 square feet. The fee is being gradually implemented between 2018 and 2021.[128]

The fee is intended to cover 20 percent of the operating costs (currently estimated at about $92 million per year[129]). The REM developer can receive a maximum of $460 million[130] in royalties over a period of 50 years, or an average of US$9.2 million per year.[131] About half of the US$4.5-billion project construction costs[132] are being financed by a private investor that manages Québec's pension plans and insurance programs.[133] The remainder of the project is being funded through a loan from the Canada Infrastructure Bank, grants from the provincial government and the local utility (Hydro-Québec), and the land value capture revenues.

The unique opportunity in West Maui is to integrate transit stations and retail complexes with redeveloped hotels and resorts that can create an economically sustainable system. This redevelopment could also occur as climate adaptation strategies are implemented, such as raising roadways and ground planes or moving development mauka. Closely integrating the visitor infrastructure with transportation would provide increased and more reliable ridership and ancillary revenue streams to support transit system operations. Such close integration, for example, could integrate transit fare payment media with hotel room keys—allowing for a seamless and efficient visitor experience.

This new visitor infrastructure could even be developed to support and manage new types of business models, such as virtual short-term rentals. Rail stations could include central check-in and key distribution facilities as well as luggage transportation services and room shuttles. Busy arteries such as Lower Honoapiʻilani Road could be transformed into shared-use pedestrian malls, with low-speed electric shuttles and service vehicles transporting people and luggage between the stations and accommodations. This could effectively replicate the experience of large resort campuses that already have internal transportation systems for guests and visitors. Such virtual resorts could enable individual homeowners to capture the income benefits of accessory dwelling units, and would create more sustainable communities.

Part IV: Moving Forward

Based on long-term trends, analysts predict that Maui's population will increase by almost 30 percent over the next 25 years to over 210,000 residents.[134] Tourism could increase by over 45 percent to about 92,000 visitors per day by 2045. These additional residents and visitors will place increased demands on mobility, housing, and services. Currently, West Maui has about 56 percent of the island's hotel rooms—about 12,000 units. Assuming that this share is maintained in the future, this could translate into another 5,500 hotel units and 7,000 more residents in West Maui. The potential implications of this type of development pressure on mobility and urban sprawl could be detrimental without proper planning and a sustainable vision for the future. With more than 80 percent of residential land in West Maui zoned for single-family homes, any future development is likely to continue current low-density patterns unless major policy changes and infrastructure investments are made.[135] A coordinated strategy to establish a light rail system and concentrating development within walkable areas around stations could go a long way towards addressing this growth in a more sustainable manner.

Community stakeholders and civic leaders could start this long journey by including consideration of a new transit corridor within other comprehensive planning efforts, such as the West Maui Community Plan or updates to the Maui Island Plan. Since 2017, Maui County officials have been engaging stakeholders to evaluate a series of different future land use scenarios.[136] These scenarios included an infill alternative that constrains development into existing areas and permitted projects, rather than expanding or dispersing growth throughout the region. In this scenario, Central Lahaina is built out more intensely, and existing open space and agricultural lands are preserved. A light rail transit corridor could be incorporated into this infill alternative. This would incentivize redevelopment and densification of areas around rail station hubs in existing built-up areas, rather than opening up new lands for development.

A more aggressive planning strategy could even eliminate on-site parking requirements or restrict the maximum amount of parking to levels that can be sustained by the existing roadway system. Landowners could also be allowed to transfer their development rights into areas around the rail stations in exchange for preserving agricultural land or open space, thus creating incentives to promote more concentrated development and reducing sprawl. Hotels could even be required to minimize or even eliminate off-street parking for both guests and employees. Combined with new forms of flexible transportation systems, this could help transform the visitor infrastructure to adopt more sustainable models of mobility.

Incremental Transit Improvements

While development of a light rail system is a long-term effort to shape land use patterns, there are a number of incremental improvements to the existing

Maui Bus system that could improve mobility while also making the case for long-term land use and mobility changes. The Maui Bus and paratransit system carried almost 6,500 passengers per day on an average weekday in 2018.[137] The West Maui routes accounted for 42 percent of the total Maui Bus system ridership between 2017 and 2018.[138] Increasing the frequency and span of service of the West Maui bus routes along with some other improvements could increase ridership and make the service much more useful.

An improved service could include more frequent buses with departures every 15 to 30 minutes instead of hourly. The hours of operation should also be expanded to include late-night service that becomes a better option for hotel workers. The current regular services run from 6:30 am to 7:30 pm, which probably starts too late or ends too early for many workers. In addition, commuter buses often lack enough capacity or miss the hotel shifts. Indeed, the two most frequently provided comments in a 2014 survey of West Maui bus riders included a desire for more frequent service (45 percent of comments) and a longer span of service (22 percent).[139] Transit planner Jarett Walker notes that high frequency and a long span of service are fundamental features of transit services that feel empowering, because they allow people to use transit whenever they want. [140] This freedom helps to promote transit-dependent lifestyles.

Another service improvement would be to develop an express service that could operate from Kapalua to the Kahului Airport. Such a route could provide a limited-stop service that would reduce travel time and make the bus more competitive with the automobile. The current trip by bus takes two hours and five minutes, with a transfer in Lahaina, a detour through Wailuku, and another transfer in Kahului. A limited-stop express service should be able to do this direct trip in about an hour. The new route could be branded as a Bus Rapid Transit (BRT) system and could cater to tourists as well as workers, as shown in Figure 5.5. Connections to new and existing park-and-ride facilities as well as major transfer stations along the Honoapiʻilani and Kūihelani Highways could also minimize the need for circuitous routes and create a faster service.

One potential model for West Maui is the VelociRFTA service that connects Aspen and Glenwood Springs in Colorado.[141] This BRT corridor operates along a 42-mile route serving a three-county area with 149,000 residents. The route takes about an hour to complete, and buses operate every 12 to 15 minutes between 4:45 am to 8:45 pm. Late-night services operate until about 2 am at reduced frequencies of every half-hour or hour. Buses are equipped with extra-cushioned seats and onboard Wi-Fi. Fare payment occurs at vending machines located at each station in order to speed boarding times. The service

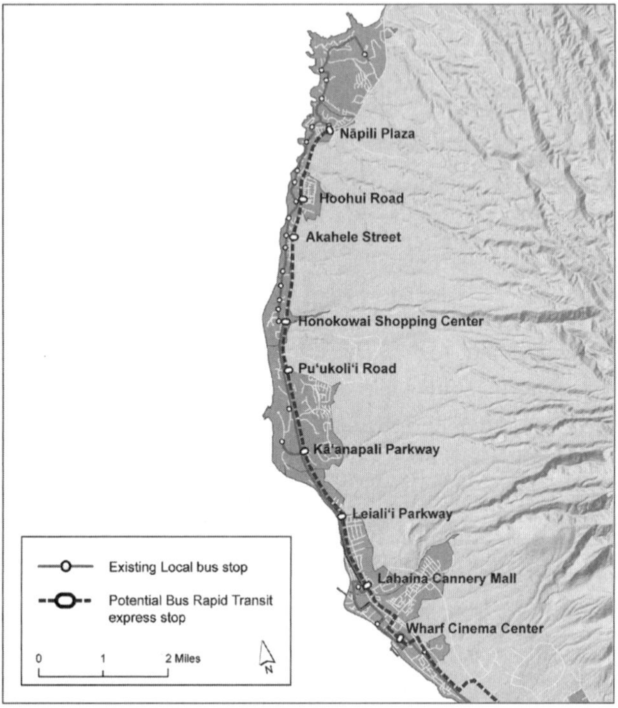

Figure 5.5. Potential interim bus rapid transit express corridor through West Maui

carried about 900,000 passengers in 2017. The Roaring Forks Transportation Authority used a $25 million FTA grant to help pay for the $46.2 million project, which included nine stations, five park-and-ride facilities, bus priority signals, bus-only lanes, and 22 compressed natural gas buses. The system opened in 2013.

Such a project could also be integrated with the development of the West Maui Greenway, which is envisioned as a 25-mile multiuse greenway utilizing abandoned agricultural roads and the old railway right of way.[142] The multiuse path could be built alongside a rail or bus transit guideway, as was done in Cambridge and Manchester in the United Kingdom. The multiuse path built as part of the busway in Cambridge was actually responsible for an 85 percent increase in cycling near the city.[143] In Colorado, a recent expansion of the VelociRFTA system is being undertaken through a property tax increase that also includes funding for multiuse trails, bikeshares, and pedestrian enhancements.[144] As noted earlier, the voter-approved SMART rail project in Sonoma and Marin counties included a parallel bicycle and pedestrian pathway as part of the rail project.

Overall, this type of integrated multi-modal approach towards creating a high frequency, highly accessible transit corridor could be a very good model for West Maui. Although buses may not necessarily have the same type of catalytic long-term land use changes as rail, they could offer a viable, incremental solution over the short to medium timeframe. This would also create a robust and adaptable pathway towards the eventual establishment of a high-capacity rail corridor. A bus rapid-transit corridor could be incrementally upgraded over time with new segments on guided surface or elevated busways. Decisions could be re-evaluated over time, and strategies could be adapted accordingly. The technologies behind electrically powered transit vehicles or autonomous guidance systems, for example, could mature and become commercially viable for integration into the transit corridor. The tourism market could also evolve and introduce additional changes to the economic and mobility needs of West Maui.

Conclusion

Shifting away from a reliance on automobile-oriented mobility could be one of the most effective ways to promote a more sustainable future for West Maui. A light rail corridor could play a catalytic role in creating tight-knit, walkable communities that could transform lifestyles—enhancing social closeness while even improving health outcomes. Denser urban communities can help to protect agricultural lands and watersheds from urban sprawl. West Maui also now has a generational opportunity to undertake such a transformation, especially as the community adapts to the realities of climate change—perhaps requiring development to shift mauka or else reconstructing buildings to accommodate sea level rise.

A light rail system could also enhance the visitor experience and help improve the overall image of the island. A well-designed system of integrated transit hubs could also reduce the reliance on car rentals and create a more relaxing experience for visitors. Hotel parking lots could be replaced with additional amenities or more units, helping to accommodate growth and minimize sprawl.

The transformation of West Maui into a corridor of walkable communities linked by rail could help to promote a modern, high technology, environmentally sustainable image for the island. Maui's rich natural, cultural, and social environment has the potential to attract and support new types of knowledge-based businesses and micro-industries. This could support economic diversification and help to ensure a more sustainable future for the island.

Notes

1. Conrad Goodwin, "Lands of the Pioneer Mill, Lahaina, Hawaii," Paper presented at the Association of American Geographers 95th Annual Meeting, March 23-27, 1999, www.academia.edu/5702708/Lands_of_the_Pioneer_Mill_Lahania_Hawaii.
2. Joseph Iao, *Map of the Island of Maui*, Hawaii Territorial Survey, June 1929. https://evols.library.manoa.hawaii.edu/handle/10524/55320.
3. "History," Sugar Cane Train Maui. *Accessed* May 9, 202. www.sugarcanetrain.com/history/.
4. Gerald M. Best, "Pioneer Narrow Gauge on Maui," in *Railroads of Hawaii* (San Marino, California: Golden West Books, 1978), 13.
5. John B. Hungerford, "Kahului Railroad: First and Last of the Hawaiian Rails," in *Hawaiian Railways: A Memoir of the Common Carriers of the Fiftieth State*. Reseda, California: Hungerford Press, 1963, 74.
6. Except Sundays.
7. Robert A. Ramsay, "Kahului Railroad—The Final Chapter," *The Railway and Locomotive Historical Society Bulletin*, No. 120 (Railway & Locomotive Historical Society, April 1969), 60–63. www.jstor.org/stable/43518271.
8. Measured at a point just south of the Kā'anapali Highway. "HDOT Highways Program Status Map," State of Hawai'i Department of Transportation. *Accessed* March 8, 2019. https://histategis.maps.arcgis.com/apps/MapSeries/index.html?appid=39e4d804242740a89d3fd0bc76d8d7de.
9. Google Maps. "Directions from Kahului, Hawaii to Lahaina, Hawaii at 4 pm on Thursday, February 6." *Accessed* May 9, 2020. https://goo.gl/maps/yJdi6CCxmmsu8tYF6.
10. Hawai'i Climate Change Mitigation and Adaptation Commission, *Hawai'i Sea Level Rise Vulnerability and Adaptation Report*, Prepared by Tetra Tech, Inc. and the State of Hawai'i Department of Land and Natural Resources, Office of Conservation and Coastal Lands, (December 2017), https://climate.hawaii.gov/wp-content/uploads/2019/02/SLR-Report_Dec2017-with-updated-disclaimer.pdf.
11. Google Maps, "Directions from Napili Market, 5095 Napilihau St, Lahaina, Hawaii to Kahului Airport at 4 pm on Thursday, February 6." *Accessed* May 9, 2020. https://goo.gl/maps/aeGL6C4EnfUNcjSJ7.
12. "Maui mayor contemplates rail, envisions more Disneyland than Honolulu," January 27, 2015. www.khon2.com/local-news/maui-mayor-contemplates-rail-envisions-more-disneyland-than-honolulu/.
13. State of Hawai'i Department of Business, Economic Development and Tourism, "Table 18.08: Vehicle Registration, By Type of Vehicle, By County: 2018," in *State of Hawaii Data Book* (November 2019). https://dbedt.hawaii.gov/economic/databook/db2018/.

14. "Table 18-10: Vehicles Available to Occupied Housing Units, by County: 2017," *State of Hawaii Data Book.*
15. Maui Metropolitan Planning Organization, *Hele Mai Maui Long Range Transportation Plan 2040 Factbook* (December 2018), 23. https://issuu.com/mauimpo/docs/hele_mai_maui_factbook_final_dec_2018.
16. Maui Metropolitan Planning Organization, *Hele Mai Maui Long Range Transportation Plan 2040 Final Plan* (December 2019), 13. https://mauimpo.org/hele-mai-maui-2040.
17. Allison Schaefers, "As impacts mount, some wonder whether 'managed tourism' is possible on Maui," *Honolulu Star-Advertiser*, August 25, 2019. www.staradvertiser.com/2019/08/25/hawaii-news/as-impacts-mount-some-wonder-whether-managed-tourism-is-possible-on-maui/.
18. County of Maui Department of Planning, "Community Profile Technical Resource Paper," West Maui Community Plan (January 2018), 29. https://wearemaui.org/technical-resource-papers-community-profile.
19. "Longitudinal Employer-Household Dynamics Origin-Destination Employment Statistics, Version 7," U.S. Census Bureau. *Accessed* November 17, 2019. https://lehd.ces.census.gov/data/.
20. State of Hawai'i Department of Business, Economic Development and Tourism, "Table 18.17: Motor Vehicle Fuel Consumption and Vehicle Miles, 1994 to 2018, and by County, 2017 and 2018," in *State of Hawaii Data Book* (November 2019). https://dbedt.hawaii.gov/economic/databook/db2018/.
21. State of Hawai'i Department of Transportation Highways Division, *Financial Statements (With Independent Auditors' Report Thereon* (June 30, 2017). https://hidot.hawaii.gov/highways/files/2019/03/Highways-Division-FY2018-Financial-Statements.pdf.
22. Includes Department of Public Works budget allocations for Highway Administration, Roads and Bridge maintenance, and Traffic Management. *Council Adopted Budget*, County of Maui, Fiscal Year 2017. www.mauicounty.gov/DocumentCenter/Index/4377.
23. AAA, *Your Driving Costs: How Much Are You Really Paying To Drive?* September 2019. www.aaa.com/AAA/common/AAR/files/AAA-Your-Driving-Costs.pdf.
24. Maui County Code, Chapter 19.36B.080 (March 23, 2020) (Adopted December 21, 2018). https://library.municode.com/hi/county_of_maui/codes/code_of_ordinances?nodeId=TIT19ZO_ARTIICOZOPR_CH19.36BOREPALO_19.36B.080LA.
25. Maui County Code, Chapter 19.56.050 (March 23, 2020) (Adopted December 21, 2018). https://library.municode.com/hi/county_of_maui/codes/code_of_ordinances?nodeId=TIT19ZO_ARTIVREMIAR_CH19.56OPSPINSY_19.56.050BOCOPA.

26. Christof Spieler, *Trains, Buses, People: An Opinionated Atlas of US Transit*. Washington: Island Press, 2018, 8–9.
27. Donald Shoup, "Unnatural Selection," in *The High Cost of Free Parking*. New York: Routledge, 2017, 22–26.
28. Maui County Code, Chapter 19.36B, (March 23, 2020) (Adopted December 21, 2018), https://library.municode.com/hi/county_of_maui/codes/code_of_ordinances?nodeId=TIT19ZO_ARTIICOZOPR_CH19.36BOREPALO.
29. Todd Littman, *Parking Pricing Implementation Guidelines* (Victoria: Victoria Transport Policy Institute, April 11, 2018). www.vtpi.org/parkpricing.pdf, 9.
30. County of Maui Department of Planning, "Table 9: West Maui Residential Zoning in Growth Boundaries," in *West Maui Community Plan Land Use Technical Resource Paper* (May 31, 2019). https://wearemaui.org/technical-resource-papers-land-use.
31. Laurence Kahn, "How Large is a Parking Space?" Franklin Street, May 23, 2019. https://franklinst.com/about-us/newsroom/news-details/2019/05/23/how-large-is-a-parking-space.
32. Nadia Balint, "As Apartments Are Shrinking, Seattle Tops New York with the Smallest Rentals in the U.S.," *RentCafe Blog,* November 30, 2018. www.rentcafe.com/blog/rental-market/real-estate-news/us-average-apartment-size-trends-downward/.
33. Shoup, "A Great Planning Disaster," in *The High Cost of Free Parking*, 144.
34. Shoup, "A Great Planning Disaster," 148.
35. Shoup, "A Great Planning Disaster," 131–132.
36. Grady Clay, "Strips," in *Close Up: How to Read the American City*. Chicago: The University of Chicago Press, 1980, 85–109.
37. Edward Glasier, Triumph of the City: How Our Greatest Innovation makes us Richer, Smarter, Greener, Healthier, and Happier. New York: Penguin Books, 2011, 207–209.
38. Donald Appleyard, "The Ecology of the Street," in Livable Streets. Berkeley: University of California Press, 1981, 29–40.
39. "National Complete Streets Coalition," Smart Growth America, accessed May 9, 2020. https://smartgrowthamerica.org/program/national-complete-streets-coalition/.
40. Resolution 12-34, Establishing a Complete Streets Policy for the County of Maui, Maui County Council (April 10, 2012). www.mauicounty.gov/DocumentCenter/View/18797/Reso-12-034?bidId=
41. Jane Jacobs, "The Need for Concentration," in *The Death and Life of Great American Cities*. New York: The Modern Library, 1993, 288–289.
42. Edward Glasier, *Triumph of the City*, 6–8.
43. David Sim, *Soft City: Building Density for Everyday Life*. Washington, D.C.: Island Press, 2019.

44. David Sim, *Soft City*, 98–102.
45. Boris S. Pushkarev and Jeffrey M. Zupan, *Public Transportation and Land Use Policy.* Bloomington: Indiana University Press, 1977, 5.
46. Pushkarev and Zupan, 5–7.
47. Pushkarev and Zupan, 173.
48. Eric Guerra and Robert Cevero, "Transit and the 'D' Word," *Access 40*. Berkeley: The University of California Transportation Center, Spring 2010. www.accessmagazine.org/spring-2012/transit-d-word/.
49. Christof Spieler, *Trains, Buses, People*, 18.
50. "Selected Housing Characteristics: DP04," 2018 American Community Census 5-Year Estimate, U.S. Census Bureau, accessed April 19, 2020. http://data.census.gov.
51. "Oahu & Neighbor Island Highlights," Department of Business, Economic Development & Tourism Visitor Statistics, accessed March 14, 2020. https://dbedt.hawaii.gov/visitor/ni-stats/maui20.xls.
52. Reconnecting America, *Transit Technologies Worksheet*, accessed March 7, 2020. www.reconnectingamerica.org/assets/Uploads/bestpractice175.pdf.
53. European Commission, "Annex 13 – Case study on tunnels," *Assessment of unit costs (standard prices) of rail projects (CAPital EXpenditure)*, Brussels, July 13, 2018. https://ec.europa.eu/regional_policy/sources/docgener/studies/pdf/assess_unit_cost_rail/annex_13_case_study_tunneling.pdf.
54. "Kaneohe—Kailua Wastewater Conveyance & Treatment Facilities Project Overview." *Accessed* April 26, 2020. www.kktunnel.org/project-overview/.
55. Japan International Cooperation Agency, JICA Preparatory Survey on Greater Cairo Metro Line No. 4 in the Arab Republic of Egypt, Final Report, Volume 3, Feasibility Study Report, June 2010. https://openjicareport.jica.go.jp/pdf/12001715_03.pdf.
56. Jae-Ho Pyeon, Trend Analysis of Long Tunnels Worldwide, MTI Report WP 12-09. San Jose: Mineta Transportation Institute, March 2016. https://transweb.sjsu.edu/research/trend-analysis-long-tunnels-worldwide.
57. "Bus Schedule Effective July 2019," Maui Bus, County of Maui Department of Transportation. *Accessed* October 6, 2019. www.mauicounty.gov/DocumentCenter/View/4353.
58. Google Maps, "Directions from Kapalua, Hawaii 96761 to Lahaina, Hawaii at 4 pm on Thursday, February 6." *Accessed* May 9, 2020. https://goo.gl/maps/GSuzW91kj138Mfpu5.
59. Note that this distance is about the length of the terminal concourse at the Kahului Airport. This distance is also equivalent to walking from Gate A13 to Gate G6 at the Daniel K. Inouye International Airport in Honolulu.
60. Trimet, *A Primer on Station Access and Park-and-Rides: A Handbook for Decision Makers, Project Partners and Community Members.* June 2019. https://trimet.org/swcorridor/openhouse/parkandride/pdf/ParkandRide-Primer.pdf.

61. Jeff McMahon, "The 4 Reasons Autonomous Vehicles Seem Stalled in the U.S.," *Forbes*, January 27, 2020. www.forbes.com/sites/jeffmcmahon/2020/01/27/the-4-reasons-autonomous-vehicles-seem-to-have-stalled-in-the-us/.
62. Ryan Tam, "Technology, Shared Mobility And The Rail System," *Honolulu Civil Beat*, September 26, 2017. www.civilbeat.org/2017/09/technology-shared-mobility-and-the-rail-system/.
63. U.S. Department of Transportation, Federal Highway Administration, *Simplified Highway Capacity Calculation Method for the Highway Performance Monitoring System*, October 2017.
64. Parsons Brinckerhoff, Inc., *Track Design Handbook for Light Rail Transit, 2nd Edition*, Transit Cooperative Research Program Report No. 155. Washington, D.C.: Transportation Research Board, 2012, 11-5.
65. Keith Barrow, "Bombardier unveils battery-electric Talent 3," *International Railway Journal*, September 18, 2018. www.railjournal.com/fleet/bombardier-unveils-battery-electric-talent-3/.
66. Allison Hirschlag, "As old diesel trains are phased out of rail networks around the world, the UK is about to test a new type of engine that could help to decarbonise railways—hydrogen-powered trains," *BBC Future*, February 27, 2020. www.bbc.com/future/article/20200227-how-hydrogen-powered-trains-can-tackle-climate-change.
67. Alon Levy, "Why It's So Expensive to Build Urban Rail in the U.S.," Citylab, January 26, 2018. www.citylab.com/transportation/2018/01/why-its-so-expensive-to-build-urban-rail-in-the-us/551408/.
68. "Light Rail Average Cost Is $202 Million/Mile," The Antiplanner, July 19, 2018. https://ti.org/antiplanner/?p=14829.
69. Reconnecting America, "Commuter Rail Transit" in *Transit Technologies Worksheet.*
70. Fort Worth Transportation Authority, "Section 2.6: Preferred Alternative Capital and Operating Costs," in *TEX Rail Final Environmental Impact Statement/Section 4(f)* Evaluation, May 2014, 2-65.
71. Dallas Area Rapid Transit Authority, "Section 7: Cost and Financial Analysis," in *Cotton Belt Regional Rail Project Final Environmental Impact Statement/Record of Decision*, November 2018, 7-3. www.dart.org/ShareRoot/about/expansion/cottonbelt/cottonbeltfeis/CottonBeltFEISandROD.pdf.
72. This assumes a double-tracked line with 60 miles of track.
73. *FY 2020 Council Adopted Budget*, Budget Documents and Ordinances, Office of the Mayor, 641–647. www.mauicounty.gov/DocumentCenter/View/120165/FY-2020-Council-Adopted-Budget.
74. Gordon Dickson, "It's been a year since TEXRail launched. Why aren't more commuters riding the trains?" *Fort Worth Star-Telegram*, January 10, 2020. www.star-telegram.com/news/traffic/article239013403.html.
75. Ray Leszcynski, "DART's $1.1 billion Cotton Belt plan about to come into public

view," *The Dallas Morning News,* March 18, 2018. www.dallasnews.com/news/transportation/2018/03/18/dart-s-1-1-billion-cotton-belt-plan-about-to-come-into-public-view/.

76. Trinity Metro, *Trinity Metro TEX Rail*, Forth Worth, TX: July 2019. https://ridetrinitymetro.org/wp-content/uploads/2020/01/TEXRail-Fact-Sheet_low-res.pdf.
77. "TEX Rail Project Profile," Current Capital Investment Grant (CIG) Projects, Updated February 11, 2020. www.transit.dot.gov/funding/grant-programs/capital-investments/tex-rail-project-profile.
78. Kevin Fixler, "SMART to begin work on extension of commuter rail to Windsor," *Santa Rosa Press Democrat,* September 19, 2018. www.pressdemocrat.com/news/8754419-181/smart-to-begin-work-on.
79. Sonoma–Marin Area Rail Transit District, *SMART 2019 Strategic Plan*, November 2019, 8. http://sonomamarintrain.org/sites/default/files/Financial%20Documents/2019%20Strategic%20Plan%20Final-Nov%202019.pdf.
80. Derek Moore, "'Concessionistas' to offer food service aboard SMART trains," *Santa Rosa Press Democrat*, July 17, 2017. www.petaluma360.com/news/7207705-181/concessionistas-to-offer-food-service.
81. Sonoma–Marin Area Rail Transit District, *SMART Train Vehicle Fact Sheet. Accessed* March 26, 2020. http://sonomamarintrain.org/sites/default/files/Documents/SMART%20Train%20Vehicle%20Fact%20Sheet.pdf.
82. "SMART Board of Directors Ridership Data Collection and Reporting," Sonoma Marin Area Rail Transit District, February 5, 2020. http://sonomamarintrain.org/sites/default/files/Board/COC%20Documents/Ridership%20Presentation_02.05.2020.pdf.
83. Kevin Fixler, "Marin-to-Solano SMART extension estimated at $1B," *Marin Independent Journal*, May 6, 2019. www.marinij.com/2019/05/05/marin-to-solano-smart-extension-estimated-at-1b/.
84. "Sonoma–Marin Area Rail Transit District Measure Q," 2008 Ballot Measures, Past Election Results and Information, County of Marin. www.marincounty.org/-/media/files/departments/rv/elections/past/2008/nov/measureq.pdf.
85. Sonoma–Marin Area Rail Transit District, *SMART 2019 Strategic Plan*, 10–12.
86. William D. Middleton, "Diesel light rail rolls at last in North America," *Railway Gazette International*, November 2002, Volume 158, Issue 11, 702.
87. New Jersey Transit, *NJ Transit Facts At a Glance: Fiscal Year 2018. Accessed* March 22, 2020. www.njtransit.com/AdminTemp/FactsAtaGlance_2018.pdf.
88. $1.4 billion in 2004 dollars. "Camden-Trenton: River Line Light Railway Gains Riders, Spurs Economic Development," Light Rail Now!, May 2004 (revised). www.lightrailnow.org/news/n_nj002.htm.
89. "Sprinter Hybrid Rail," North County Transit District. *Accessed* March 26, 2020. www.gonctd.com/services/sprinter-hybrid-rail/#.

90. "Sprinter Fact Sheet," North County Transit District. *Accessed* March 26, 2020. https://gonctd.com/wp-content/uploads/2019/03/SPRINTER_Fact_Sheet.pdf.
91. "BART to Antioch: East Contra Costa BART Extension," Bay Area Rapid Transit. *Accessed* March 26, 2020. www.bart.gov/about/projects/ecc.
92. Trimet, *WES Commuter Rail Tour Fact Sheet*, August 2012. https://trimet.org/pdfs/history/railfactsheet-wes.pdf.
93. Keaton Thomas, "10 years in, WES ridership proving to be a 'big, serious problem' for TriMet," September 2, 2019, KATU2.com. https://katu.com/news/following-the-money/10-years-in-wes-ridership-proving-to-be-a-big-serious-problem-for-trimet.
94. Guerra and Cevero, "Transit and the 'D' Word."
95. "About the Program," FTA Capital Investment Grant Program. *Accessed* March 8, 2020. www.transit.dot.gov/funding/grant-programs/capital-investments/about-program.
96. *Annual Report on Funding Recommendations* (Washington: Federal Transit Administration, February 2020, www.transit.dot.gov/funding/grant-programs/capital-investments/about-program.
97. For large projects that cost over $300 million, the FTA can reimburse up to 60 percent of the total project cost. For smaller projects that are less than $300 million, the FTA can reimburse up to 80 percent of the total project costs. The FTA funds up to 80 percent of the costs for a request of less than $100 million, or up to 60 percent of the costs for a request of over $100 million.
98. U.S. Department of Transportation, Federal Transit Administration, *Capital Investment Program Guidance and Application Instructions, FTA Circular C 9300.1B*, November 1, 2008. /www.transit.dot.gov/regulations-and-guidance/fta-circulars/capital-investment-program-guidance-and-application.
99. *Hele Mai Maui Long Range Transportation Plan 2040 Final Plan.*
100. Taotao Deng and John D. Nelson, "Recent Developments in Bus Rapid Transit: A Review of the Literature," *Transport Reviews*, Volume 31, No. 1, January 2011, 71.
101. "Yutorito Line Nagoya." *Accessed* May 9, 2020, www.japanvisitor.com/japan-transport/yutoritoline.
102. "Monorail in China's Chongqing runs through residential blocks," *The Asia Times*, April 17, 2018. https://asiatimes.com/2018/04/monorail-chinas-chongqing-runs-residential-blocks/.
103. Michael J. Coren, "Monorails Are Back," Quartz.com, December 14, 2017. https://qz.com/1152121/monorails-are-back/.
104. Larry Higgs, "Big money fixes coming to Newark airport's monorail, PATH stations," *NJ.com,* October 24, 2019. www.nj.com/traffic/2019/10/big-money-fixes-coming-to-newark-airports-monorail-path-stations.html.
105. Magic Ears Dudebro, "Why Are There No Monorails Outside Of The Disney Parks?" *Medium.com,* January 7, 2018. https://medium.com/@the

_disney_dudebro/why-are-there-no-monorails-outside-of-the-disney-parks -30f3374b76ac.

106. "Project Profile: Las Vegas Monorail," U.S. Department of Transportation, Federal Highway Administration, Office of Innovative Program Delivery. Accessed May 2, 2020. www.fhwa.dot.gov/ipd/project_profiles/nv_lasvegas_monorail.aspx.
107. "Las Vegas Monorail Company, 2017" *National Transit Database, Transit Agency* Profiles, U.S. Department, Federal Transit Administration. *Accessed* May 2, 2020. www.transit.dot.gov/ntd/transit-agency-profiles/las-vegas-monorail-company.
108. Richard F. Post, "Toward More Efficient Transport: The Inductrack Maglev System" (presentation at Advanced Transportation Workshop, Stanford, October 10, 2005). https://gcep.stanford.edu/pdfs/ChEHeXOTnf3dHH5qjYRXMA/09_Post_10_11_trans.pdf.
109. U.S. Department of Transportation, Federal Transit Administration, *Capital Investment Program Guidance and Application Instructions, FTA Circular C 9300.1B.*
110. U.S. Department of Transportation, Federal Transit Administration, Capital Investment Program Guidance and Application Instructions, FTA Circular C 9300.1B, V-6 and V-7.
111. Full Funding Grant Agreement, Honolulu Rail Transit Project, HI-0-0047-02, United States Department of Transportation, Federal Transit Administration, October 1, 2012. http://hartdocs.honolulu.gov/docushare/dsweb/Get/Document-16914/20121219-full-funding-grant-agreement.pdf.
112. "Section 4(f) of the Department of Transportation Act," U.S. Department of Transportation, Federal Transit Administration. *Accessed* May 9, 2020. www.transit.dot.gov/regulations-and-guidance/environmental-programs/section-4f-department-transportation-act.
113. "Historic Resources and Section 106," U.S. Department of Transportation, Federal Transit Administration. *Accessed* May 9, 2020. www.transit.dot.gov/regulations-and-guidance/environmental-programs/historic-resources-and-section-106.
114. "Buy America," U.S. Department of Transportation, Federal Transit Administration. *Accessed* May 9, 2020. www.transit.dot.gov/buyamerica.
115. U.S. Department of Transportation, Federal Transit Administration, Capital Investment Program Guidance and Application Instructions, FTA Circular C 9300.1B, V-13.
116. "Population, End-2019," Census and Statistics Department, the Government of the Hong Kong Special Administrative Region. Accessed February 23, 2020. www.censtatd.gov.hk/hkstat/sub/so20.jsp.
117. "Quick Facts, Maui County, Hawaii," U.S. Census Bureau. Accessed May 9, 2020. www.census.gov/quickfacts/mauicountyhawaii.
118. Hong Kong's unique land ownership structure means that all land is owned by the government, but is leased out on a long-term basis, and has made it possible to transfer land ownership to the transit agency.

119. Matthew Keegan, "How public transport actually turns a profit in Hong Kong," *The Guardian*. March 19, 2020. www.theguardian.com/cities/2019/mar/19/how-public-transport-actually-turns-a-profit-in-hong-kong.
120. Connecting Communities: MTR Annual Report 2018. Hong Kong: MTR Corporation Limited, 2019. www.mtr.com.hk/en/corporate/investor/2018frpt.html.
121. About $5 billion Hong Kong dollars (HKD).
122. About $2.5 billion HKD.
123. About $5 billion HKD.
124. About $1.9 billion HKD.
125. About $9.2 billion HKD.
126. $10 Canadian dollars (CAD).
127. $769,000 CAD.
128. Autorité régionale de transport métropolitain, *ARTM By-Law Respecting Transportation Dues regarding the Réseau Express Métropolitain Application Guide*, December 21, 2018. https://artm.quebec/wp-content/uploads/2019/01/GuideApplication_ed03_EN.pdf.
129. $120 million CAD.
130. $600 million CAD.
131. $12 million CAD. Andre Dubuc, "Redevances immobilières: déjà 23 millions dans les coffres du REM," *La Presse*. Montréal, September 11, 2019. www.lapresse.ca/affaires/201909/10/01-5240686-redevances-immobilieres-deja-23-millions-dans-les-coffres-du-rem.php.
132. $6.3 billion CAD.
133. Canada Infrastructure Bank, *Canada Infrastructure Bank invests in Réseau express métropolitain project with $1.28 billion, 15-year loan*, August 22, 2018. https://cib-bic.ca/en/canada-infrastructure-bank-invests-in-reseau-express-metropolitain-project-with-1-28-billion-15-year-loan/.
134. State of Hawaii Department of Business, Economic Development, and Tourism Research and Economic Analysis Division, *Population and Economic Projections for the State of Hawaii to 2045*, June 2018, 2-3. http://files.hawaii.gov/dbedt/economic/data_reports/2045-long-range-forecast/2045-long-range-forecast.pdf.
135. County of Maui Department of Planning, "Table 9: West Maui Residential Zoning in Growth Boundaries," *West Maui Community Plan Land Use Technical Resource Paper*, May 31, 2019. https://wearemaui.org/technical-resource-papers-land-use.
136. County of Maui Department of Planning, *West Maui Community Plan Update Maui County Planning Department Draft*, July 11, 2019. https://wearemaui.konveio.com/draft-west-maui-community-plan.
137. "2018 Annual Database Service," U.S. Department of Transportation, Federal Transit Administration. *Accessed* March 8, 2020. www.transit.dot.gov/ntd/data-product/2018-annual-database-service.

138. Maui Metropolitan Planning Organization, Hele Mai Maui Long Range Transportation Plan 2040 Factbook, 25.
139. SSFM International, Maui Short-Range Transit Plan, Appendix C (Wailuku: County of Maui Department of Transportation, 2016), http://mauicounty.us/wp-content/uploads/2017/09/Maui-Short-Range-Transit-Plan.pdf.
140. Jarrett Walker, Human Transit: How Clearer Thinking about Public Transit Can Enrich Our Communities and Our Lives. Washington: Island Press, 2012, 85.
141. Dan Blankenship, "VelociRFTA: The Nation's First Rural Bus Rapid Transit System" (presentation at the American Planning Association Colorado Conference, Snowmass, Colorado, October 4, 2012). www.apacolorado.org/sites/default/files/2012-10-04%20coapa_rfta%20brt_final%20%5BCompatibility%20Mode%5D.pdf.
142. Maui Bicycling League, *West Maui Greenway Phase 1 Conceptual Plan*, March 2016. www.mauibike.org/west-maui-greenway/.
143. "Joining the dots on infrastructure in UK: spotlight on the Cambridge Guided Busway." London: Royal Institute of British Architects, July 17, 2018. /www.architecture.com/knowledge-and-resources/knowledge-landing-page/joining-the-dots-spotlight-on-the-cambridge-guided-busway.
144. Roaring Forks Transportation Authority, *RFTA Destination 2040. Accessed* January 2, 2020. www.rfta2040.com/wp-content/uploads/2018/10/18040_rfta2040brochure.pdf.

Chapter 6

AROUND KAHAKULOA

Albert Perez

West Maui is known for its natural beauty, world-class beaches, and popular resort areas. Lahaina, in the middle of this region, contains important cultural sites and historic buildings. Millions of visitors are drawn to West Maui every year. Due to the fact that there are thousands of West Maui residents who work and shop outside of Central Maui, and thousands of employees who commute to West Maui to work in resorts and other businesses, there is a significant demand for daily transportation.

Almost all of this travel occurs along a single main roadway, the Honoapi'ilani Highway (Hawaii State Route 30), which runs from Wailuku, through Lahaina, and all the way around the northernmost tip of West Maui. It is possible to travel to Central Maui via Kahekili Highway (consisting of Maui County Route 340 and Hawai'i State Route 340), but that roadway is substandard, dangerous, and has a very low traffic capacity (see Figure 6.2).[1]

Kahekili Highway (see Figure 6.3) was one of the last roads to be built on Maui. Kahakuloa, the only real village in this vicinity, is one of the last remaining places on Maui where a Hawaiian subsistence lifestyle is practiced. There are many cultural sites in the area, and there is a good likelihood that additional cultural features would be disturbed during any roadway expansion. Given the known opposition by local residents to improvement of the roadway, impact to cultural features would surely be an issue during environmental review. Many residents value the fact that the roadway is difficult to traverse because it reduces the amount of traffic and makes it less likely that outsiders will be willing to try to buy land or build houses in the area.

Most traffic between Central and West Maui currently passes through "The Pali," which is what local residents call the portion of Honoapi'ilani

Figure 6.1. Aerial view of Kahakuloa

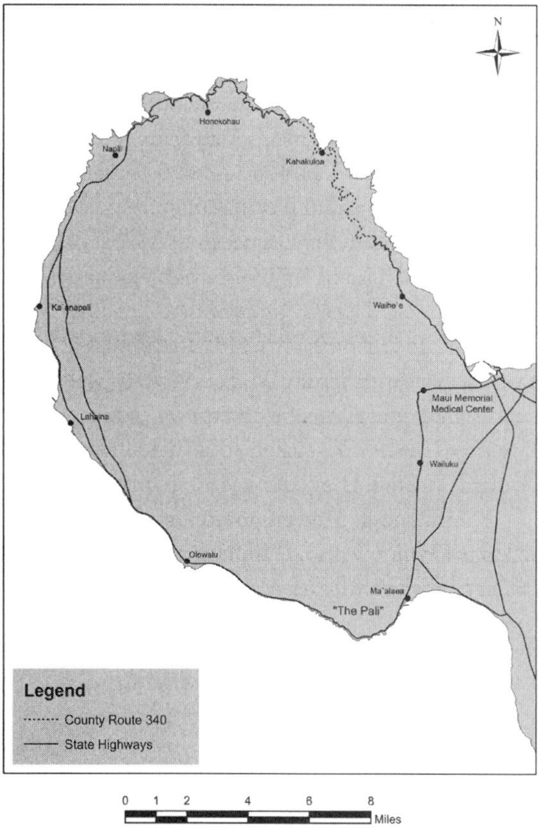

Figure 6.2. West Maui Highways

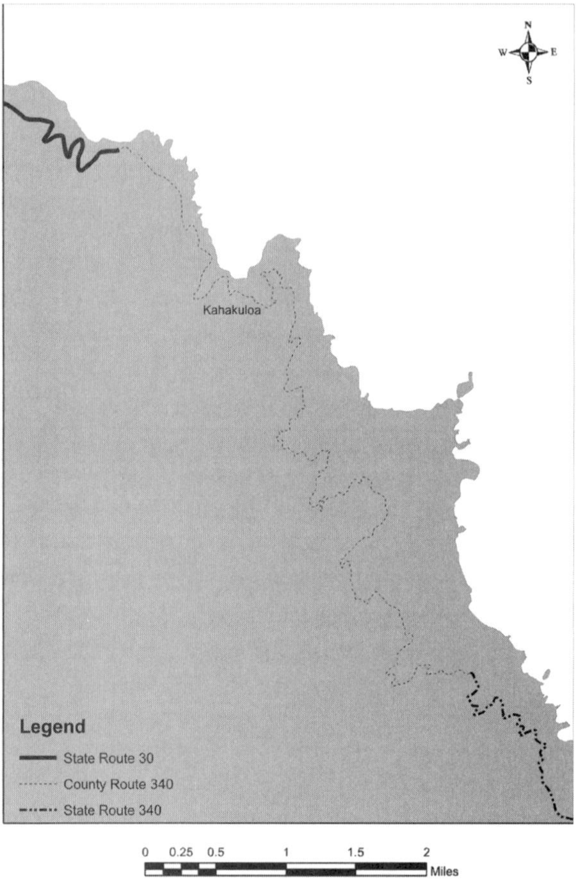

Figure 6.3. Kahekili Highway

Table 6.1. Functional Classification of Roads in Hawaiʻi

PRINCIPAL ARTERIALS	OTHER ROADWAYS
Urban Interstate	Urban Minor Arterial
Rural Interstate	Rural Minor Arterial
Urban Other Freeway/Expressway	Rural Major Collector
Urban Other Principal Arterial	Rural Minor Collector
Rural Other Principal Arterial	Urban Collector
	Local Urban
	Local Rural

Source: Federal Aid Functional Classification Update: Policy and Procedures, December 2012, Page 3. Prepared for State of Hawaiʻi Department of Transportation, Highways Division, Planning Branch, by CH2MHill.

Highway between Pāpalaua Beach Park and Mā'alaea. Annual average daily traffic (AADT) through The Pali is currently 27,900 vehicles per day. According to the Hawai'i State Department of Transportation, this section of Honoapi'ilani Highway is classified as an "Urban Other Principal Arterial" (see Table 6.1), which means that it comprises a significant portion of statewide highway mileage and carries a significant portion of statewide traffic.

Honoapi'ilani Highway is subject to occasional closure due to wildfire, flooding, or traffic accidents. The resulting backups can be massive, with closures sometimes lasting for days. During these incidents, residents and visitors can become stranded on both sides of a road closure. Since lodging is often expensive and unavailable on short notice, those who cannot stay with relatives or friends may end up sleeping in their vehicles.

Whenever Honoapi'ilani Highway is closed for any length of time, some in the community begin to suggest alternative routes, including the possibility of improving "the back way," or Kahekili Highway, which runs around the far north side of West Maui from Honokōhau to Waihe'e. Due to its substandard, narrow, and dangerous condition, the county portion of Kahekili Highway is not nearly as well traveled as "The Pali" section of Honoapi'ilani Highway. Although it is known that many residents of the Kahakuloa area are opposed to improvement of Kahekili Highway, the topic of providing alternate access to Central Maui via Kahekili Highway keeps coming up. This chapter is intended to discuss the considerations that would be involved in improving Kahekili Highway, including planning, environmental and cultural impacts, cost estimates, prioritization, and funding. It is hoped that the information provided here will facilitate a productive discussion of options based on factual information.

Honoapi'ilani Highway: A Baseline for Comparison

The first task in evaluating options for improvement of Kahekili Highway as a transportation alternative is to characterize the route to which those options will be compared. Honoapi'ilani Highway (State Highway 30) is a modern roadway that starts at Main Street in Wailuku and continues for about 42 miles around the north tip of West Maui (see Figure 6.2). It runs through Waikapū, Mā'alaea, Olowalu, Lahaina, Kā'anapali, Kapalua, Honolua, and Honokōhau, with speed limits ranging from 20 to 55 miles per hour. This highway is for the most part a two-lane roadway, with the exception of stretches through Lahaina and Kā'anapali that consist of four lanes, and three separate one-lane bridges between Honolua and the end of the state highway. Honoapi'ilani Highway has guardrails and good signage, adequate shoulders in most places, acceleration and deceleration lanes, left-turn storage lanes, center striping and edge striping, and rumble strips in many places to get the attention of distracted or sleepy drivers. Shortly after Mile Marker 39, a cattle guard structure built into the pavement across the road signals the potential for livestock to be in the driving lanes, which can be hazardous, especially at night. There are occasional stretches of road that are marked by "Falling Rock" signs. Honoapi'ilani Highway ends about 0.7 miles past Mile Marker 41, where the road jurisdiction changes to the County of Maui.

Maui County Route 340

Continuing in the Wailuku direction, the road becomes County Route 340, the county portion of Kahekili Highway. In contrast to State Route 30, this road is classified as a "Rural Minor Collector," meaning that it is not designed to connect major population centers or handle significant amounts of traffic. County Route 340 continues around the north end of West Maui, through the village of Kahakuloa, and onward toward Waihe'e, where Route 340 continues as the state portion of Kahekili Highway.

About 0.6 miles from the northern terminus of Honoapi'ilani Highway, the first visible mile marker on the county portion of Kahekili Highway is numbered 16, and the mile marker numbers decrease thereafter as one proceeds toward Waihe'e. This roadway continues until just after Mile Marker 7, near Mendes Ranch and the turnoff to the Waihe'e Ridge Trail. Here, the roadway widens back to two lanes, and the designation changes to State Route 340, which then runs through Waihe'e and Waiehu on its way to Wailuku. To be clear, State Route 340 is also referred to as Kahekili Highway; where specificity is needed in referring to the (mostly) one-lane county road, this chapter will refer to "the county portion of Route 340" or "the county portion of Kahekili Highway."

Speed limits on the county portion of Route 340 vary between five and 20 miles per hour, but because it is a one-lane roadway for most of its length, progress along this road can be even slower, especially for those who are unfamiliar with its challenges. Drivers must often stop at informal pullouts to wait for oncoming vehicles to pass before they can proceed.

Although this roadway does not meet current highway standards, it is sometimes used by the Maui Police Department (when The Pali section of Honoapi'ilani Highway is closed) to direct traffic out of West Maui. This is accomplished by restricting the highway to traffic going in one direction at a time. Recent practice has been to allow Waiheʻe-bound traffic to proceed during the day, and the direction of flow has been reversed at night.

In order for Kahekili Highway to serve as a realistic alternative to Honoapiʻilani Highway, significant capacity and safety improvements would need to be made to the one-lane county portion. Between Mile Markers 4.29 and 13.819, the AADT on the county portion of Route 340 is currently 1,300 vehicles per day, which is only 4.7 percent of the AADT on the Pali section of Honoapiʻilani Highway.[2] In other words, the capacity of the county portion of Route 340 would need to be increased by more than a factor of 21 in order for it to handle as much traffic as The Pali. Such a project would be challenging and expensive enough on level ground with no obstacles, but Kahekili Highway is among the most dangerous and challenging roads on Maui, with steep cliffs above and below the one-lane road, and many blind curves. Falling rocks, which are not unusual, add to the danger of traversing this roadway.

Following is a list of some of the serious incidents that have occurred along Kahekili Highway:[3]

- In 1929, one person was killed and two others injured when their vehicle plunged to the bottom of a 150-foot gulch.
- In 1971, two people died in an accident on the highway.
- In 2001, two people were killed when their vehicle went off the road at Makamakaʻole Gulch and plunged to the rocks below.
- In 2006, a driver apparently missed a curve and dropped 300 feet onto the rocks below.
- In 2007, one person died when their vehicle plunged into the ocean after dropping 140 feet.
- In 2012, a vehicle carrying two people went over a 100-foot cliff; fortunately, they suffered only minor injuries.
- In 2014, one person suffered fatal injuries when their vehicle dropped 100 feet off a cliff.
- In 2016, one person died when their vehicle went over an embankment and down a 200-foot cliff.
- In 2017, a Seattle couple stopped on a narrow portion of the road and were backing up to make room for a school bus when their vehicle went over the edge, falling about 40 feet. Fortunately, they were uninjured.
- In 2018, an elderly couple pulled over to the side of the road to make way for a passing car and got stuck on the edge of the cliff. Fortunately, there were no injuries, but this was a very close call.

The known history of terrifying plunges and resulting fatalities, the lack of traffic capacity, substandard roadway construction, and the fact that much of Kahekili Highway is a one-lane road on which drivers may have to back up along a cliff, have all helped to give this roadway a reputation as being one of the most dangerous roads in the world.[4] In 2009, the West Maui Transportation Access Plan Working Group recommended that visitors be restricted from driving this route.[5]

In order for Kahekili Highway to be made suitable for an alternate northern route to Central Maui by way of Kahakuloa—with similar capacity to Honoapiʻilani—the current roadway would need to be largely abandoned, major bridges built, and additional right-of-way acquired. When the possibility of such a project was raised with state and county transportation professionals, the unanimous reaction was that the idea was extremely unrealistic, would be prohibitively expensive, and would fall much lower on the priority list than other projects.

Existing County Roadway

The county portion of Kahekili Highway between Mile Marker 15.5 and Mile Marker 6.9 is particularly challenging and dangerous, and would need to be significantly improved to make it a safe route for either regular driving or emergency access. There are also bridges with weight limits as low as three tons[6] (one of which is signed "No Truck") that would need to be improved or replaced to enable use of this roadway for transportation of truck freight. Steep cliffs mauka of the roadway have loose rock and dirt, but the roadway below is only sometimes posted with "Falling Rock" signs. There are periodic rockslides during and after heavy rains. This a serious concern that will continue unless some type of rockfall protection, such as netting or terracing, is installed.

There are also quite a few very sharp turns on this roadway (see Figure 6.4) that obscure any view of oncoming vehicles; some of these have "Sound Horn" signs posted. Many turns lack guardrails or adequate reflectors, which makes them especially dangerous at night. Fatalities have occurred when drivers have run off the road, plunging over steep cliffs with nothing to stop them. There are occasional yellow turn-warning signs with cautionary speed limits from five to 20 miles per hour, some yellow caution signs that say "No Shoulder" or "One Lane Road, 5 MPH," and a few other yellow signs that say "Narrow Winding Road, 15 MPH." There are also a number of red and white "Yield" signs posted

Figure 6.4. Aerial view of narrow, winding Kahekili Highway

before one-lane roadway sections or one-lane bridges, but there is sometimes no way to see to the end of the one-lane section to determine whether there is another vehicle there to yield to.

Proceeding in the Wailuku direction, about a mile after the county highway begins and just before Kahakuloa Bay comes into view, the roadway narrows down to one lane and stays that way for the next 8.5 miles. Shortly before entering Kahakuloa Village, a "Narrow Roadway" sign lets drivers know that the one-lane road is about to get even narrower. Within the village, the road becomes so narrow that it resembles a driveway more than a highway (see Figure 6.5). Here, another sign asks people to "Please Drive Slow." Since the land parcel boundaries in this vicinity do not appear to coincide with the roadway, some right-of-way acquisition might be required in order for any widening to be done (see Figure 6.6).

After Kahakuloa Village the roadway widens somewhat, but still consists of one lane with only occasional pullouts. After about another mile, very narrow one-lane sections begin to appear. Some of these segments have steep cliffs below the roadway. A few have wide enough shoulders, or pullouts, to allow two vehicles to squeeze by each other, but others are too narrow. These are the sections on which one or more of the cars traveling in opposite directions will have to back up—a maneuver requiring skill that not all drivers possess. The ease of backing up is dependent on the size of the vehicle. It is also influenced by rear visibility factors such as window configuration, blind spots, the adequacy of

Figure 6.5. Kahekili Highway through Kahakuloa Village

Figure 6.6. Parcel boundaries in Kahakuloa Village

vehicle mirrors, the presence of backup cameras, or the lack of any of these. A mistake in backing up in the vicinity of a cliff can be fatal.

Rules of the Road

When two vehicles meet on this winding, one-lane roadway, and there are no pullouts available, one of them needs to back up in order to allow the other to pass. Drivers who are experienced with this road are constantly vigilant, stealing quick glimpses of the roadway ahead to see if another vehicle is approaching, while being careful not to drive off a cliff. If another vehicle is seen, the courteous driver can look for the nearest pullout, and wait for the other driver to pass. Visitors and others who are unfamiliar with the county portion of Route 340 often fail to take these precautions, with the result being frustration for regular drivers due to consequent single-lane faceoffs.

The informal rules for "who backs up" seem to vary, depending upon the situation, and depending on whom one asks. Some say that in the event two vehicles meet along a one-lane section, if there are no pullouts nearby, the driver in the Wailuku-bound lane is supposed to back up because the cliff edge is on the driver's side, and the driver can see it better. Others who drive the road say that the real rule is that the person who has lived the longest out Kahakuloa way has priority. The reality is that what happens on the road depends on the situation and the people involved.

These types of conflicts were not that common when traffic counts were lower, but with the massive increase in tourism over the years, and with overall increases in the West Maui population, these encounters have become more frequent. Tourists who drive slowly and cause other vehicles to queue up behind them make the single-lane backup procedure much more difficult and dangerous to execute; five cars backing up together makes for a much more complicated and precarious situation than one car backing up alone. A driver who lacks experience on rural roadways may panic in the presence of cliffs that present the very real possibility of going over the edge and plummeting to one's death. Aside from giving hand signals, honking their horns, or getting out of their cars and talking, drivers have no way to communicate with each other, and disagreements regarding who will back up are not uncommon. Language barriers between people from different countries can add to the confusion. Clearly, this roadway that has served the rural Kahakuloa area for decades has been overwhelmed in recent years by the number of tourists who now attempt to use it along with the area residents for whom it is a lifeline.

Emergency Operations

As described previously, the county portion of Route 340 is treacherous and has very limited capacity compared to Honoapiʻilani Highway; it is not currently an adequate alternative route. However, when The Pali is closed due to fire, flood, or accident, Kahekili Highway is sometimes used as an emergency route under the supervision of the Maui Police Department (MPD). Depending on the circumstances, MPD may close the road between Kapalua and Waiheʻe (although residents who live between these points are allowed to proceed). Alternatively, police units may be posted near Mile Marker 7 at the end of State Route 340 in Waiheʻe, and near Mile Marker 38 on State Route 30. One-way traffic is then allowed to proceed at intervals in opposite directions on the one-lane roadway until Honoapiʻilani Highway is reopened.

Objectives

The main goal of this chapter is to examine the feasibility of providing an alternative transportation route around the north end of West Maui. Three possible objectives will be considered:

1. Increased Traffic Capacity. This would take some of the daily load off of Honoapiʻilani Highway and would provide an alternate route in case of closure of The Pali.
2. Reduced Travel Time. This would make this northern route more acceptable for emergency transport and more attractive as an alternate route.
3. Increased Safety. This would reduce injuries and fatalities on what is now a dangerous roadway.

Increased Daily Traffic Capacity

The current average annual daily traffic for the county portion of Highway 340 is 1,300 vehicles per day. The Pali portion of Honoapiʻilani Highway currently has an AADT of 27,900 vehicles per day. The type of improvements to the county and/or state roadways, and the degree to which such improvements induce additional growth, will determine the degree to which traffic on Honoapʻilani Highway is alleviated.

Improved Emergency Transport Time to Central Maui via Kahekili Highway

Fires, floods, motor vehicle accidents, and other incidents that pose a threat to life, health, property or the environment occur on West Maui with regularity. Whenever these occurrences cause Honoapiʻilani Highway to be closed, the lack of an alternative transportation route is itself life-threatening to anyone who cannot access emergency medical care at Maui Memorial Medical Center (MMMC) in Kahului—the only acute-care hospital on the Valley Isle.[7] On a typical day, there are about 10,000 residents, 20,000 workers, and 34,000 visitors in West Maui, for a total daytime population of 64,000 people; this makes for a large potential patient population.[8]

Although there are several urgent care clinics in Lahaina and Kāʻanapali, the only emergency medical or trauma care available on the west side of Maui is from Emergency Medical Services (EMS) providers or the Maui County Department of Fire and Public Safety. EMS and fire department personnel can perform some emergency services in the field, but in order to receive acute care, patients must be transferred to MMMC in Kahului. Since timely access to emergency care after a traumatic injury can increase the odds of successful treatment, closure of Honoapiʻilani can mean the difference between life and death. Although an EMS helicopter is now providing enhanced 911 service for all of Maui, it is subject to availability and has a limited capacity.

If Honoapiʻilani Highway is open, a patient in Kāʻanapali can be driven to MMMC in about 40 minutes, depending on traffic. If Honoapiʻilani Highway is closed, a comparable trip via Kahekili Highway takes about 90 minutes, depending on traffic (more than twice as long). Not only are the speed limits much lower on Kahekili Highway, but the current distance is 37 miles, compared to 23 miles on Honoapiʻilani. If any oncoming vehicles are encountered on the one-lane sections along the way, this travel time can be even greater.

Increased Safety

Highway systems exact high prices in terms of human injury and death. Road traffic injuries are the leading cause of unintentional deaths, and Kahekili Highway is not exempt from this. Any improvements to this roadway will need to comply with modern highway standards, which will very likely reduce associated injuries and deaths.

Cost Estimation

Usually, when the topic of improving the road around Kahakuloa is brought up, the reaction is amusement that someone could actually be asking such a question. None of the transportation professionals who were consulted for this chapter considered this to be a serious option, especially in consideration of other needs. As an example of another, much higher priority that continues to be deferred, the addition of two lanes to the Pali section of Honoapiʻilani Highway between Māʻalaea and Pāpalaua Park has widespread community support, and would likely have access to federal highway funds, but is so expensive that it has not been completed for decades.

The idea of constructing a modern roadway around Kahakuloa, although suggested by a few people, is staunchly opposed by residents of the area. In addition, as a Rural Minor Collector, such a project would be very unlikely to be able to access federal transportation funds.

Estimating the cost of a highway project is a complex undertaking that involves much uncertainty. For purposes of this chapter, we are not so much concerned with accuracy as we are with obtaining some idea of the financial magnitude of such a project. If the cost of an alternative route is comparable to that of other options, then future efforts at refining those cost estimates may be worthwhile. On the other hand, if the estimated cost is clearly beyond the financial capacity of the county government, even with possible state or federal assistance, then refinement of those estimates will be unnecessary.

Highway cost estimation involves a combination of experience and art. Not all inputs to the estimate may be known, especially in the early stages, and circumstances may change before a decision is made to fund a project. If all goes as planned, then a cost estimate may be accurate, but if new or unexpected factors arise, the cost is likely to be much higher. What we should expect from an estimate, then, is a range of costs; we should also expect that this range will change as time goes on. Formal cost estimate reviews for highway projects are generally done at the end of the environmental review process, and then again before the start of construction.

Unfortunately, the Maui County Department of Public Works, which is responsible for county roadways, is currently understaffed, and was not able to provide answers to questions about the county portion of Kahekili Highway. Accordingly, cost and other information for this chapter had to be gathered from other sources. Since one of the purposes of this chapter is to compare the relative costs of several alternatives, accurate cost calculation methodology is not necessary.

The addition of a second lane to the existing county highway to increase capacity would be considered a modernization project; this category of project receives a lower priority than preservation and maintenance of existing roads. Due to the current scarcity of funds for transportation improvement, few modernization projects are being undertaken. Therefore, comparable cost estimates are difficult to find.

The Maui Metropolitan Planning Organization (Maui MPO) is a government agency that was formed in 2016 by the State of Hawaii and County of Maui to facilitate comprehensive planning for federally funded or regionally significant transportation systems on the Island of Maui.[9] When selecting and prioritizing projects for the Maui Island portion of the State Transportation Improvement Program, the Maui MPO must consider agency policies for asset management, construction readiness, public input, and availability of local matching funds.[10] Neither an alternative capacity route nor an improved emergency route around Kahakuloa are included in the State Transportation Improvement Program at this time, nor does such a project appear to be on the Maui MPO's radar in the short or long term. If it were to be considered, a county Kahekili Highway project would first need to be well defined, and a full cost estimation process would need to be completed. Only then could such a project be compared with all of the other projects being seriously considered for funds.

Since there are no similar projects currently under consideration that would help with the goal of providing an estimated range of cost, it is necessary to look for projects that share some aspects of the alternatives to be examined in this chapter.

Maui County has recently estimated costs for two projects that involve roadway reconstruction along the two-lane Kaupakalua Road.[11] Due to the terrain, these projects do not involve significant rockfall mitigation. The cost varies, but it can be averaged to $1.6 million per mile for purposes of a ballpark estimate. Due to the fact that the existing roadbed is reused for these undertakings, the cost is less than what would be required for the creation of an additional lane. On the county portion of Kahekili Highway, the addition of another lane also would involve blasting out the cliff on the mauka side, building out over the steep cliffs, or both.

An undertaking that bears similarities to the Kahekili Highway situation is the Keʻanae Road Safety Improvements project. Although it does not involve the construction of an additional lane, it does involve rockfall mitigation and roadway improvements. The scope of work includes rock slope scaling, rock bolts, concrete barrier construction, rockfall fencing, rockfall netting, and other associated work. The roadway improvements include pavement reconstruction, pavement resurfacing, metal guardrail installation, pavement striping and markers, roadside signs, and other associated work. The inflation-adjusted cost for just 0.3 miles of this type of work, on terrain that is somewhat similar to that on the county portion of Kahekili Highway, would be $13.3 million per mile (not including the cost of building a roadway out over steep cliffs).

Adding together the Kaupakalua Road costs of $1.6 million per mile for lane creation and $13.3 million per mile for rockfall mitigation, we get a cost of $14.9 million per mile (not including the cost of blasting another lane out of the hillside, building out over the existing cliff, or both). For 8.5 miles, this would come to $126.7 million.

On the south side of Maui, emergency projects were performed for rockfall mitigation and to provide support for undermined cliff faces at three locations along the one-lane portion of Piʻilani Highway near Kaupō. The cost for this work was $10.8 million in 2008. Adjusting for inflation, the cost today would be about $13.2 million for about 0.3 miles of work, which works out to about $44 million per mile.

The topography along Kahekili Highway is not exactly the same as that along Kaupakalua Road, Piʻilani Highway in Kaupō, or across The Pali, but in view of the above state and county projects, the cost to add an additional lane and providing rockfall protection along the county section of Kahekili Highway could range widely—from $4.8 million to $111 million per mile. Taking the midpoint of this number, $57.9 million per mile, and multiplying by 8.5 miles gives us a total ballpark project cost of $492 million to attain a two-lane roadway around the north side of Maui. This roadway would be safer, but would still be very curvy, and would not even begin to approach the traffic capacity of Honoapiʻilani Highway across The Pali.

Other Considerations

- Existing traffic levels already bother residents along this highway; many do not want any more traffic, and want to leave the road "as is."
- The existing "highway" through Kahakuloa village is more like a narrow, local street, with widths as small as ten feet. The location of the right-of-way may not be consistent with the actual location of the road.[12] Widening through this area could require acquisition of prop-

erty and/or removal of existing structures, both of which would be disruptive to this small community (see Figure 6.6).

- Increased road capacity and safety improvements on Kahekili Highway could lead to more development along this currently rural road, along with population increases and increased demand for public infrastructure, including schools, parks, solid waste disposal, police and fire services, and medical facilities. Associated increases in demand for water and wastewater facilities could also be expected.
- Additional capacity on this highway could result in increased impact on the environment, including noise impacts, air quality impacts, water quality impacts, impacts to sensitive habitats, impacts to scenic views, and increased strain on fisheries and other natural resources.
- Safety improvements and/or a two-lane roadway could cause tourists to feel more comfortable driving on this scenic roadway. This would lead to an increase in tourist traffic, possibly offsetting the anticipated capacity benefits of increasing the roadway to two lanes.

Design Options

The location and shape of a roadway are typically selected during the design phase while considering the characteristics of vehicles likely to use it, and how these factors interact to meet modern safety and performance standards. Roadway design is a field in itself, and is beyond the scope of this chapter. Nevertheless, there are some considerations worth discussing that would clearly affect the cost and practicality of improving the road around the north side of West Maui.

Topography must be taken into account and would be a critical concern for any capacity upgrade on the county portion of Route 340. Steep cliffs along much of this part of Kahekili Highway would need to be cut into, or the roadway would need to be built out over the cliffs on some type of support system.

Other factors, such as estimated traffic volume, desired speed limit, the number of lanes, lane width, shoulder width, roadbed depth, required sight distances, and drainage all interact with each other and determine the responses and reactions of drivers to the roadway. These factors also determine the durability of the roadway and its maintenance costs. With so many variables, a preliminary examination such as this one needs to make some assumptions. Since we are mainly seeking to examine whether any of the options are feasible, we will consider three alternatives.

Project Categorization and Priority

One of the main challenges with improving the road around Kahakuloa is that there is so little funding for new roadways or additional lanes. Roadway system preservation takes priority and exhausts most of the available funds. Every additional lane-mile that is constructed is another lane-mile that will then require preservation, so transportation agencies are very careful about where new or expanded roads are put in. In the past, the federal government provided much more of the funding than it does presently, so funds are even harder to come by.

Projects that increase capacity are categorized as "Modernization." The addition of a lane to the county portion of Route 340 would likely receive a lower priority than projects that would preserve or maintain existing roadways unless a new funding source can be found. In fact, new funding has recently been allocated through the Rental Car Surcharge, but there are many projects, such as the Pāʻia Bypass and the Lāhaina Bypass Extension to Kāʻanapali, that are already identified for funding in the Maui County Metropolitan Planning Organization's Transportation Improvement Program.

Due to the extremely dangerous nature of the existing one-lane roadway, it is possible that a Kahakuloa project could be considered under the category of "Safety Improvements." This is what was done in the case of the Honoapiʻilani Highway Realignment from Olowalu to Pāpalaua Park. However, even if a Kahekili Highway project were to be reclassified accordingly, it would still need to go through the prioritization process.

In addition, federal policy directs states to establish a classification of roads based on function so that roadways can be improved appropriately as funding opportunities arise. Functional classification is used in determining federal, state, regional and local priorities for roadway resurfacing or reconstruction (see Figure 6.2).[13] While the Pali section of Honoapiʻilani Highway is classified as an "Urban Other Principal Arterial," the county portion of Kahekili Highway is currently classified as a "Rural Minor Collector Roadway," which is not considered a Federal Aid Highway; therefore, Kahekili Highway would not normally be eligible for State Transportation Plan funds. Unless a major transportation modernization or safety project were somehow to be funded by the state, the cost of any improvements to the county portion of Route 340 would very likely fall on the County of Maui.

Alternatives Considered

In order to give broad consideration to the issues involved in coming up with an alternative route between West Maui and Central Maui it is helpful to consider a range of options, some of which are "out of the box." It would not be helpful to simply avoid considering options just because the prevailing wisdom says that they are unrealistic. Accordingly, this chapter will consider the following three options:

Option 1: Duplicate the Capacity of Honoapi'ilani Highway

This option would involve the creation of a highway similar to the Pali portion of Honoapi'ilani Highway. The winding one-lane county portion of Kahekili Highway would be replaced with a modern two-lane highway. Curves would be straightened, and major bridges built. Many portions of the roadway would need an additional lane cut into the hillside, or an additional lane would need to be built out over the cliffs. In addition to widening the 8.5-mile one-lane county roadway around Kahakuloa, improvements would need to be made to other portions of Honoapi'ilani and Kahekili Highways to enable speed limits to be increased to 40 mph from Kapalua all the way to Waihe'e.

Option 2: Widen the One-lane Section of Kahekili Highway to Two Lanes

This option would widen only the 8.5-mile county portion of Kahekili Highway to two lanes. It would address the current problem of vehicles coming from opposite directions on a one-lane roadway, with one of them having to back up. Widening of the roadway to two lanes would need to comply with modern standards, so safety would also be improved. Although this option would result in some improved capacity, it would not be comparable to that of the Pali section of Honoapi'ilani Highway.

Option 3: Signalize One-Lane Road Sections

The purpose of a traffic signal is to allocate shared right-of-way. The addition of traffic signals to the one-lane county portion of Kahekili Highway would in itself be a significant change. These signals would supplant the existing informal methods of determining who can proceed and who needs to wait when there are two or more vehicles needing to use a single lane. The effectiveness of this solution would depend on community acceptance. Drivers would need to accept the necessity of this change, and would need to trust the fairness of a signal's allocation decisions.

Alternatives Analysis

Option 1: Two-lane, 40 mph Roadway

TRAFFIC CAPACITY

Traffic to and from West Maui is limited by the capacity of Honoapi'ilani Highway, which consists of two lanes on the Pali segment between Olowalu and Mā'alaea. The current AADT along that stretch is 27,900 vehicles per day. Portions of this roadway were already over capacity and operating at Level of Service F in 2007,[14] and travel demand was predicted to increase 30 percent by 2035.

A modern two-lane roadway around the north side of West Maui that could handle the same number of vehicles per day as Honoapi'ilani Highway from Pāpalaua Park to Mā'alaea would likely reduce some of the traffic on The Pali, especially during peak traffic hours. However, there are significant financial, environmental and cultural hurdles that would have to be cleared in order for this to occur.

EMERGENCY OPERATIONS

Even if improvements could be made to portions of State Highway 30, County Route 340, and State Highway 340 that would allow speeds similar to those along Honoapi'ilani, the trip time would only be reduced to about 64 minutes as compared to the 40 minutes that a similar trip currently takes via The Pali. However, in the event of closure of The Pali, a modern two-lane roadway around the north side of West Maui would allow faster patient transport to Maui Memorial Medical Center than can be achieved on the existing roadway.

Construction of an emergency facility located somewhere between Lahaina and Kā'anapali would reduce patient transport time to 20 minutes or less from most parts of West Maui. Recently, Maui Health System announced its intent to establish a 24-hour urgent care center in West Maui in the near future, and a 24-hour emergency department several years after that.[15] The estimated cost is $5 to $7 million, which would be vastly less expensive (and could be accomplished much more quickly) than building new roadways.

SAFETY

Construction of a modern two-lane roadway would need to comply with current highway standards. This would include installation of guardrails, good signage, adequate road shoulders, center striping and edge striping. These improvements would increase safety along the route.

CONSTRUCTION COST

In 2017, the estimated cost for adding two lanes on the Pali portion of Honoapiʻilani Highway between Māʻalaea and Pāpalaua Park ranged from $500 million to $1 billion, not including possible additional costs associated with environmental, cultural and historic impacts.[16] This would be a distance of about 4.5 miles, depending on the exact project extent, which means that the project would cost between $55.5 million and $111 million per lane mile. The challenging terrain on The Pali is similar to that on the north side of Maui in that it has many valleys and steep cliffs. The cost of this project may be representative of what would be required for a two-lane highway around Kahakuloa, if the current roadway were to be largely abandoned and the road were to be designed for speeds of 40 miles per hour—similar to the existing Honoapiʻilani Highway around The Pali. The two-lane portions of State Routes 30 and 340, which are currently posted at 25 to 35 miles per hour, would still need to be upgraded in order to improve travel time between Kāʻanapali and MMMC.

If the cost of a project around The Pali were indeed representative of the cost of going around the north side of West Maui, a 26-mile project from Kapalua to Waiheʻe would be between $1.4 and $2.9 billion. As with the cost of adding two lanes to The Pali, this would not include possible additional costs associated with environmental, cultural and historic impacts.

PRIORITIZATION AND FINANCING

Construction of Option 1 is not being considered at this time. Even though the addition of two lanes on the Pali portion of Honoapiʻilani Highway between Māʻalaea and Pāpalaua Park has been discussed for decades, that project has taken a back seat to other more pressing needs. For example, realignment of Honoapiʻilani Highway from Olowalu to Pāpalaua Park at a cost of $150 million is urgently needed to prevent the highway that provides access to all of West Maui from being undermined and cut off by coastal erosion and sea level rise. Another example of a higher priority is the building of the next segment of the Lāhaina Bypass from Keawe Street to Kāʻanapali at a cost of $49 million. Note that each of these projects required special funding from the Rental Car Surcharge that was passed by the Hawaiʻi State Legislature. The high price tag for a modern two-lane highway around Kahakuloa would mean that the combined cost of these other two projects would have to be accumulated for over 25 years. Given the many other transportation priorities on Maui, it is extremely unlikely that public support for such a project could be maintained over that long a period of time.

ENVIRONMENTAL IMPACT

Option 1 would involve massive changes to the relatively isolated northern part of West Maui. Large amounts of earth-moving and rock-blasting would create noise impacts for years. The logistics of moving construction materials in and out of the area on a one-lane rural roadway would be extremely disruptive to local residents. Social and cultural impacts would be extreme, and the historic and cultural context of the village of Kahakuloa would be irretrievably damaged.

Due to the number and type of potentially significant environmental impacts, it is quite certain that a full Environmental Impact Statement (EIS) would need to be prepared. The EIS would need to fully discuss significant impacts of the proposed project, including impacts on flora and fauna, air quality, noise, archaeological resources, cultural resources, scenic resources, population, housing, economic impacts, fiscal impacts, public facilities, traffic, utilities, energy, climate change, drainage, water resources, and wastewater. It would also need to discuss cumulative and secondary impacts, and would need to examine consistency with state and county plans and policies. An EIS would also need to consider reasonable alternatives to the project, including the No Action alternative, and alternatives that might enhance the quality of the environment in the project area. It would further need to discuss any secondary population and growth impacts resulting from the proposed action and its alternatives, would need to discuss possible mitigation strategies for identified impacts, and finally, would need to discuss any unresolved issues. At a minimum, this process would take several years.

Due to the complexity of evaluating a project of this magnitude, and due to the fact that there are people on Maui who would adamantly oppose any such action, it is likely that one or more legal challenges would be filed should such an EIS ever be accepted. If this type of legal challenge were to occur, Option 1 could be delayed for many years.

Option 2: Widen the One-Lane Section of Kahekili Highway to Two Lanes

TRAFFIC CAPACITY

Addition of another lane to the one-lane section of the county portion of Kahekili Highway would eliminate the problem of one-lane faceoffs. This would remove one of the most dangerous aspects of this road, and would make many more people feel comfortable with driving this way.

However, this northern route would still be slower than via The Pali. Due to the winding nature of the road between Kapalua and Waiheʻe, a trip via

Kahekili Highway to Central Maui would take about 90 minutes instead of the current 40 minutes via Honoapi'ilani Highway.

Existing AADT at the northern terminus of Honoapi'ilani Highway (just before the county portion of Kahekili highway begins) is 4,000 vehicles per day. AADT on the county portion of Kahekili Highway is 1,300 vehicles per day, while AADT on the state highway on the Waihe'e side of the County highway is 6,800 vehicles per day. For purposes of this analysis, we will make a conservative assumption that the elimination of the one-lane bottleneck on the County highway will result in an increase of AADT to 6,800 vehicles per day on all sections of the northern route from West Maui to Central Maui. This would only amount to about 36 percent of the AADT currently handled by The Pali section of Honoapi'ilani Highway, but it would be a 523 percent increase over existing AADT through Kahakuloa.

EMERGENCY OPERATIONS

Addition of a lane to the one-lane section of the county portion of Kahekili Highway would eliminate the delay associated with single-lane conflicts. Travel time from Kā'anapali to Maui Memorial Medical Center would be about 90 minutes, as compared to the 40 minutes that a similar trip currently takes via The Pali. However, in the event of closure of Honoapi'ilani Highway, having two lanes all the way around the north side of West Maui as an alternative would at least allow for (slower) patient transport to that emergency facility.

SAFETY

Addition of a lane to the winding, 8.5-mile low-speed county portion of Kahekili Highway would need to comply with modern highway standards. This would include installation of guardrails, good signage, adequate shoulders, center striping and edge striping. These improvements would likely increase safety along the currently dangerous one-lane roadway.

CONSTRUCTION COST

In the foregoing Cost Estimation section of this chapter, a review of state and county projects similar to this one estimated that the cost of adding an additional lane and providing rockfall protection along the county section of Kahekili Highway could range from $4.8 million to $111 million per mile. Taking the midpoint of this number, $57.9 million per mile, and multiplying that by 8.5 miles gives us a total ballpark project cost of $492.1 million to achieve a two-lane roadway around the north side of Maui.

PRIORITIZATION AND FINANCING

Construction of Option 2 is not being considered at this time; there is already a backlog of other, more urgent projects, such as the realignment of Honoapiʻilani Highway from Olowalu to Pāpalaua Park at a cost of $150 million, and the building of the next segment of the Lāhaina Bypass from Keawe Street north to Kāʻanapali at a cost of $49 million. Each of these projects required special funding from the Rental Car Surcharge that was passed by the Hawaiʻi State Legislature. The $492 million cost for adding another lane to the 8.5-mile county portion of Kahekili Highway would be more than twice the combined cost of these two higher-priority projects. Given the many other transportation priorities on Maui, community opposition to road improvement around Kahakuloa, and limited benefits, it is unlikely that there would be much public support for Option 2.

Since Federal Highways Adminstration funding categories for Federal-Aid Highways do not include Rural Minor Collectors, roads such as Kahekili Highway are not normally eligible for State Transportation Planning funds. This means that the state and/or county would most likely need to come up with the money for any improvements.

ENVIRONMENTAL IMPACT

Although less impactful than Option 1, Option 2 would still impose massive changes on the isolated northern coast of West Maui. Large amounts of earth-moving and rock-blasting associated with the creation of an additional lane would create noise impacts for years. As with Option 1, the logistics of moving construction materials in and out of the area on a one-lane rural roadway would be extremely disruptive. Social and cultural impacts would be considerable, and the historic and cultural context of the village of Kahakuloa would be significantly altered.

As with Option 1, it is certain that an EIS would need to be prepared, entailing all of the same impacts and issues, and would take several years to complete.

The complexity of evaluating a project of this scale and local opposition would make it likely that one or more legal challenges would be filed if such an EIS were to be accepted. As with Option 1, if this type of legal challenge were to occur, Option 2 could be delayed for many years.

Option 3: Install Traffic Signals on One-Lane Road Sections

If stop/go signals were to be installed at each end of the 8.5-mile one-lane county portion of Kahekili Highway, a driver waiting for a car to traverse the entire length of that section could be waiting for 45 to 60 minutes. This would clearly not be practical. If instead traffic signals were to be installed at the beginning and end of each of the one-lane road sections that have no turnouts, the delays could be reduced to just a few minutes, during which motorists would be less likely to become impatient. These signals would reduce delays and fuel consumption.

Due to the remoteness and intermittent nature of traffic on Kahekili Highway, fixed-time traffic signal systems would very likely be ignored by impatient drivers. Instead, adaptive traffic controls would be much more likely to be valued and respected. These signals would have the capability of automatically changing (stop or go) in response to the presence or absence of a vehicle traversing their respective one-lane sections. Adaptive signals would require deployment of traffic detectors.

Automated traffic signals at the beginning and end of each one-lane section would increase safety by eliminating single-lane conflicts. Signals would reduce the number of accidents associated with drivers misjudging cliff edges when they are backing up or pulling to the side to make room for oncoming drivers. These traffic signals could be activated permanently, or they could be used only during emergencies, depending on community preference.

However, the potential for vandalism of these remote signals and their support systems, whether random or purposeful, cannot be ignored. The Hawaiʻi Department of Transportation has already experienced theft of components of portable road alert signs in remote areas. In order to prevent this, support systems such as solar energy generation and storage facilities would need to be protected with vandalproof walls and/or fencing. This would increase the footprint of the facilities, which would in turn add to their space requirements, their visual impact, and their expense.

Option 3 would not address the substandard nature of the existing roadway. Due to the reduction of delay, it would provide a small amount of capacity improvement, but not as much as Option 2, and would not come anywhere close to providing the capacity of Option 1.

TRAFFIC CAPACITY

By resolving the issue of single-lane conflicts, the placement of automated traffic signals at the beginning and end of each one-lane section would alleviate one of the main dangers associated with Kahekili Highway, and would make more people comfortable with driving this way. However, it would still remain a substandard, dangerous roadway, with inadequate guardrails and shoulders, steep cliffs, and poor signage.

Option 3 would not remove a significant amount of traffic from the Pali segment of Honoapi'ilani Highway. Even if the current AADT of 1,300 were to double to 2,600 as a result of traffic signal installation, that would be only nine percent of the 27,900 AADT of The Pali.

EMERGENCY OPERATIONS

By resolving the issue of single-lane conflicts, the placement of automated traffic signals at the beginning and end of each one-lane section could eliminate the delay experienced by emergency vehicles on the way to Central Maui; this would be ensured if emergency personnel were given the ability to override the automated signals to give themselves priority. Travel time from Kā'anapali to Maui Memorial Medical Center would still be about 90 minutes, as compared to the 40 minutes that a similar trip currently takes via The Pali. However, in the event of closure of Honoapi'ilani Highway, the ability to travel all the way around the north side of West Maui without unnecessary delay would provide an alternative for (slower) patient transport to that emergency facility.

SAFETY

Installation of automated traffic signals at the beginning and end of each one-lane section on Kahekili Highway would eliminate the single-lane conflicts that lead to dangerous (and sometimes fatal) maneuvers on this roadway. However, it would still remain a substandard, dangerous highway, with inadequate guardrails and shoulders, steep cliffs, and poor signage, so the safety improvement of Option 3 would not be as great as those of Options 2 or 3.

CONSTRUCTION COST

The cost of Option 3 would depend on the number of one-lane sections of roadway that need to be signalized. For estimating purposes, we will assume that there are 10 such sections.

Each roadway section would need two signal stations, two vehicle sensors, and two power supplies. There would also need to be a way for each signal station to communicate with the other in order for syncronized operation to occur. All of this equipment would need to be secured to prevent theft and/or vandalism. A rough estimate of the cost of this type of system is $4 million. Even if this estimate were off by a factor of 10, the cost would still be far lower than that of Options 1 or 2.

PRIORITIZATION AND FINANCING

Construction of Option 3 is not being considered at this time. There is already a backlog of other, more urgent projects, such as those mentioned under Options 1 and 2. However, the relatively low cost of Option 3 might make it attractive to members of the community, depending on whether they view resolution of the one-lane conflicts issue as positive or negative. The estimated $4 million cost of signalizing the one-lane portions of Kahekili Highway would be just a fraction of the cost of these higher-priority projects. If classified as a safety project, it might receive priority.

ENVIRONMENTAL IMPACT

Installation of automated traffic control systems would create minimal disruption as compared to Options 1 and 2. At least some Kahakuloa area residents have expressed support for a project like this. However, it is likely that there are others who prefer the current situation and do not want it to change.

Other than a No Action alternative, Option 3 would involve the fewest changes to the isolated northern coast of West Maui. However, social and cultural impacts to this wider northern part of West Maui could still be significant. Due to increased traffic and a different mix of road users, the historic and cultural context of the area would still be at risk.

Option 3 could have a substantial adverse effect on the social welfare and/or the relatively intact Hawaiian cultural practices of the Kahakuloa-area community. Due to the creation of a less challenging commute from employment centers, it could also generate secondary impacts, such as population growth. For these reasons, it is unlikely that an Environmental Assessment (EA) presuming no significant impacts would suffice. As with Option 2, if attempted, an EA would likely be challenged, and a full Environmental Impact Statement (EIS) would very likely need to be prepared. The EIS would need to fully discuss significant primary, cumulative and secondary impacts of the proposed project. including secondary population and growth impacts, and would need to discuss possible mitigation strategies. This process would take several years.

Due to the fact that there are people on Maui who would adamantly oppose any such action, it is likely that one or more legal challenges would be filed should such an EIS ever be accepted. As with Options 1 and 2, if this type of legal challenge were to occur, Option 3 could be delayed for many years.

A comparison of Options 1, 2, and 3 is shown in Table 6.2.

Summary

There are three main conclusions that can be drawn from this chapter's analysis:

- Given the constraints regarding funding; priority relative to other projects; and likely environmental, social and cultural impacts, a capacity-improvement project around the north end of West Maui that would provide traffic relief to the Pali section of Honoapiʻilani Highway is unlikely to be completed in the foreseeable future.
- The distance involved in going around the north side of West Maui makes it difficult to achieve an effective emergency route to Maui

Table 6.2. Evaluation of Alternatives

EVALUATION FACTORS	OPTION 1	OPTION 2	OPTION 3
Description	Two-lane 40 mph highway on new alignment from Kapalua to Waiheʻe	Add a lane to existing county portion of Kahekili Highway	Automated traffic signals at ends of one-lane road sections
Reduce daily load on The Pali	Significant	Marginal	No
Provide alternate route in case of closure of The Pali	Yes	Yes	Yes
Reduce emergency transport time	Marginal	No	No
Increase safety	Yes	Yes	Somewhat
Cost	$1.4 to $2.9 billion	$492 million	$4 million
Cultural impact	Very High	High	Medium
Environmental impact	Very High	High	Low
Priority	Low	Low	Medium–Low

Memorial Hospital that would reduce travel time for victims of trauma. None of the options considered would significantly improve travel time to the emergency facility at Maui Memorial Medical Center in Kahului. Construction of an emergency facility located somewhere between Lahaina and Kāʻanapali would be a much better solution; it would reduce patient transport time to 20 minutes or less from most parts of West Maui, and would still be vastly less expensive (and completed much more quickly) than building new roadways.

- The No Action option may be the most appropriate, given that it would be self-limiting. This option would continue to limit the impact on social and environmental systems in the Kahakuloa area associated with higher traffic counts.

Notes

1. Federal Aid Highways 2035 Transportation Plan for the District of Maui, Prepared for State of Hawaiʻi Department of Transportation Highways Division, CH2M-Hill, July 2014.
2. HDOT Highways Program Status, https://histategis.maps.arcgis.com/apps/MapSeries/index.html?appid=39e4d804242740a89d3fd0bc76d8d7de.
3. The Index to *The Maui News*, 1951–1973, compiled and edited by Gail Ainsworth, Maui Historical Society, Wailuku, Maui, 2010.
4. www.dangerousroads.org/north-america/usa/643-kahekili-highway-usa.html.
5. West Maui Transportation Access Plan, 2009. West Maui Transportation Access Plan Working Group, Department of Transportation, State of Hawaiʻi.
6. Another sign on the county portion just before MM 7 bears conflicting information regarding the weight capacity of the bridges. It reads, "All Bridges Weight Limit 10 Tons."
7. For purposes of this chapter, the term "emergency" refers to a life-threatening situation that requires immediate action. This definition does not include inconvenient situations, such as when residents are unable to make it to a concert in Central Maui, or tourists miss their flights. Those situations are regrettable and may cause financial loss, but in comparison to potential loss of life, they must be considered less important.
8. https://wearemaui.org/technical-resource-papers-community-profile, County of Maui, Department of Planning, 2017, page 11.
9. https://mauimpo.org/about-maui-mpo. *Accessed* December 22, 2019.
10. Transportation Improvement Program Policies and Procedures - Final, Maui Metropolitan Planning Organization, November 22, 2017.
11. www.mauiCounty.gov/1844/Current-Future-Projects.

12. Screenshot from the County of Maui Real Property website (qpublic.schneidercorp.com), showing parcel boundaries and aerial pictometry as of 2014.
13. Federal Aid Functional Classification Update: Policy and Procedures, December 2012. Prepared for State of Hawai'i Department of Transportation, Highways Division, Planning Branch, by CH2MHill.
14. Level of Service (LOS) describes operating conditions in six letter-grade categories from A to F, with LOS A representing conditions with little or no delay, and LOS F indicating poor operations with long wait times or extreme congestion. LOS F is typically unacceptable; Federal Aid Highways 2035 Transportation Plan for the District of Maui, Prepared for State of Hawai'i Department of Transportation Highways Division, CH2MHill, July 2014. Pp. 3–10.
15. *Lahaina News*, February 6, 2020. www.lahainanews.com/page/content.detail/id/566375/Maui-Health-System-plans-to-establish-urgent-care-center-in-West-Maui-this-year.html.
16. *Maui News*, May 14, 2017. www.mauinews.com/news/local-news/2017/05/solutions-for-pali-traffic-woes-elusive/.

About the Contributors

Lauren Armstrong is the Executive Director of Maui Metropolitan Planning Organization (MPO) which exists to hear the voice of the people and ensure that their concerns and feedback are part of the transportation planning process for Maui. Lauren holds a bachelor's degree in Environmental Science from Middlebury College in Vermont, and a master's degree in Urban and Regional Planning from University of Hawaiʻi at Mānoa. Prior to Maui MPO, she worked as a planner for Townscape Inc. on Oʻahu, then for Marin County Planning Department in California, with a focus on climate change adaptation and public engagement in community planning. Born and raised on Maui, Lauren lives in Waiehu with her husband.

Lance D. Collins is an attorney in private practice on the island of Maui. He also holds a PhD in Political Science from the University of Hawaiʻi at Mānoa. He was the compiler and indexer of the seventeen-volume *Proceedings of the Charter Commissions of the County of Maui* (1966–2012). He coedited *Tourism Impacts West Maui* (2016) and *Social Change in West Maui* (2019) and edited *Civil Society in West Maui* (2021). His research interests focus on the Philippines, Hawaiʻi, American colonialism in the Pacific, and legal and political history.

Dawn Hegger-Nordblom previously worked for the state Department of Land and Natural Resources, Department of Defense, Hawaii Community Development Authority, and the Honolulu Authority for Rapid Transit. She has a master's degree in Urban and Regional Planning and two bachelor's of arts degrees in Environmental Analysis and Design and Psychology and Social Behavior from the University of California, Irvine. In addition to championing ongoing and current environmental causes, Dawn serves on the state Marine and Coastal Zone Advocacy Council and the West Maui Community Plan Advisory Committee. She is the principal for Ke Kai Planning LLC that does pro bono work yearly, and assists clients with Climate Change, Sea Level Rise,

Land Use, Environmental Planning, Transit Oriented Development, Affordable Housing, and Sustainability issues.

Bianca K. Isaki is a writer, solo legal practitioner, community activist, and a director of the North Beach-West Maui Benefit Fund. She received her PhD from the University of Hawaiʻi at Mānoa Department of Political Science for research on Asian settler colonialism and plantation labor organizing, completed a postdoctoral fellowship at the University of Illinois at Urbana-Champaign, returned to Hawaiʻi to teach Women's Studies, and then graduated summa cum laude from the William S. Richardson School of Law. She has contributed to the following West Maui oriented books: *Tourism Impacts West Maui* (2016), *Social Change in West Maui* (2019), *Civil Society in West Maui* (2021), and *Water and Power in West Maui* (2021).

Albert Perez is Executive Director of the Maui Tomorrow Foundation, and was one of its three original codirectors. Born and raised in Hawaiʻi, he earned a master's degree in Urban and Regional Planning from the University of Hawaiʻi at Mānoa. Albert has worked at the State of Hawaii Office of Coastal Zone Management, the Washington State Department of Transportation, and the County of Maui. He has previously been involved with Sierra Club of Hawaiʻi, The Wilderness Society, and Life of the Land. Albert spent fifteen years as a Geographic Systems Analyst/Programmer, and 8 years in photovoltaic systems design, installation, and sales. His publications include work in habitat connectivity, remote sensing, environmental analysis, watershed delineation and characterization, scenic resources, helicopter noise analysis, and carrying capacity.

Ryan Tam is the Director of Planning, Environmental Compliance, and Sustainable Mobility for the Honolulu Authority for Rapid Transportation. He also serves as an adjunct graduate faculty member in the Department of Urban and Regional Planning at the University of Hawaiʻi at Mānoa and has a doctorate from the Massachusetts Institute of Technology. Ryan is a descendant of a Chinese merchant in Makawao, who would spend a whole day or more to haul goods back from Kahului Harbor in the late 1800s—a trip that now takes 20 to 25 minutes by car.

Benjamin Treviño and Victoria Larson Treviño have combined experience in the transportation, urban planning, hospitality, and human resources sectors. Ben currently serves as the Sustainability Planner for the Honolulu

Authority for Rapid Transportation and previously was the founding president and COO of Bikeshare Hawaii, the nonprofit that oversees the BIKI bikeshare system on Oʻahu. Victoria is on the staff of the Oahu Metropolitan Planning Organization and previously worked for Marriott Hotels in human resources and guest services on Oʻahu and Maui.

MASON M. YAMAKI has over ten years of experience as an attorney in private practice on the island of Hawaiʻi. His specialties include commercial litigation and real property. He is also a licensed professional engineer in Hawaiʻi and California and, prior to his legal career, worked as a project manager, construction manager, and design engineer throughout the West Coast, Japan, and Hawaiʻi. Prior to his engineering career, he worked for the late Congresswoman Patsy T. Mink.

Index